# TAMBOUR BEADING

*techniques and projects*

Hannah Mansfield

# TAMBOUR BEADING

*techniques and projects*

THE CROWOOD PRESS

# CONTENTS

Introduction 7

CHAPTER 1 Materials and Equipment 11

CHAPTER 2 Preparing Fabric for Embroidery 23

CHAPTER 3 Transferring a Design to Fabric 29

CHAPTER 4 Chain Stitch 33

CHAPTER 5 Applying Beads 51

CHAPTER 6 Applying Sequins 69

CHAPTER 7 Advanced Tambour Techniques 83

CHAPTER 8 Designing for Tambour 103

CHAPTER 9 Projects 111

Appendix: Patterns for the Projects 203

Stockists 222

Index 223

Bibliography 224

Acknowledgements 224

# INTRODUCTION

Tambour beading is a specialist embroidery technique that uses a tool called a tambour hook to quickly apply beads and sequins to fabric. The tambour hook creates a chain stitch, which can be simply used as a decorative stitch on its own, or beads and sequins can be added to the chain stitch. The chain stitch can be formed very quickly with the tambour hook, which makes tambour beading a much faster way of applying beads and sequins to fabric as opposed to using a needle and thread. For this reason, it is a much more preferable technique to use because it reduces the time-consuming nature of beading. The beauty of tambour beading is the endless possibilities of the embroidery designs and items you can create with glittering sequins, shimmering beads and glossy threads.

Tambour beading is also known as 'crochet de Lunéville' or 'Lunéville embroidery'. This is due to its origins in the French town of Lunéville in the nineteenth century, when it was developed by embroiderers to speed up the process of applying beads. However, there may have been an earlier version of tambour that is believed to have originated in India in the

seventeenth century. It can probably be assumed that this version of tambour was closer to aari, which is a technique similar to tambour beading that is still used in India today. There are some key differences between tambour beading and aari. Tambour beading is worked on the wrong side of the fabric and aari is worked on the right side. The hooks used for tambour and aari are also different. The aari hook is finer and longer, and whereas the tambour hook has a screw to hold the hook in place, this is not a feature of an aari hook, in which the hook is fixed so cannot be removed. The aari hook must be removed from the working loop of thread to pick up several beads or sequins. These are placed directly onto the hook and then dropped onto the thread one by one to be secured by a stitch. In tambour beading, many beads are strung onto the thread at the same time and then pushed up the thread, to the fabric, to be secured by a stitch. This does make tambour beading slightly quicker than aari because you can transfer many more beads to the thread for tambour than you can fit beads onto the hook for aari, meaning that with tambour you do not need to regularly stop embroidering to pick up more beads.

The technique of tambour beading is still better known and more frequently used in France than the UK. However, it is now present in the embroidery techniques used and taught in many countries across the world. Today tambour beading is used extensively in haute couture embroidery. It is seen as an haute couture technique because it is highly specialized and requires a certain amount of skill to master. There are many videos showing tambour beading being used to embroider exquisitely detailed garments by fashion houses such as Dior and Chanel. These can serve as an insight into how tambour beading is used in fashion and as a great source of inspiration. Much of the tambour beading you see in couture fashion will have been embroidered by specialist hand-embroidery ateliers such as Lesage and Vermont.

From the start point to the finish, a line of beads applied with the tambour hook is applied with one continuous thread. This makes the process of applying beads much less time consuming. However, this can pose a slight challenge to beginners – an unfortunate combination of a wrong movement of the hook, causing the thread to be dropped from the hook, and an acciden-

A tambour-beaded floral design featuring decorative chain stitch, beads and sequins.

tal tug on the thread can cause the entire section of embroidery to be very swiftly undone. Conversely, when a mistake is made in the embroidery, the swift way in which it can be undone is a blessing.

Although tambour beading appears to be a complicated technique and can take a while to master, it is in fact fairly simple once the technique has been learnt. Unlike many other embroidery techniques, which incorporate numerous different stitches, there is only one stitch that forms the basis of all tambour techniques, which is chain stitch. Once you are confident with working a chain stitch with the tambour hook, you will be able to use this stitch to apply beads and sequins, and embroider more advanced techniques with the tambour hook, such as cutwork and vermicelli.

This book will guide you through the materials, equipment and processes required to learn tambour beading, beginning with the basic chain stitch, then moving on to applying beads and sequins. Each of the technique chapters includes a small design intended to help you practise the technique. Once these techniques have been mastered, you can move on to learning more complex tambour techniques. After these technique chapters, there is advice to help you begin creating your own designs for tambour. The projects chapter (Chapter 9) demonstrates how the techniques detailed in the book can be used in a variety of embroidery designs and shows how these can be made into different items, including a bag, cushion and framed embroideries. You can follow the step-by-step instructions to make these projects, or these projects can serve as inspiration for your own designs.

One of the most important things to remember when learning tambour beading is the need to practise. It can take a while to get used to using a tambour hook and becoming familiar with the hand movements required to form stitches. In addition, the requirement to use both your hands to carry out different actions at the same time can be challenging for beginners. If at first it seems impossible, persevere and practise as much as possible and you will be surprised how, in time, using a tambour hook becomes second nature.

A sample combining tambour beading and goldwork embroidery. The base fabric is made of several layers of honey-toned organza that are embroidered with a honeycomb pattern using the tambour cutwork technique. Sections of the honeycomb are highlighted with beads and the goldwork bees are embroidered on top.

This sample features organza that has been hand embroidered with raised needlework flowers and tambour-beaded flowers. Three-dimensional sequin flowers have been formed by embroidering the petals individually on a separate piece of organza. The petals were cut out and applied to the base embroidery to form flowers.

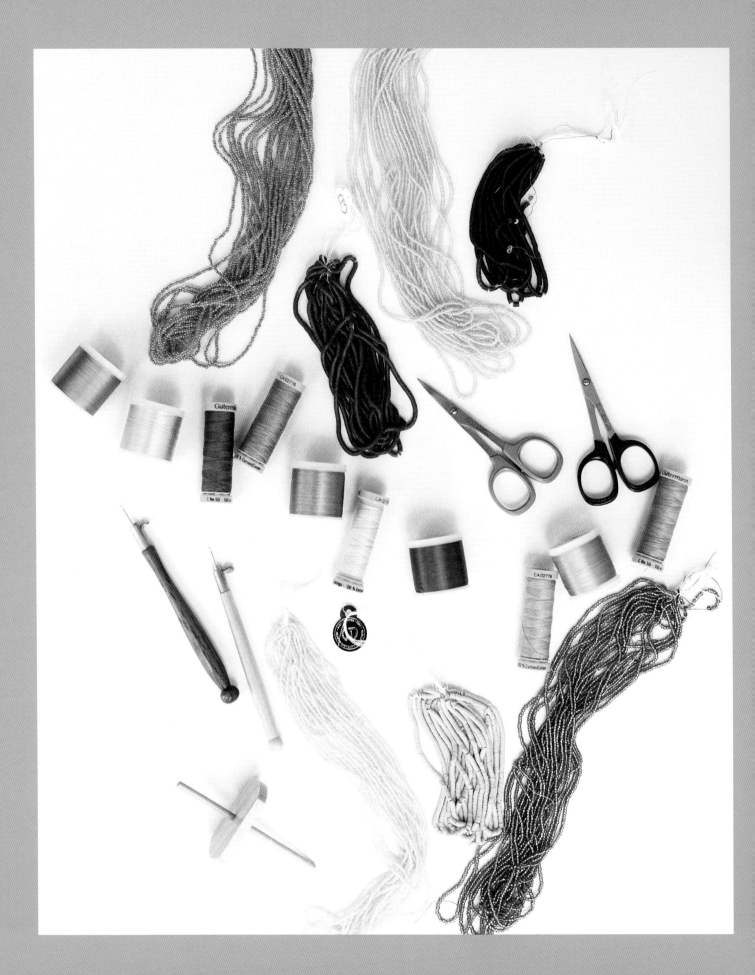

# CHAPTER 1

# MATERIALS AND EQUIPMENT

A benefit for the embroiderer is that tambour beading requires very little equipment. In fact, except from the tambour hook, there is no specialist equipment required to get started. Of course, as you progress with the technique, you may wish to invest in more costly equipment such as a slate frame to improve the tensioning of the fabric. To begin with, however, you may find you already have much of the equipment required. There is a great variety of threads, beads and sequins that you can use for tambour. To get started with practising the techniques, you may prefer to use loose beads and sequins before sourcing the more specialist category of pre-strung beads and sequins that are used specifically for tambour beading.

A selection of the main tools and materials required for tambour beading. This includes a tambour hook, threads, scissors, an embroidery hoop, a measuring tape, pins, pencils, a screwdriver and pliers.

# TAMBOUR HOOK

A tambour hook is a tool that is comprised of a wooden handle and a metal hook. The hook has a sharp pointed end, which is used to pierce the fabric and is held in the handle with a screw. The tambour hook should be positioned in the handle facing towards the screw, which indicates the direction in which the hook is facing when it has been inserted through the fabric. This allows you to know which way to turn the hook so it faces the right direction when it is brought back up through the fabric.

The tambour hook is used to make a chain stitch, which is the basis of all tambour techniques. The sharp pointed end of the tambour hook easily pierces the fabric.

Tambour hooks are available in several different sizes. A size 90 hook is the standard size that you should use for applying beads and sequins with a standard sewing thread. The hook size increases with the number – for example, a size 100 hook is larger than a size 90. You can purchase hooks separately from the handle or as a complete tambour hook including a handle and hook. Many tambour hooks are sold in this way, as a handle with a hook. When this is the case, the hook included will normally be the standard size.

Using different sizes of tambour hooks allows you to use a variety of thicknesses of thread. You need to choose the appropriate hook size for the thread you are using. A variety of different hook sizes can be bought separately from the handle, which can be useful when you want to experiment with using threads of different thicknesses. When buying hooks separately, they will sometimes need to be cut down to size to fit in the handle, but make sure you check the length of the hook in the handle before making any adjustments.

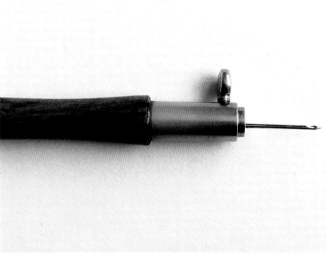

The tambour hook should be positioned pointing towards the screw and should be firmly secured in the handle. The screw is an important indicator of which way the hook is facing when it is inserted into the fabric and is not visible. This means that you can easily see which way you need to turn the hook to form the stitch.

# THREAD

You need to use a thickness of thread that is suitable for the hook size you are using. The hook size you use will be dependent on which technique you are using. If you are applying beads and sequins, you can use a standard sewing thread, such as the type you would use in a sewing machine; this type of thread is usually comprised of either cotton or polyester. Polyester thread can be slightly more prone to splitting and catching in the hook than cotton thread. Usually, it is good practice to match the thread composition to the fabric composition. For example, if you are embroidering onto silk organza, it makes sense to use cotton thread as they are both comprised of natural fibres. Make sure to choose a good-quality thread as this will make a difference as to how easy it is to use, and to the finished look of the embroidery. Poor-quality thread is more likely to wear and break easily. Standard sewing thread is the

Standard sewing threads are a suitable thickness to use for chain stitch and applying beads and sequins. *Fil à gant* thread is specially made for use with the tambour hook. It can be used for decorative chain stitch as well as applying beads and sequins. Metallic threads can also be used for decorative chain stitch or to apply beads and sequins.

perfect thickness for applying beads and sequins, and will be suitable for the standard hook size that you would use for this technique.

If you wish to use chain stitch decoratively, you may want to use a thread that is more decorative. *Fil à gant*, otherwise known as gloving thread, is the perfect type of thread for a fine chain stitch. It is about the same thickness as a regular sewing thread but it has a smoother appearance and a slight sheen, as the thread has been mercerised. *Fil à gant* is designed specially for use with a tambour hook and can also be used to apply beads and sequins. It is also available in metallic colours. Rayon thread is also a lovely choice for tambour, especially decorative chain stitch, because it has a reflective quality that creates a nice sheen.

You can experiment with using any type of thicker thread to create decorative chain stitch. However, there are a couple of points to keep in mind when choosing a thicker thread. First, you are limited by the size of your largest hook as to how thick your thread can be; you need to be able to fit the whole diameter of the thread in your hook so that you do not split the thread with the hook when working with it. You also need to use a thread that is smooth and has an even thickness along its length, as this means it can be pulled through the fabric easily with the hook.

## METALLIC THREAD

Metallic threads can be used for chain stitch, either decoratively or to apply beads and sequins. Metallic threads are constructed from a soft flexible core that is wrapped with a flat metallic strip. They are highly reflective, which can add interest

to an embroidery. However, some metallic threads will not be suitable to use with tambour. Some metallic threads can be quite rough, which can make them abrasive to the fabric, especially to a fabric with a fine weave, such as organza. If the metallic thread is not smooth it can be prone to splitting or becoming damaged, as the thread is more likely to catch on the fabric. There is slightly less chance of this being an issue with tambour because, unlike hand sewing, you are not passing the entirety of the thread through the fabric each time you make a stitch. However, do make sure that you choose a metallic thread that is smooth, such as *Fil à gant*, and use the thread with care to avoid damaging it with the hook as you work.

## PRE-STRUNG BEADS AND SEQUINS

In a tambour embroidery, the focus is on the beads, sequins and threads, so choosing high-quality beads and sequins will greatly enhance the appearance of your embroidery. High-quality beads and sequins will also be easier to use and you will be able to achieve a neater finish. For example, when selecting beads for tambour beading, it is best to choose good-quality glass beads that are consistently sized as this makes the spacing of the beads easier.

Beads and sequins that are going to be used for tambour beading need to be pre-strung, which means the beads or sequins are strung onto thread. You can buy beads and sequins that are pre-strung specifically for use with tambour. Pre-strung beads and sequins are hard to source in the UK but it is easy to find a huge variety of pre-strung beads and sequins from France. In the UK, beads and sequins are typically sold loose,

Beads need to be pre-strung to be used for tambour beading. Good-quality pre-strung glass beads can be obtained from France. They have a good uniformity in size, meaning they are easier to use and can achieve a neater finish. Pre-strung beads are available in a variety of different sizes, shapes and finishes.

and you would need to string them onto thread by hand in order to be able to use them for tambour. This can be done by simply using a needle threaded onto the end of a reel of thread. To speed up the process of stringing loose beads onto thread, you can use a bead spinner (*see* Bead Spinner section). Loose flat sequins can also be threaded using a bead spinner, but cup sequins, or sequins that have a right and wrong side, can only be strung by hand because you need to string all the sequins onto the thread in the same direction. This ensures that when you apply the sequins to the fabric with a tambour hook, the right side of the sequins will be visible.

The only remaining French producer of sequins is Langlois Martin. They produce pre-strung sequins in many colours and finishes, which are supplied to couture houses and individuals for use in tambour beading. Langlois Martin's sequins are very high quality; they have a great uniformity in colour and size. Today the majority of sequins available are produced in Asia. These will usually be sold loose and are not as high quality as French-made sequins, which are specifically designed for use in tambour beading.

Many of the pre-strung beads available are Czech-made, and are of excellent quality and uniformity in size. These qualities are shared by Japanese seed beads such as Toho and Miyuki, although these are only sold as loose beads so will need to be strung before use.

Sequins need to be pre-strung for use with tambour beading. Pre-strung sequins are sold in bunches that contain a large number of sequins. French-made sequins are the best quality and will usually be sold as pre-strung sequins. Langlois Martin is the only remaining French producer of sequins; their sequins are specifically made for tambour beading.

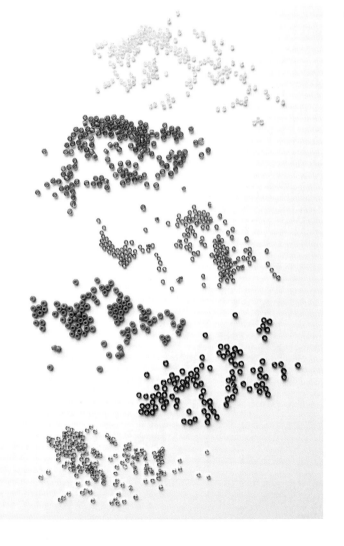

Japanese seed beads, such as Toho and Miyuki, are uniform in size. These are sold as loose beads and will need to be strung to be used for tambour beading. This can be done by hand with a needle and thread, or a tool called a bead spinner can be used to speed up the process.

## BEAD SHAPES, FINISHES AND SIZES

Beads for tambour are available in several different shapes. This includes round beads, cut beads and bugle beads, all available in varying sizes. Round beads are smooth, curved beads. They are not completely spherical; instead they have a slightly flattened doughnut-like shape. Cut beads are short tube-shaped beads with cuts in the surface of the bead. These cuts create facets, which make the beads appear more sparkly because the flat surfaces created from the cuts reflect the light at different angles. Cut beads are available with different numbers of cuts; a three-cut bead has more cuts in the surface than a two-cut bead. Bugle beads are short or long tube-shaped beads. Bugle beads may be faceted or smooth. If they are smooth, this will be referred to as 'round'.

Beads are available in different finishes, such as opaque, glossy and lined. Opaque beads have no transparent quality to them, meaning that they are a solid colour. Glossy beads have a shiny finish.

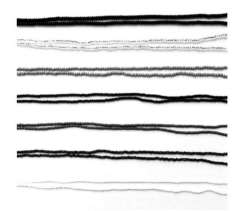

There are various different sizes of beads, which are indicated by a system of numbers. The smaller the number is, the larger the bead. In this illustration, the beads shown are size 10 at the top, 12 in the middle and 13 at the bottom. This means the largest size beads are at the top and the smallest are at the bottom.

Lined refers to beads that are either transparent or coloured and have a different colour in their centre. This type of bead finish is sometimes referred to as 'tosca'. Silver-lined is a common type of lined bead. These have a silver-coloured or genuine silver core, which gives a metallic effect to the beads. Other types of bead finishes include Ceylon and AB (aurora borealis). Ceylon beads have a shiny pearl appearance. Beads with an AB finish applied to them have an iridescent quality, which means they reflect a number of different colours.

Beads are sized according to numbers. This can be a little tricky to understand, as the numbers do not refer to their size in millimetres. The smaller the number is, the larger the bead. For example, a number 10 bead is larger than a number 11 bead. Pre-strung beads are commonly available in sizes number 9 to number 16. These sizes are all fairly small, with none of these beads being more than a few millimetres in size. Whenever you purchase a different size of bead, it is useful to add a couple to a sheet of paper and label them with their size so that in the future you can compare the bead sizes and understand exactly which size you are ordering.

The length of bugle beads will usually be indicated in millimetres, but the length is sometimes also indicated by numbers. When the bugle bead size is given as a number, there will normally also be an approximate size in millimetres given in the product description.

Vintage pre-strung beads, if you are lucky enough to find some, can be a great source of material for a tambour embroidery.

## SEQUIN SHAPES, FINISHES AND SIZES

There are two main types of sequins: flat sequins or cup sequins. Cup sequins have a sort of inverted faceted appearance. Sequins are available in many different finishes, such as metallic, matt, pearlescent and iridescent, and can be completely opaque or slightly transparent.

Most strung sequins are sourced from France; because of this, many of the finishes are labelled in French. Many of the French words for the finishes are similar to the words in English so are easy to trans-

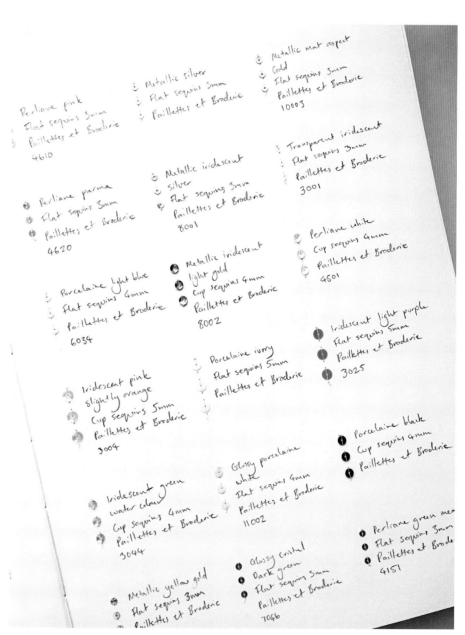

There are two main sequin shapes: flat and cup sequins. They are available in a range of different sizes. Sequins are sized in millimetres. Sequins can be opaque or slightly transparent, and feature many different finishes such as metallic, matt, iridescent and pearlescent. These finishes can be used to create different effects in an embroidery.

late. The following list contains some of the most common types of sequin finishes with their French names and English translations, where applicable, and a description of the finish.

*Metallic*: A highly reflective finish that is fully opaque.

*Métallic Irisé*: Iridescent metallic, a highly reflective finish that reflects multiple colours. This is a fully opaque sequin.

*Métallic mat*: Matt metallic, a metallic sequin with a matt finish. This is a fully opaque sequin.

*Étincelle*: Spark, similar to metallic sequins, this is a highly reflective finish. This is a fully opaque sequin.

*Nacrolaque*: A shiny finish on top of a matt finish, which gives a slight sheen to the sequin. This is a slightly transparent sequin.

*Oriental*: A shiny iridescent finish. This is an opaque sequin.

*Irisé*: Iridescent, a shiny finish that reflects multiple colours. This is a transparent sequin.

*Porcelaine*: Porcelain, a shiny finish. This is a fully opaque sequin.

*Porcelaine lustreé*: Glossy porcelain, a higher sheen finish than porcelain sequins. This is a fully opaque sequin.

*Cristal lustreé*: Glossy crystal, a shiny finish. This is a semi-transparent sequin.

*Perliane*: Pearl, a subtle sheen finish. This is a semi-transparent sequin.

Sequins are sized in millimetres, which makes it easy to determine the size of the sequin. The size in millimetres refers to the diameter of the sequin. Pre-strung sequins are commonly available in 3mm, 4mm and 5mm diameters.

# FABRIC

Tambour beading is most often worked on sheer fabrics such as organza or tulle. This is because, when applying beads and sequins with a tambour hook, you work from the wrong side of the fabric. Using a sheer fabric means that even though you are facing the wrong side of the work, you have some idea of how the embroidery is looking on the right side. For example, you can see how far apart you are spacing the beads or sequins and whether you have inadvertently applied two beads or sequins at the same time.

When selecting fabric to use for tambour, the type of fabric you use depends on your skill level. It is best for beginners to use only sheer fabrics, but once you become more advanced you may wish to experiment with using opaque or semi-opaque fabrics. However, it can be challenging to find opaque fabrics that are suitable to use for tambour beading. This is because any fabric you use must be easily punctured with a tambour hook. A smooth fabric with a fine, looser type of weave usually works best. The weave of loosely woven fabric, such as a fine muslin, is able to be parted with the tambour hook to allow the hook to pass through it without catching on the fabric. Thick fabrics with uneven or tight weaves can often cause the hook to catch and snag the fabric. The fabric must also be able to withstand being punctured with a tambour hook; some fabrics can be dam-

aged when pierced with the hook, which ruins the appearance of the fabric, so these types of fabric must be avoided.

In order to avoid the difficulty of using an opaque fabric, tambour beading is frequently worked on a sheer fabric and then cut out and applied to an opaque fabric using appliqué. This means that tambour beading can be applied to any type of fabric.

## SILK ORGANZA

Silk organza is the ideal and most widely used fabric for tambour beading. It is sheer, and although it is a very fine fabric, it does have strength and can hold up to being repeatedly punctured with the tambour hook. It is also sturdy enough to hold the weight of beads and sequins, which can become rather heavy when applied densely or over a large area. Silk organza varies between manufacturers – some organza will be stiffer and some will be softer and more fluid.

Silk organza is often easier to work with than synthetic organza, as it tends to be easier to part the weave of the fabric with

Silk organza is a highly suitable fabric for tambour beading. The fabric can be pierced easily with the tambour hook and it is sheer, which makes applying beads or sequins easier as you can see what is happening on the right side while you work. This makes it a good fabric for beginners to use when learning tambour beading.

the tambour hook. You can usually avoid snagging or catching the hook in the fabric when using silk organza, especially when you are comfortable with using the tambour hook. When the hook punctures the fabric, it easily parts the threads that make up the fabric weave to make a small hole that the hook can then pass back through when you pull the hook up. Using several pieces of silk organza layered up is a good way to practise working on semi-opaque fabrics while still using a fabric that is well suited to tambour. Silk organza has been used for most of the examples of work and projects in this book.

## TULLE

Tulle is another fabric that is frequently used with tambour beading. There are many different types of tulle available, but most commonly tulle is made from nylon or polyester. Tulle with a synthetic composition is not particularly well suited to using with tambour beading as it can break easily when tensioned in a slate frame or when snagged with a tambour hook. It is worth sourcing a cotton or silk tulle, as these are

more durable. However, care does need to be taken when working with any type of tulle, especially when tensioning the fabric. If you are working with a particularly fine tulle, or are having issues with the delicacy of the fabric, you can layer two pieces of tulle together to create a stronger fabric.

The standard type of tulle is a fine net that forms small holes all over the fabric. When working on tulle, the tambour hook is placed through the holes in the fabric to form the stitches. This means you do not have as much freedom about where you place your tambour hook to make the stitches.

## OPAQUE FABRICS FOR LAYERING

If you have created a tambour embroidery on organza, you can use almost any type of fabric underneath to make an opaque backdrop for your embroidery. There are a wide variety of silk fabrics available that work really well for this. These include silk satin, dupion and crêpe de chine. You will notice that layering has been used for many of the projects in this book. For example, the butterfly clutch bag and summer flowers framed embroidery have had opaque silk fabrics placed underneath them to increase

the colour intensity of the background fabric, to hide the seams of the bag and to cover the mount board that is used in the process of mounting an embroidery for framing.

## FRAMES, HOOPS AND CLAMPS

When working with tambour beading you need the use of both hands, one above the fabric and one below. This means that you need to be able to tension your fabric in a frame or hoop that is supported by a stand so that you do not have to hold it in one of your hands. It is also important that your fabric is tensioned well, as this will make it easier to work with and will reduce puckering of the fabric when you remove it from the frame or hoop.

### SLATE FRAME

The optimum method for tensioning fabric for tambour beading is in a slate frame. A slate frame is comprised of four wooden sections – two roller bars that are opposite each other and two slats that are threaded through the roller bars at each end to create a square- or rectangular-shaped frame. The fabric is sewn into the frame and tensioned by gradually stretching the fabric, securing it with pegs that are inserted into holes in the slats and lacing the sides of the fabric around them. Stretching the fabric along each straight edge tensions the fabric evenly and does not distort the weave. If set up correctly, the tension of the fabric will be retained for a very long time in this type of frame without needing adjustment.

There is another type of slate frame that varies slightly from the type previously described. Because of the differences in the frame, the tensioning of the fabric

Tulle is another fabric that is frequently used for tambour beading. It is best to use cotton or silk tulle as they have more strength than synthetic tulle, which can tear easily under tension. You can also layer up two pieces of tulle to create a stronger fabric, which can be easier to work with.

Opaque fabrics can be layered underneath an embroidery that has been made on organza to create a solid background colour that is not see-through. Most fabrics are suitable but silk fabrics, of which there is much variety, work particularly well.

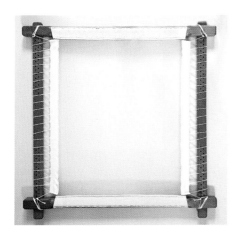

A traditional slate frame is the best way to tension fabric for tambour beading. The fabric is tensioned evenly along all four straight edges. This reduces puckering of the fabric because the weave is not distorted under tension. It is important to achieve a tightly tensioned fabric for tambour beading as this makes it easier to work on.

requires a slightly different method. Instead of rounded roller bars, this type of frame has flat bars with several holes at either end. The slats have a long rectangle cut out from them. The slats are placed on top of the flat bars; screws are placed through the holes in the flat bars and the cutout rectangles in the slats to attach the pieces of the frame together. The fabric is stretched by pulling the flat bars further apart and securing them by tightening the screws. The sides of the fabric are tensioned with lacing around the slats. After a while in this type of frame, the tension of the fabric will loosen slightly and will need to be tightened by loosening the screws to pull the flat bars further apart and then retightening the screws to hold the tension.

This book will focus on using the first type of slate frame described because it is the most widely available type of slate frame. It is also slightly easier to set up and retains the tension of the fabric for longer than the second type of slate frame.

Slate frames are often large and a little heavy, so they need to be supported by being placed on two surfaces. You can use trestles for this or two tables of the same height to support either side of the slate frame. With the frame supported in this way you can then sit between the supports with your legs underneath the frame as you would sit at a desk.

There are no-sew versions of slate frames available but these are not suitable for tambour beading. Instead, when looking to purchase a slate frame, you should seek one labelled as a 'traditional' slate frame or one where you can see there is webbing or fabric tape attached to the roller bars. A good-quality traditional slate frame, although costly, is worth the investment as it will be sturdy and will not warp when under tension. If you can, source a handmade slate frame because these are made by skilled woodworkers from good-quality materials.

The disadvantages of using slate frames are that they are usually expensive and take up a lot of room when in use. They can also take a considerable amount of time to set up.

Several additional items are required to set up a slate frame. These include a standard sewing needle and a large tapestry or curved needle, a heavy-duty thread, such as buttonhole thread, for sewing the fabric into the frame, herringbone tape for the sides of the fabric and string for lacing up and tensioning the sides of the fabric.

## Embroidery Hoop

A more affordable and smaller alternative to a slate frame is an embroidery hoop. An embroidery hoop is very simple to use and quick to set up. However, there are some disadvantages of using an embroidery hoop to tension your fabric. It is very difficult to stretch the fabric evenly, which causes the weave of the fabric to distort. This means that you are more likely to have issues with the fabric puckering when it is removed from the hoop. A hoop can mark the fabric, leaving a circular indentation in the fabric, which is often impossible to completely remove with an iron. You are also constrained by the circular shape of the hoop as you need to be able to fit your design within the hoop, which can be limiting.

## Clamps

When using an embroidery hoop to tension your fabric, you will need either a seat clamp, table clamp or floor stand to hold the hoop. Each of these clamps attach to the hoop or frame at the top, but to hold them steady a seat clamp is placed under one of your legs, a table clamp is attached to the edge of the table and a floor stand is placed on the floor and has a wide base to steady it. Some clamps come with a hoop that is permanently attached to the clamp. This means that you cannot change the size of the hoop you use with the clamp.

The best type of clamp to use is one that is made of hard wood. A clamp made from hard wood will be more expensive but it will last much longer. This is because of the screw at the top of the stalk, which is used to hold the hoop at the desired angle. On a clamp made of soft wood, the wood compresses each time the screw is tightened, which eventually results in the screw not

being able to be tightened enough. This means it does not hold the hoop in position, which can become very frustrating because the hoop will constantly be slipping downwards when you are working.

## Other Items

### Spool Holder

A spool holder is a small wooden tool that holds the thread while you are working. One end of the thread holder is placed through one of the holes in the slate frame and a spool of thread is placed on the other end. This stops the spool of thread from rolling away while it is in use.

## Bead Spinner

A bead spinner can be used to quickly string loose beads and some sequins onto thread. It is a tool comprised of a wooden bowl on a spindle. Loose beads are placed in the bowl and the bowl is rotated using the spindle. A long needle with an eye that can be threaded at one end and a curved pointed end at the other is held in the bowl to collect the beads. The bowl is spun by turning the spindle. As the bowl spins, beads are pushed onto the needle, which can then be moved up the length of the needle and onto the thread. When using a bead spinner, the needle should be placed in the bowl facing against the direction the bowl is spinning. You need a fairly significant amount of loose beads in the bowl for the

A bead spinner can be used to speed up stringing loose beads onto thread. It is comprised of a wooden bowl on a spindle, which is used to spin the bowl. The bowl is half filled with beads and a long needle with a curved end is placed in the bowl. When the bowl is spun, beads are pushed onto the needle.

bead spinner to work effectively; usually the beads should fill about half of the bowl.

You can also use a bead spinner to string loose sequins, but you can only use it with sequins that do not have a right side. Sequins that have a right side need to all be strung onto the thread in the same direction so that the right side of every sequin shows when it is applied to the fabric.

## SCISSORS

You will need two pairs of scissors, one for cutting fabric and the other for cutting threads. For cutting threads, choose a pair of small embroidery scissors. They must be sharp so the threads can be cut cleanly and easily. A pair of embroidery scissors with a fine point to the blades will mean you can cut threads close to the fabric. For cutting fabric, you will need a pair of fabric scissors. These have long sharp blades. You can choose between fabric scissors with a standard smooth blade or a serrated blade. Either are suitable but serrated blades are better suited to cutting fine, delicate fabrics, so you may prefer to use these for the type of fabrics you will be using with tambour beading. Always have scissors dedicated to specific purposes; never use your embroidery or fabric scissors to cut paper or any tough material because this will blunt the blades.

## MEASURING TAPE/RULER

A measuring tape is required for measuring lengths of fabric and marking where a piece of fabric should be cut. A rigid ruler is useful for drawing straight lines onto fabric that can be followed when cutting a piece of fabric for embroidery.

## PINS

Dressmaking pins can be used when sewing fabrics together to hold them in place. General-purpose bobble-headed pins are used when mounting an embroidery for framing.

## GLUE

You will need glue for finishing off the thread ends. This helps to make sure the thread ends are very secure so your embroidery will not unravel. Glue is also used to secure mount board together to make a stable surface to mount embroidery on. Conservation polyvinyl acetate (PVA) glue is best to use for these purposes. It has a neutral pH, which will ensure that your embroidery is not damaged by acidity from the glue in the future. Conservation PVA can be very easily found online. However, you can also use regular PVA or fabric glue if you are not so concerned about long-term conservation of the embroidery.

## PLIERS

A pair of flat-nose pliers will allow you to remove damaged or imperfect beads from the thread easily, without having to cut the thread.

## PENCILS AND PENS

For drawing designs onto fabric, you may need several different mediums with which to do this. These can include a hard leaded pencil such as a 2H, which is less prone to smudging, or a white-coloured pencil or white chalk pencil. You should avoid using

any kind of pen on your fabric except a gel pen. Some inks can run on fabric. Ink is also very permanent and visible whereas pencil lines are fainter and more easily covered by embroidery.

## PRICK AND POUNCE

If you are transferring a design to fabric using the prick and pounce technique, you will need a pricker, loose pounce powder, a pouncer and either a water-based paint or gel pen. A pricker is used to create holes in a paper design, which the pounce powder is pushed through to transfer the design to the fabric. You can create your own pricker by swapping the hook in your tambour handle for a fine sewing needle. This allows you to easily and quickly prick holes in a paper design.

Prick and pounce sets can be bought that provide you with white, grey and black loose pounce powders and a pouncer. A pouncer is a rolled-up piece of fabric that is dipped in the pounce powder and rubbed over the design. You can make a pouncer by rolling up a thick fabric such as felt and stitching the end down to secure it.

To permanently mark the design onto the fabric, you can use a water-based paint such as watercolour or a gel pen. If using paint, you will need a small paintbrush to ensure you can create very fine lines to mark the design onto the fabric.

These items are required when using the prick and pounce method of transferring a design to fabric. They include a pricker, a pouncer and pounce powder in white, grey or black. For marking the design onto the fabric, a water-based paint such as watercolour and a fine paintbrush or a gel pen are needed.

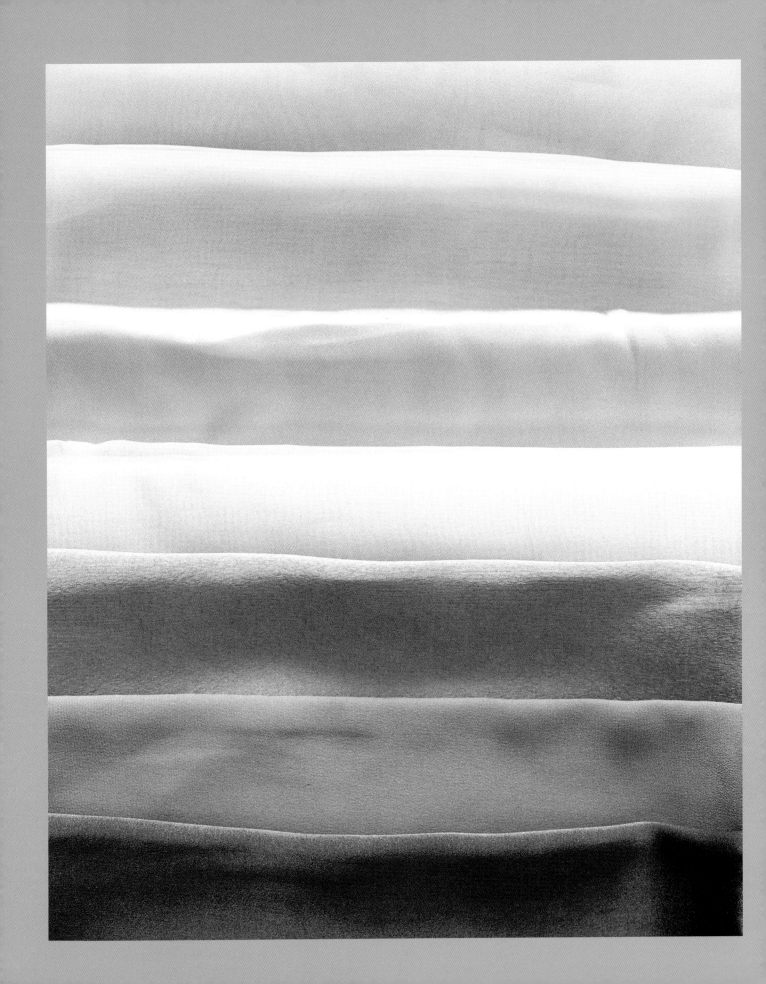

# CHAPTER 2

# PREPARING FABRIC FOR EMBROIDERY

It is very important to properly tension your fabric for tambour beading. Properly tensioned fabric should be drum tight and should distort the fabric weave as little as possible. If your fabric is not tightly tensioned, it will mean that your tambour hook will be more likely to catch on the fabric, making it more difficult to form the stitches, and the fabric is likely to be badly puckered when removed from the frame or hoop.

Always iron your fabric before tensioning it in a frame or hoop. It is important to remove any creases from the fabric before it is embroidered because you will not be able to iron the fabric once beads or sequins have been applied. Even if you have only used decorative chain stitch on a fabric, it cannot be ironed because an iron can flatten the thread.

## SETTING UP A SLATE FRAME

Fabric that is to be tensioned in a slate frame must be cut with as straight lines as possible. When a piece of fabric has straight edges, it will be possible to tension it evenly all the way along the fabric edges. When using silk organza, an easy way of achieving straight edges is to rip the fabric. If you cut into the edge of the fabric by a few centimetres and then pull the fabric either side of the cut, the fabric will easily rip along the grain line.

When using a fabric that does not rip, you will need to ensure that your fabric is ironed to make it as flat as possible. Then lay the fabric right-side down, making sure it is completely flat. You also need to make sure the fabric is laid out so the weave is straight; use the selvedge (the selvedge is the uncut edge of the fabric that is formed at the sides of the fabric as it is woven) of the fabric as a guide, making sure it is straight and then smoothing the rest of the fabric out from the selvedge. If the fabric is fluid or slippery and will not stay in position, you can use masking or washi tape to carefully secure the fabric to the surface onto which you are laying the fabric out. Once the fabric is neatly laid out, mark the desired size onto the fabric with a pencil or a chalk/white-coloured pencil and a ruler. Carefully cut along the lines you have marked with a pair of fabric scissors.

There are different methods to use for setting up a slate frame and there are varying types of slate frames that require different methods to set up. The following instructions apply to a slate frame that has holes in the slats into which pegs are placed to hold the tension of the fabric.

The first time you use a slate frame, you need to mark the centre point on the webbing. To do this, measure from the end of the wooden roller bar to the other end and mark the centre point onto the webbing with a pencil. Then take your fabric and fold it in half; place a pin at the edge of the fabric at the centre point.

At the centre point of the fabric, fold the edge of the fabric over by about 1.5cm (½in). Match up the centre points of the fabric and the webbing and place a pin through both to attach them together.

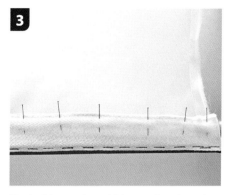

Pin the fabric to the webbing, working from the centre point to one end of the webbing first. Turn the fabric edge over by about 1.5cm (½in) as you go.

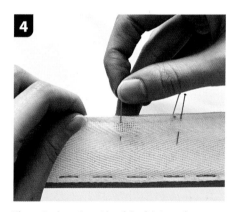

Then pin the other side of the fabric to the webbing, again working from the centre point to the end of the webbing.

Thread a needle with a single length of heavy-duty thread and, beginning about 2cm (¾in) before the centre point, begin to stitch the fabric and webbing together.

Sew towards the end of the webbing.

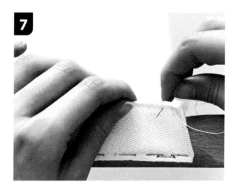

When you reach the end, work a few stitches back for about 2cm (¾in).

Repeat the process of stitching the fabric and webbing together on the opposite side. When you begin, overlap the centre point by 2cm (¾in) so that you are stitching over the previous stitches.

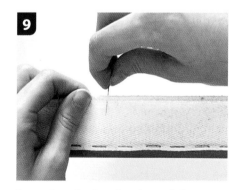

Repeat Steps 5 to 8 on the other end of the fabric.

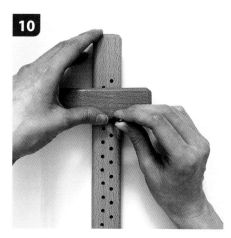

**10**

Using the pins in the slats, begin to tension the fabric by gradually moving the pins up the holes, one hole at a time, until the fabric cannot be stretched any further. You may need to use your foot on the end of the roller bars to help push the bar down so that you can move the peg to the next hole.

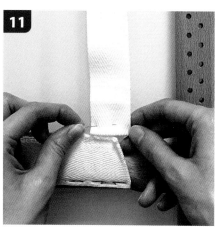

**11**

Fold the end of the herringbone tape over and pin it to the edge of the fabric so it slightly overhangs the edge of the fabric.

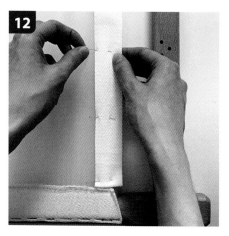

**12**

Continue pinning the tape up the side of the fabric. Then pin tape to the other edge of the fabric.

**13**

Thread a needle with a single length of thread and, beginning at one end of the tape, make a couple of long stitches over each other.

**14**

Then, working along the length of the tape, make diagonal stitches to secure the ribbon to the fabric.

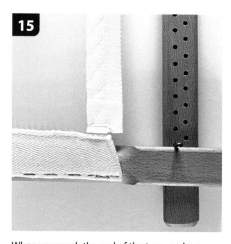

**15**

When you reach the end of the tape, make a few stitches over each other and make a knot to secure the thread. Repeat Steps 13 to 15 to stitch the ribbon to the other side of the fabric.

*continued on the following page…*

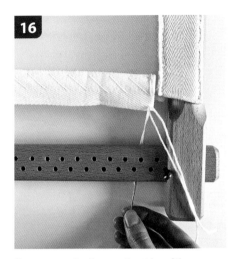

Now you need to lace up the sides of the fabric to tension them. Thread a thick tapestry needle or a curved needle with string. Bring the needle down through the end of the tape and underneath and over the slat.

Bring the needle down through the tape, about 2cm (¾in) away from the last point you brought the needle down. Then bring the thread underneath and over the slat again.

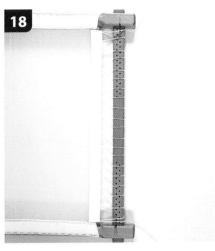

Repeat Step 17 to lace the side of the fabric to the slat until you reach the end of the tape. Then repeat Steps 16 to 17 to lace the other side of the fabric to the other slat.

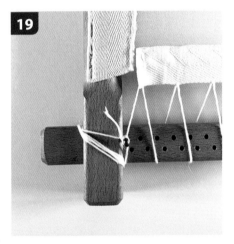

Then wrap one end of the string around the frame and tie it around the peg to secure it. Do the same with one end of the string on the other side of the frame.

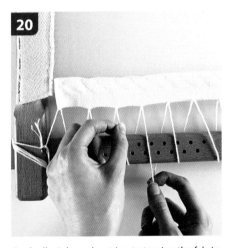

Gradually tighten the string to tension the fabric from either side. Pull the string tighter on both sides of the fabric a little bit each time to evenly tension the fabric. When both sides of the string are pulled tight enough, wrap the end of the string around the frame and tie it around the peg to secure it.

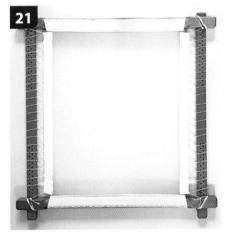

The fabric is now tensioned in the slate frame and ready for embroidery. It will need to be propped on two trestles or similar supporting surfaces.

## Avoiding Tearing Fabric When Tensioning

Although fabric needs to be tightly tensioned for tambour, it can be overstretched, and fine fabrics such as a single layer of organza will begin to tear if stretched too much. When you are moving the pins up the holes, if you start to hear the fabric tearing or see small holes starting to appear where the fabric has been stitched to the webbing, do not stretch the fabric any further.

## USING AN EMBROIDERY HOOP

Although tensioning fabric in an embroidery hoop may seem uncomplicated and self-explanatory, there are a couple of points to note if you will be using a hoop to tension fabric for tambour beading. The fabric needs to be tensioned very carefully to avoid distorting the weave. This is difficult when tensioning fabric in a hoop but try to pull the fabric with as equal a tension as possible from opposite edges of the fabric at the same time. Wrapping the inner hoop with strips of an inexpensive cotton fabric will help the hoop grip the fabric and prevent the tension from being lost as you are embroidering.

Remember that the whole of your embroidery design needs to fit within the size of your hoop. You will not be able to move the hoop around your fabric to embroider other areas of your design because you cannot position the hoop over areas to which you have applied beads or sequins.

## HOW TO TENSION A PIECE OF FABRIC IN AN EMBROIDERY HOOP

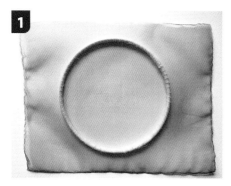

Loosen the screw slightly so the outer hoop slides off the inner hoop. Place the fabric over the inner hoop.

Place the outer hoop on top of the fabric and push it down over the inner hoop. Push the top of the hoop down first where the screw is and then push the bottom of the hoop down.

Tighten the screw slightly but not all the way, and gently pull the fabric from both sides at the same time, trying to avoid distorting the weave of the fabric as much as possible.

The fabric should be tensioned to the point that it is drum tight. When this has been achieved, tighten the screw with a screwdriver as tightly as possible.

## HOOP CLAMPS

Remember you will need to place your hoop in a clamp so you have both hands available for tambour beading. There are several different options of clamps available, including a seat, table or floor clamp. Choose whichever option suits you best and feels the most comfortable for you to work with, and attach the clamp to the top of the hoop.

# CHAPTER 3

# TRANSFERRING A DESIGN TO FABRIC

When working with a design, you need to transfer the design to the fabric. This is very easy to do when working with a sheer fabric such as organza but becomes more challenging when using an opaque fabric, especially a dark-coloured fabric.

Avoid using water-soluble or air-soluble fabric pens, as these can be difficult to completely remove from the fabric. When rinsing an embroidery to remove water-soluble pen, the ink can often spread to other areas of the fabric. It is also often best to avoid water coming into contact with beads and sequins, as it could affect the finishes on them. Air-soluble pens are often not long lasting enough and can disappear before the embroidery is finished. Although the pigment is no longer visible, the ink is still present on the fabric and can reappear in certain weather conditions such as very cold climates.

Always transfer a design after the fabric has been tensioned. When the fabric is tensioned, it is very smooth, and if correctly tensioned, the weave of the fabric will be straight, which will ensure the design is applied accurately. It is important to note that when a fabric is tensioned it is slightly larger than when it is removed from the frame or hoop. Usually a fabric will stretch by a few millimetres when it is tensioned in a slate frame. This means that once the design has been embroidered and the fabric is removed from the frame or hoop, the design will shrink slightly. This is not normally noticeable, except when you are embroidering a design to specific dimensions where the embroidery goes right up to the edges. It is impossible to predict how much the fabric will shrink when removed from tension as it varies each time and for different fabrics.

## TRACING TECHNIQUE

When you are using a sheer fabric that can be easily drawn on, such as organza, you can simply trace the design onto the fabric. You can do this by printing your design onto paper and placing it on the underside of your fabric. You can hold the paper in place or pin it to the fabric. Then you can trace the design onto your fabric by drawing over the design lines on the paper. Use a hard leaded pencil for this, such as a 2H, because this will not smudge, unlike a softer leaded pencil. The pencil lines are also likely to be lighter when using a hard leaded pencil, which means they are less likely to be visible in the finished embroidery. When using a dark sheer fabric on which pencil lines would not be visible, you can use a white-coloured pencil or white chalk pencil. These may be more prone to smudging, so take care when using them.

Beads and sequins are applied with the wrong side of the fabric facing you. When tracing the design onto the fabric, you need to trace it onto the wrong side of the fabric. This means that you need to reverse your design so that the design will be the correct orientation on the right side of the fabric. If you are embroidering a design completely with decorative chain stitch, you can transfer the design to the right side of the fabric, as decorative chain stitch is worked with the right side of the fabric facing you. In this case you do not need to reverse your design.

A design created digitally that has been printed out to use for tracing the design onto a sheer fabric such as organza. The paper design will be pinned to the underside of the fabric and then the design can be drawn onto the fabric with a hard leaded pencil, which is less prone to smudging.

# Prick and Pounce

Prick and pounce is a traditional technique that has been used for centuries to transfer designs to fabric. It involves pricking holes in the paper design and then using a pouncer to push loose pounce powder through the holes to create dots on fabric that indicate the design lines. These can then be permanently marked onto the fabric using either paint or a pen. This is a very versatile way of transferring the design onto fabric as it can be used on any colour of fabric. Pounce powder is available in three colours: white for dark fabrics, grey for medium-toned fabrics and black for light-coloured fabrics. It is also a very accurate method as it is easy to transfer the design lines thinly so that they are not visible on the finished embroidery.

**1** To prepare your design for prick and pounce, you need to prick holes in the design. Print your design on paper or tracing paper.

**2** Place the design on a soft surface, such as a towel or piece of thick felt on top of a cutting mat. Using a fine needle, prick holes along the lines of the design. Make the holes a couple of millimetres apart.

**3** Place your design onto the fabric where you want the design to be transferred. Secure it in place with a few pins.

**4** Dip the pouncer in the pounce powder and tap off the excess.

**5** Rub the pouncer over the design using circular motions. This will push the pounce powder through the holes in the design. Ensure that you cover the whole design with the pouncer, dipping the pouncer in the pounce powder to pick up more as needed.

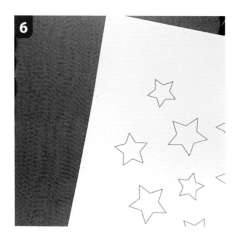

**6** Carefully lift the design straight up and away from the fabric. You should now have dots of pounce powder on the fabric indicating the design.

**7** Using a fine paintbrush, paint over the dots to mark the design lines on the fabric. Alternatively, use a gel pen to draw over the dots.

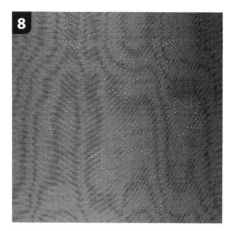

**8** You can paint lines between the dots to create a full outline for your design or you can just paint over the dots as has been done here.

# CHAPTER 4

# CHAIN STITCH

Chain stitch is the stitch type that is formed by the tambour hook. All tambour techniques are variations on this basic chain stitch. It is important, as a beginner, to learn chain stitch first by using only a standard sewing thread and the tambour hook before moving on to using chain stitch to apply beads and sequins. Practise until you are completely comfortable with manipulating the thread with the hook to confidently make a chain stitch in all directions.

In the Appendix, you can find patterns for the shapes used to demonstrate the techniques in this chapter, and for the spring flower design at the end of this chapter.

When the direction 'wrap the thread around the hook' is given in the instructions, you need to wrap the thread all the way around the hook. You can imagine this as the thread making a full circle around the hook. This ensures the thread will catch in the hook when the hook is pulled up through the fabric, to form a loop of thread on the top of the fabric.

It is important to differentiate between what is meant when the 'right' or 'wrong' side of the fabric is specified as opposed to the 'top' or 'bottom' side of the fabric in the instructions. The 'top side' of the fabric refers to the side of the fabric that is currently facing you when you are embroidering, and the 'bottom side' refers to the underside of the fabric as it is currently facing you. 'Right side' refers to the side of the fabric that the front of the embroidery is on and 'wrong side' refers to the back of the embroidery.

Remember that tambour requires you to use both your hands. Your dominant hand will be above the fabric to control the hook and your other hand will be below the fabric to control the thread. The instructions have been written from the perspective of a right-handed person but if you are left-handed you will need to reverse the instructions.

# STARTING STITCH

There is only one way to start your thread with the tambour hook and this same method is used whether you are making a chain stitch or applying beads or sequins. The stitch that is used to start the thread is referred to as a starting stitch. A starting stitch is a small stitch that is worked at the beginning of a line of chain stitch to secure the thread. A starting stitch is comprised of two stitches, one worked forwards and another stitch worked backwards over the top of the previous stitch. You need to make a starting stitch at the beginning of every line of chain stitch you make.

**1**

Begin by forming a loop in your thread by wrapping it around your finger.

**2**

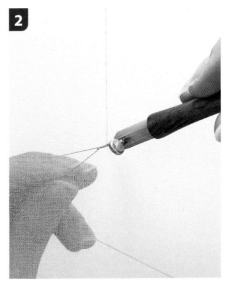

Insert the hook into the fabric where you want to start your line of chain stitch; slide the loop of thread down the hook so that it catches in the hook.

**3**

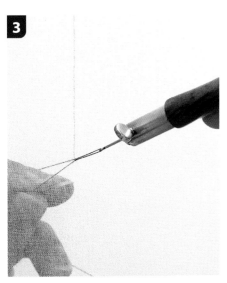

Pull the hook back up through the fabric to pull the thread loop to the right side of the fabric.

**4**

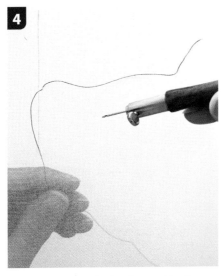

Pull the entire thread tail to the top side of the fabric.

**5**

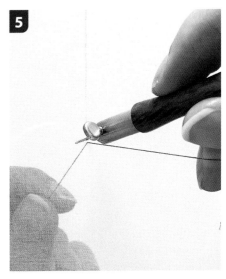

Hold the thread tail in between your fingers and push the hook into the fabric about a millimetre away from where you brought the thread tail up through the fabric.

**6**

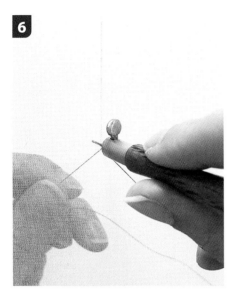

You should push the hook into the fabric with the screw pointing away from you.

**7**

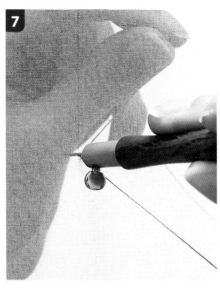

Wrap the thread around the hook in an anticlockwise direction, and at the same time, turn the hook in an anticlockwise direction so the screw is pointing towards you.

**8**

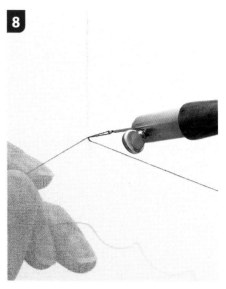

Pull the hook up through the fabric. As you pull the hook up, the thread that you just wrapped around the hook should catch in the hook, which allows it to be pulled through the fabric. There should now be a loop on the right side of the fabric.

**9**

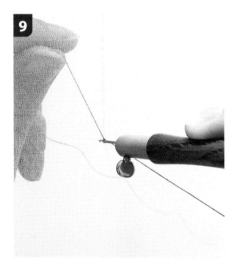

Push the hook into the fabric in the same hole as where you brought the thread tail up through the fabric. The screw should still be pointing towards you.

**10**

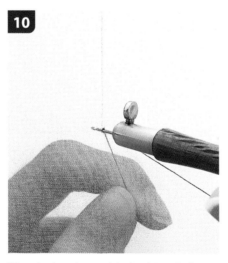

Wrap the thread around the hook in a clockwise direction and turn the hook so the screw points away from you.

**11**

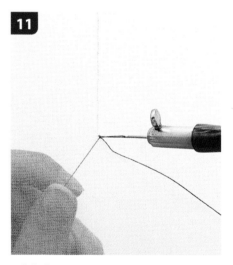

Pull the hook up through the fabric to complete the starting stitch.

### The Angle of the Tambour Hook and the Direction of the Screw on the Tambour Hook

When you insert the hook into fabric and when you are bringing it up through the fabric, you should do this with the hook at a 90-degree angle to the surface of the fabric. This means the hook will be able to pass easily through the fabric without catching on the fabric. It also helps to pay careful attention to which way the screw on the tambour hook is pointing, as this enables you to form the stitches correctly.

# How to Make a Chain Stitch with the Tambour Hook

After you have made a starting stitch you can begin to work a chain stitch. You are going to work the chain stitch away from yourself.

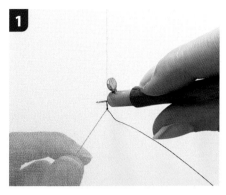

To make the first chain stitch, push the hook into the fabric with the screw pointing away from you. Where you push the hook into the fabric will determine the length of the chain stitch; the chain stitch can be as long or short as you like.

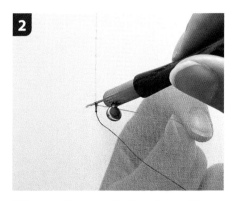

At the same time, wrap the thread around the hook in an anticlockwise direction and turn the hook in an anticlockwise direction so that the screw is pointing towards you.

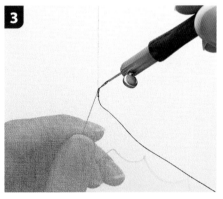

Bring the hook up through the fabric to complete the first chain stitch.

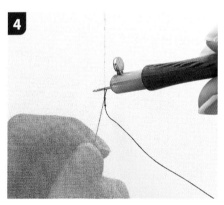

To make a second chain stitch, push the hook into the fabric with the screw pointing away from you. To do this, you should turn the hook while ensuring that the loop of thread remains caught in the hook. Try to make this chain stitch the same length as the previous chain stitch.

Then wrap the thread around the hook in an anticlockwise direction and turn the hook so that the screw is pointing towards you.

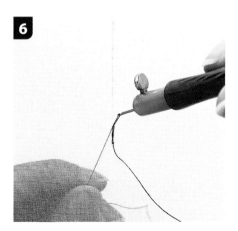

Pull the hook up through the fabric to complete the chain stitch.

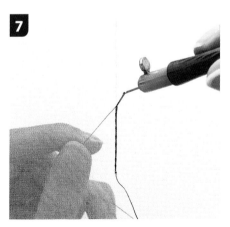

To make more chain stitches, repeat Steps 4 to 6. Remember when you are working chain stitch away from yourself to always wrap the thread around the hook and turn the hook in an anticlockwise direction.

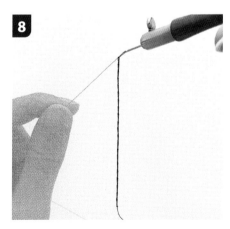

Continue making chain stitches until you have reached the end of the line.

# FINISHING STITCH AND FINISHING THE THREAD ENDS

## MAKING A FINISHING STITCH

A finishing stitch is simply a small chain stitch that secures the end of a line of chain stitch so that the stitching does not unravel.

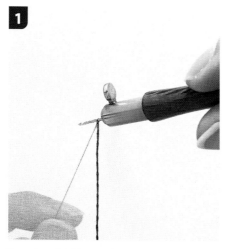

To make a finishing stitch, push the hook into the fabric about 1–2mm away from the end of the line of chain stitch. The screw should be pointing away from you.

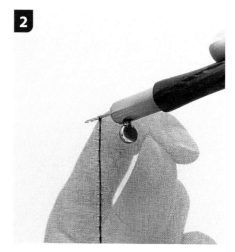

Wrap the thread around the hook and at the same time turn the hook so the screw is pointing towards you.

Bring the hook up to form the finishing stitch.

Cut the thread, leaving a tail of about 10cm (4in). Then pull the whole thread tail to the top side of the fabric.

## HOW TO FINISH THE THREAD ENDS

Once you have finished a line of chain stitch, you will be left with two thread tails at the start and end of the chain stitch. These ends need to be neatly finished to further ensure the chain stitch will not unravel. There are several different ways to finish the thread ends; the following method is perhaps a little more time consuming and fiddly than most but it is also the neatest and most secure.

If you have two thread ends close to each other, for example if you have started and finished the chain stitch into the same point, you can finish both of the thread ends at the same time.

### Bringing the Thread Ends to the Wrong Side of the Fabric

The first stage of finishing the thread ends is dependent on whether you are finishing the thread ends of chain stitch or beads or sequins because thread ends need to be finished on the wrong side of the fabric. With a line of beads or sequins, the thread ends will already be on the wrong side. However, with a line of decorative chain stitch, the thread ends will be on the right side of the fabric so you need to take them to the wrong side.

**1**

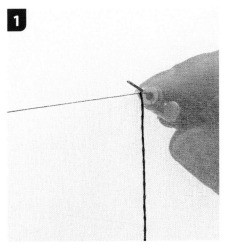

If you need to bring the thread ends to the wrong side of the fabric, place the fabric with the right side facing you and from underneath the fabric insert the hook at one of the ends of the chain stitch.

**2**

Then take the thread end and wrap it around the hook.

**3**

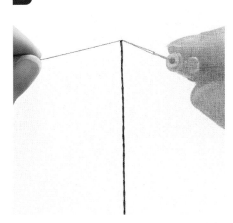

Pull the hook down through the fabric to pull the whole thread end to the wrong side of the fabric.

**4**

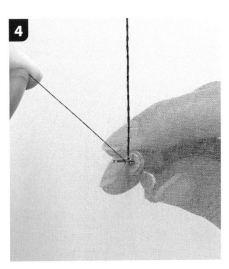

Repeat Steps 1 to 3 with the thread tail at the other end of the chain stitch line.

**5**

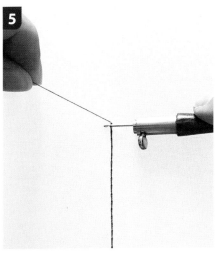

Turn the fabric over so the wrong side is facing you. Slide the hook underneath the back of the last chain stitch.

**6**

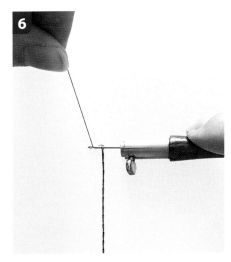

Bring the thread tail underneath and over the hook.

**7**

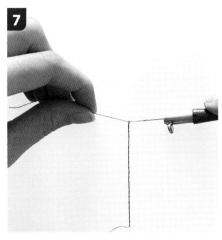

Pull the hook backwards to slide it out from under the chain stitch to pull the thread tail through the chain stitch to make a loop.

**8**

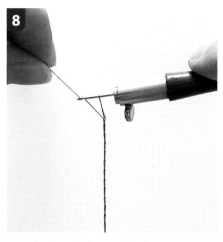

Wrap the thread tail around the hook.

**9**

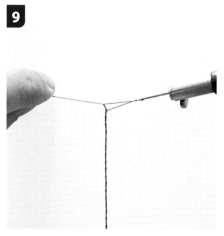

Angling the hook downwards, slide the hook backwards to pull the thread tail through the loop.

**10**

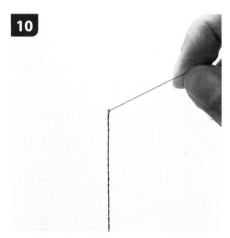

Pull the thread tail all the way through the loop and pull the tail to tighten the loop. This creates a locking stitch with the thread tail.

**11**

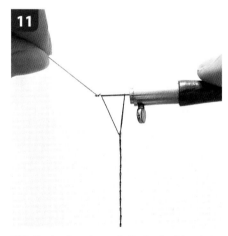

Slide the hook underneath the back of the chain stitch once again and repeat Steps 5 to 10.

**12**

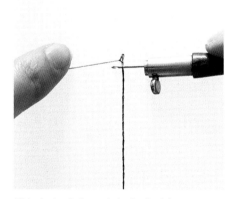

Slide the hook through the back of the next chain stitch and repeat Steps 5 to 10 to make the final locking stitch.

**13**

Cut the thread tail close to the stitching and apply a small dab of glue to the thread end to secure it.

**14**

Then repeat Steps 5 to 13 with the other thread tail. You should now have a completed line of chain stitch.

## Practising Chain Stitch

### Practising How to Make a Chain Stitch in All Directions

It is important to know how to work chain stitch in all directions, as when you are working a design, more often than not, you will need to work chain stitch in many different directions. Practising working chain stitch around a variety of shapes will help you to become familiar with the direction in which you need to wrap the thread around the hook and twist the hook when working in different directions. A good way to practise chain stitch in different directions is to work a chain stitch around a variety of shapes.

### Working Chain Stitch towards Yourself

To practise working chain stitch in different directions, begin with working a straight line of chain stitch towards yourself. To do this you need to do the reverse of the directions you used when working a line of chain stitch away from yourself.

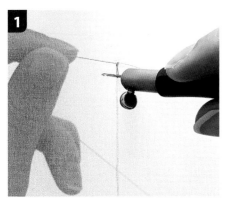

After making a starting stitch, make the first chain stitch by pushing the hook into the fabric with the screw pointing towards you.

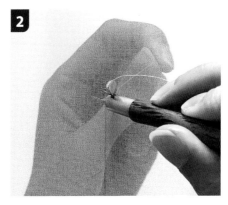

At the same time, wrap the thread around the hook in a clockwise direction and turn the hook in a clockwise direction so that the screw is pointing away from you.

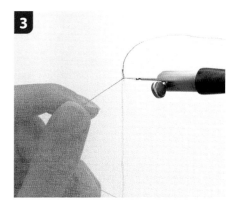

Bring the hook up through the fabric to complete the first chain stitch.

To make a second chain stitch, push the hook into the fabric with the screw pointing towards you. To do this, you should turn the hook while ensuring that the loop of thread remains caught in the hook. Try to make this chain stitch the same length as the previous chain stitch.

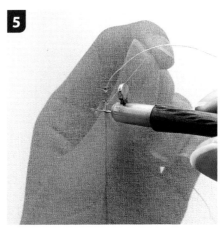

Then wrap the thread around the hook in a clockwise direction and turn the hook so that the screw is pointing away from you.

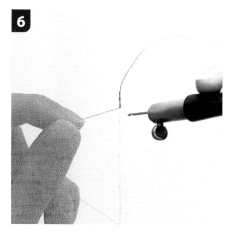

**6**

Pull the hook up through the fabric to complete the chain stitch.

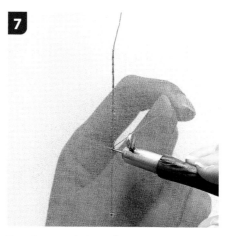

**7**

To make more chain stitches, repeat Steps 4 to 6. Remember when you are working chain stitch towards yourself to always wrap the thread around the hook and turn the hook in a clockwise direction.

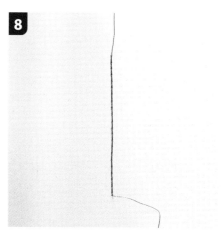

**8**

Continue repeating Steps 4 to 6 to make more chain stitches. Then make a finishing stitch at the end of the line of chain stitches.

## CHAIN STITCH AROUND A CIRCLE

Working chain stitch around a circle is a brilliant way to use chain stitch in every possible direction. Practise this as many times as you like until you are confident with how to create a chain stitch in every direction.

When figuring out which way to turn the hook and wrap the thread around the hook, it can help to view the circle in two sections: for the right section you need to reference working a line away from yourself; for the left section you can reference working a line towards yourself.

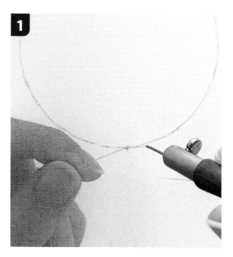

**1**

Trace a circle onto your fabric. Begin the chain stitch by making a starting stitch at the bottom centre of the circle.

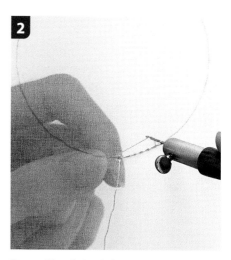

**2**

Start making chain stitches, paying attention to the direction in which you are wrapping the thread around the hook and turning the hook to make the chain stitches.

*continued on the following page…*

**3**

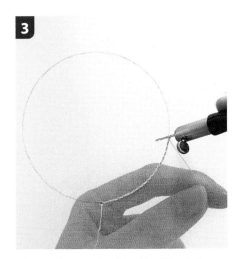

When working up the right side of the circle, you can wrap the thread around the hook in an anticlockwise direction and turn the hook in an anticlockwise direction to make the chain stitches.

**4**

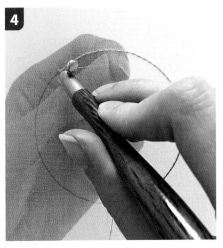

When you reach the top of the circle and start working down the left side of the circle, you can wrap the thread around the hook in a clockwise direction and turn the hook in a clockwise direction.

**5**

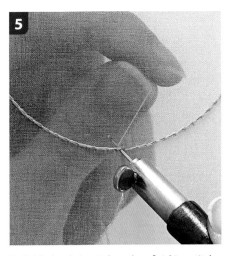

To finish the chain stitch, make a finishing stitch into the same hole as where you began the chain stitch.

**6**

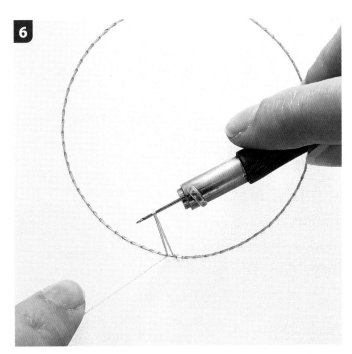

Finish the thread ends on the wrong side of the chain stitch to complete the circle.

**7**

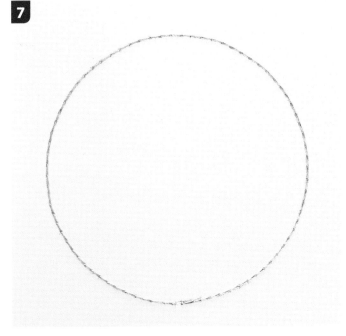

The circle of chain stitch is now complete.

# How to Make Sharp Corners with Chain Stitch

In a design that contains corners, you need to pay special attention to how you work the chain stitch at the corners to create a sharp, defined corner. This is achieved by making a small locking stitch at a corner.

## Chain Stitching a Star

Making sharp corners with chain stitch can be practised by working a chain stitch around a star shape.

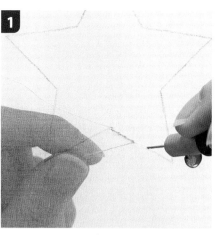

Trace a star onto your fabric and make a starting stitch. Then work chain stitch towards the corner.

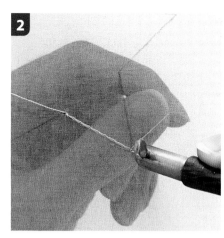

When you reach the corner, push the hook down a short distance away from the last chain stitch you made to make a tiny chain stitch. This makes a locking stitch at the corner.

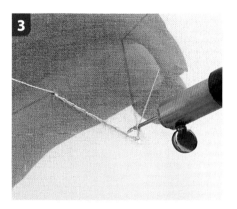

You can then draw the loop of thread in the hook back to begin working along the next line, and make a chain stitch of the normal length.

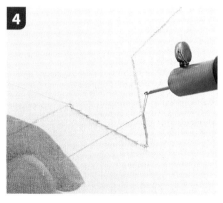

The tiny chain stitch that you made at the corner should anchor the corner in place to create a defined corner.

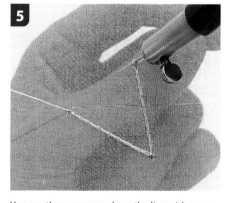

You can then progress along the line with more chain stitches until you reach the next corner. Work this corner in the same way as before, creating a tiny chain stitch at the corner.

Then continue creating normal-sized chain stitches up to the next corner and repeat the process of making a tiny chain stitch at each corner until the shape is complete.

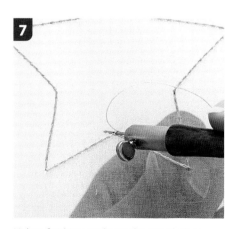

Make a finishing stitch into the same hole as where you started the chain stitch.

Finish the thread ends on the wrong side of the star to complete the chain stitch star.

# FILLING A SHAPE WITH CHAIN STITCH

Filling a shape with chain stitch is a lovely way to use the stitch decoratively. You can practise filling a shape with chain stitch with this simple heart shape.

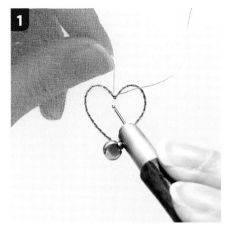

Outline the heart with chain stitch. Remember to make a locking stitch at the point at the bottom of the heart. When you reach the point where you started, make a locking stitch into the same hole as your first chain stitch.

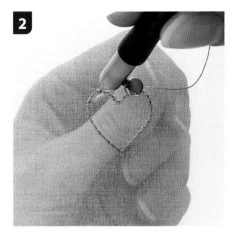

Now begin making chain stitches inside the outline. At the top of the curve, you need to make the chain stitches very close to the chain stitched outline, otherwise as you move around the curve, the lines of chain stitches will pull apart, which will leave a gap between them.

Continue around the heart, making sure your lines of chain stitch are close together so there is no gap between them. Make a locking stitch at the top of the heart.

Continue making chain stitches inside the previous chain stitches to gradually fill the shape. Keep making sure there are no gaps between your lines of chain stitches.

Continue filling the heart until you have only a small space left. As the shape gets smaller, the curves on the heart change into points; you will need to make locking stitches at the top of these points.

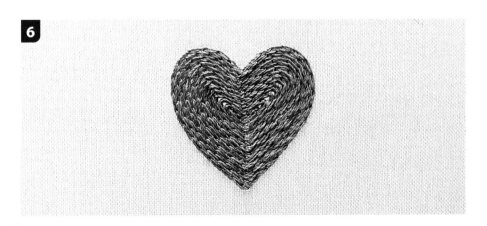

Continue until the heart is completely filled, then pull the thread ends to the wrong side and finish them to complete the heart.

# PRACTICE DESIGN – SPRING FLOWERS PART 1

## CHAIN STITCH LILY OF THE VALLEY

This small flower design allows you to practise your chain stitch skills. It is a great way to practise working chain stitch in all directions and features a variety of shapes that are either outlined or filled with chain stitch. When embroidering this design, you should pay attention to the length of your chain stitches and try to keep them as even as possible. This chain stitch lily of the valley is the first part of a larger design that is continued at the end of Chapter 5: Applying Beads and Chapter 6: Applying Sequins. You can choose to work the practice designs at the end of the next two chapters to complete the design or embroider the lily of the valley as a single practice flower.

Before you begin the embroidery, you need to transfer the design to the fabric by tracing it with a pencil. Then turn the fabric over to the right side for the embroidery.

### Materials
White silk organza
White rayon thread
Light green *Fil à gant* thread

The finished practice design part 1. Featuring a chain stitch lily of the valley, this practice design will help you to solidify the chain stitch skills you have learned in this chapter. When combined with the other two practice designs at the end of the next two chapters, this makes up one design featuring three spring flowers.

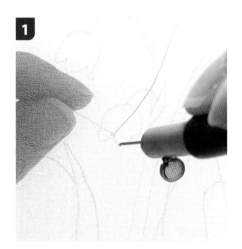

Starting with the lowest flower on the stem, using the white rayon thread, make a starting stitch at the top of the petal.

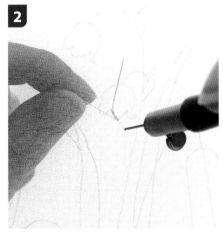

Make chain stitches along the outline of the flower, down to the point of the petal, and then make a locking stitch at the point.

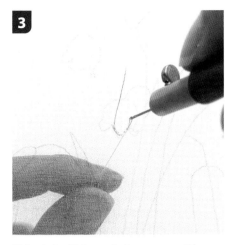

Make chain stitches up to the corner and then make a locking stitch.

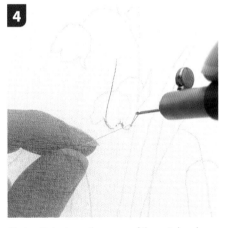

Chain stitch along the curve of the petal and make a locking stitch at the point of the petal.

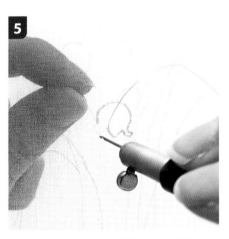

Make chain stitches around the curve of the top of the flower and then make a locking stitch when you reach the bend in the outline.

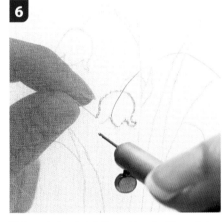

Make a chain stitch followed by a locking stitch at the next bend in the petal.

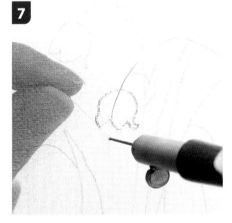

Make one chain stitch and then a locking stitch at the corner.

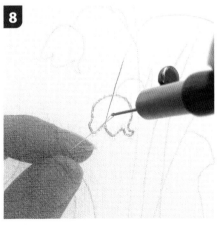

Chain stitch along the remaining outline until you reach the point where you made the starting stitch. Then make a locking stitch into the same hole as the starting stitch.

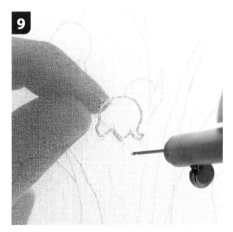

Then begin working another line of chain stitch very close to the chain stitch you made around the outline. Remember to make a locking stitch at the change of direction.

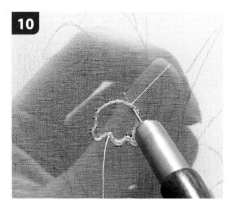

**10**

When you are making the chain stitch along the curve at the top of the flower, make sure you push the hook in as close as you can get to the previous chain stitches to ensure you do not get a large gap between the lines of chain stitch.

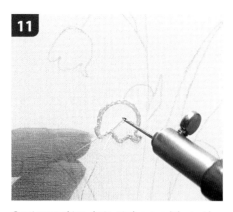

**11**

Continue making chain stitch around the inside of the previous line of chain stitch until you reach the point where you started.

**12**

Continue making chain stitch inside the previous lines of chain stitch, working around the shape in a spiral.

**13**

Chain stitch around the outline of the next flower above the flower you have just filled with chain stitch. Make a finishing stitch into the same hole as your starting stitch.

**14**

Fill the flower above the previous one with chain stitch.

**15**

Chain stitch around the outline of the next flower.

**16**

Fill the remaining flower with chain stitch.

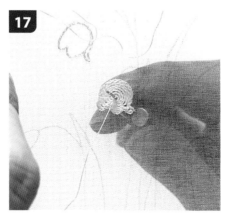

**17**

Insert the hook up through the fabric to bring the thread tails to the wrong side of the fabric.

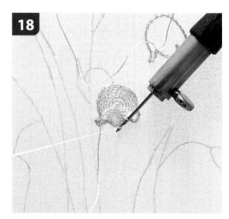

**18**

Turn the fabric over to the wrong side and insert the hook through the back of the chain stitches to finish the thread tails.

*continued on the following page…*

With the green thread, make a starting stitch at the bottom of the stem.

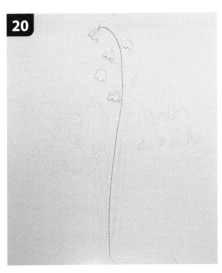

Then chain stitch all the way up the stem until you meet the flower. Make a finishing stitch very close to the flower.

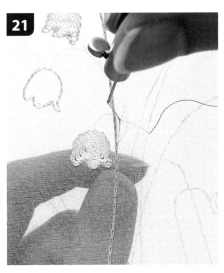

To embroider the stem for the bottom flower, make a starting stitch at the end of the stem that is furthest away from the flower.

Chain stitch along the stem and make a finishing stitch very close to the flower.

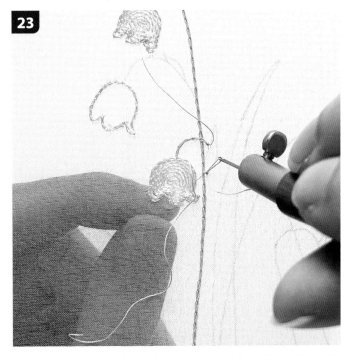

Next make a starting stitch very close to the stem at the bottom of the leaf.

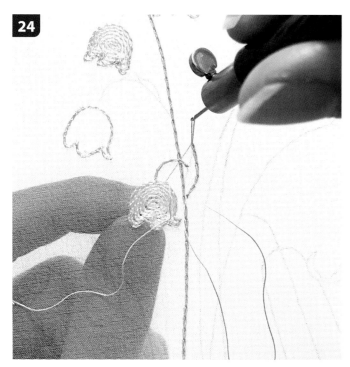

Then make chain stitches up the right side of the leaf and make a locking stitch at the tip of the leaf.

Chain stitch down the other side of the leaf and make a finishing stitch very close to the stem.

Chain stitch the other two leaves in the same way, starting at the bottom of the leaf each time.

Starting at the end of the stem that is closest to the main stem each time, chain stitch the three remaining sections of the stem. Bring the thread tails to the wrong side of the fabric and finish them on the back to complete the embroidery.

# CHAPTER 5

# APPLYING BEADS

Beads are applied to the fabric using the tambour chain stitch. The beads are strung onto the thread that will be used to apply them. The beads are then pushed up the thread one by one with the hand that controls the thread underneath the fabric, and each bead is secured in place with a single chain stitch.

When you are applying beads with the tambour hook, you will be working with the wrong side of the fabric facing you. The beads are applied to the right side of the fabric, which while you are working, is the underneath of the fabric. This means you need to get used to the feel of the beads and learn how to recognize if you have picked up more than one at a time. Of course, when working on a sheer fabric, you will be able to see the beads through the fabric, but it is faster to be able to do this by touch.

In the Appendix, you can find patterns for the shapes used to demonstrate the techniques in this chapter, and for the spring flower design at the end of this chapter.

## TRANSFERRING STRUNG BEADS TO THE WORKING THREAD

To apply beads with the tambour hook, you first need to transfer your strung beads to the thread that you will be using to apply the beads to the fabric. If you are working with loose beads, you will need to string these onto thread first.

**1**

Take a length of strung beads and the end of the thread that you will be using to apply the beads. Tie the end of the thread that contains the strung beads around the thread with which you will be applying the beads with a simple knot.

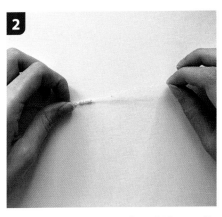

**2**

Leave a long tail of the thread, to which you will transfer the beads, to ensure it does not fall out of the knot, and fold the thread tail back on itself.

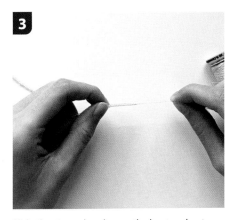

**3**

Slide the strung beads over the knot and onto the thread. As you do this, be very careful not to detach the two threads from each other, as this is easily done and can mean that a lot of the beads fall off the thread and then need to be restrung.

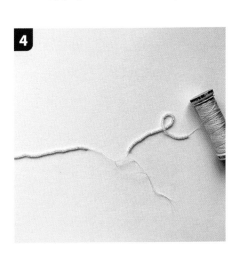

**4**

Continue sliding beads over the knot from one thread to the other until you have transferred enough beads to work with.

Slide the knot from the strung beads off the thread and your beads are now ready to be applied to fabric.

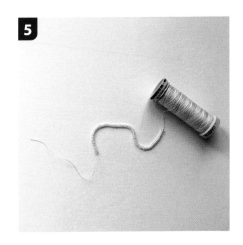

**5**

## IF THE THREAD CONTAINING THE BEADS IS NOT LONG ENOUGH TO TIE IN A KNOT

If the thread onto which the beads is strung is too short to tie in a knot to attach to the thread that you will be applying the beads with, you can use your tambour hook to attach the two threads together to allow you to easily transfer the beads from one thread to the other.

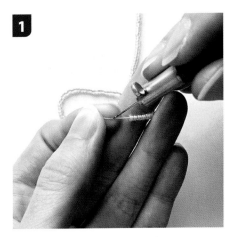

**1**

Push the hook through the thread containing the beads to pierce it.

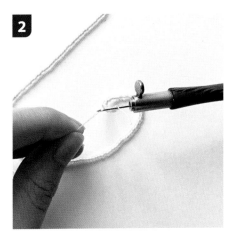

**2**

Take the thread that you will be using to apply the beads and make a loop. Catch this loop in the tambour hook.

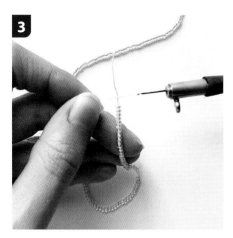

**3**

Pull the tambour hook back to pull the loop of thread through the thread containing the beads.

Begin sliding the beads onto the thread. Continue transferring beads until you have enough and then remove the thread from the centre of the thread containing the strung beads.

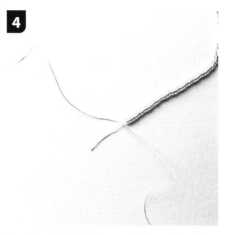

**4**

The thread with which you will be applying the beads should now be attached to the thread onto which the beads are strung.

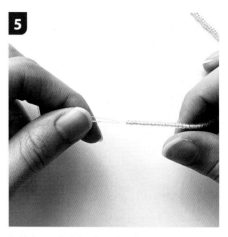

**5**

Fold the end of the thread with which you will be applying the beads back on itself.

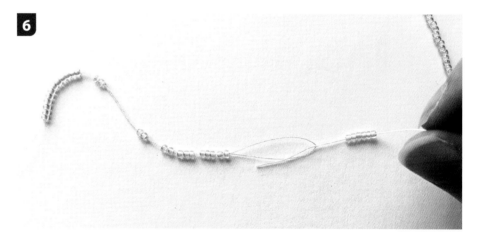

**6**

## REMOVING BROKEN OR DAMAGED BEADS

Before you start transferring beads to the thread with which you will be applying them, you should check the string of beads to make sure there are no damaged or flawed beads. It is especially important to check bugle beads because these are more likely to be damaged. Often bugle beads are chipped at the ends, which makes them very sharp; if you apply these broken beads to your fabric, they can break the thread, which will cause your embroidery to unravel.

If there are damaged beads, instead of cutting the thread to slide the bead off, you can remove the damaged bead individually. Using a pair of flat pliers, place the pliers over the bead and carefully squeeze the pliers together to crush the bead. The bead will shatter into several pieces, removing it from the thread. Cover the end of the pliers with your other hand while you are breaking the bead to catch the pieces of the bead and to stop any sharp pieces from hitting your face. This will only work with glass beads, which will shatter under the pressure fairly easily; plastic beads are stronger and often more resistant to breaking. Only break beads on the thread that they are strung onto *before* you transfer them to another thread and start applying

the beads to your fabric. This is because crushing the beads can damage or break the thread.

If you need to remove beads that you have applied to your fabric, place a pin through the centre of the bead you want to remove and then crush the bead with pliers. The pin protects the thread and prevents it from breaking. The stitch that was made to apply the bead will be left on the fabric. This can be useful if you are able to cover the stitches left behind with embroidery because it means rather than undoing a whole line of beads you can retain the beads you want to keep and save the work you have done in applying them.

# HOW TO APPLY BEADS WITH THE TAMBOUR HOOK

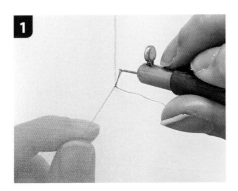

Draw a straight line on your fabric and begin by making a starting stitch.

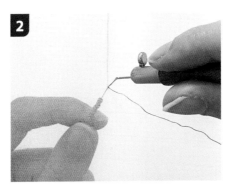

On the underside of the fabric, with the hand that is controlling the thread, take several beads and slide them up the thread, leaving a small gap from the fabric. Hold these beads in your hand as you work. When all these beads have been used, slide several more beads up the thread and keep doing this as the beads are used up.

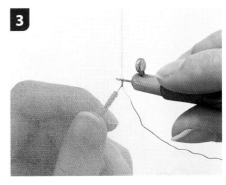

Insert the hook into the fabric, with the screw pointing away from you, to make a chain stitch slightly longer than the length of the bead.

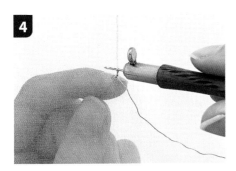

With your finger, slide one bead up the thread so that it is touching the fabric.

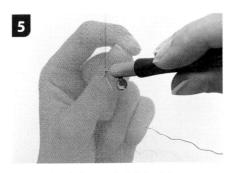

Hold the bead close to the fabric while you wrap the thread around the hook in an anticlockwise direction and turn the hook in an anticlockwise direction so that the screw is pointing towards you.

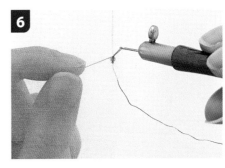

Pull the hook up to form the chain stitch. You should now have one bead that is held in place by the chain stitch.

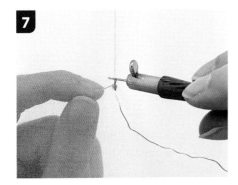

Push the hook into the fabric with the screw pointing away from you. Make sure this chain stitch is the same length as the previous one.

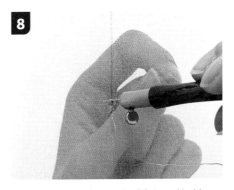

Slide another bead up to the fabric and hold it there while you wrap the thread around the hook in an anticlockwise direction and turn the hook in an anticlockwise direction.

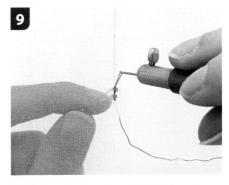

Pull the hook up to make a chain stitch and secure the bead.

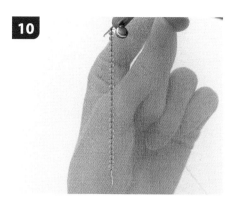

**10**

Repeat Steps 4 to 7 to continue applying beads to the fabric and make a finishing stitch at the end of the line of beads.

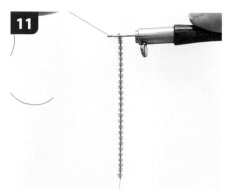

**11**

Finish the thread ends at the back of the beads.

**12**

The line of beads is now complete.

## PERFECTING THE SPACING OF BEADS

When applying beads to the fabric, you must make the chain stitch slightly longer than the length of the bead to leave a small gap between each bead. This is because when you remove the fabric from tension, the fabric relaxes and contracts a little bit. This decreases the space between the beads and pushes them together slightly. If you have not left enough space between the beads when you apply them, this will mean that the beads are too close together. This will cause the beads to push against each other, which will mean that what was a straight line when the fabric was under tension will become a wobbly line when the fabric is released from tension.

## APPLYING BUGLE BEADS

Although bugle beads can often be much longer than other types of beads, they are applied using the same method. As with all other types of beads, make the chain stitch slightly longer than the length of the bugle bead to leave a small gap between the beads. This will ensure that a straight line of bugle beads will remain straight when the fabric is removed from tension.

As you work through all the techniques in this chapter and practise the skills, keep in mind the spacing of your beads. There should be a little space between them to ensure they do not become too close together when the embroidery is removed from the tension of a frame or hoop.

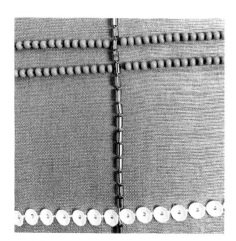

Bugle beads are available in numerous different lengths, from quite short or very long. However, as is done in this line of bugle beads featured on a cushion, no matter the length of the bugle bead, you should keep the spacing between the beads the same as if you were applying round beads.

# How to Make a Corner with Beads

Sharp corners can easily be achieved with beads by making a series of small chain stitches to position the beads so that they create a neat corner.

## Applying Beads to a Triangle

Creating corners with beads can be practised when applying beads to a triangle shape. This allows you to practise applying beads to a right-angle corner as well as a sharper corner.

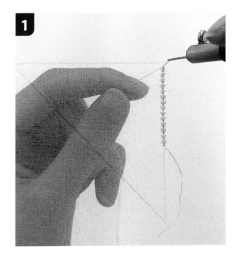

Trace a triangle onto your fabric and make a starting stitch in the centre of one of the edges of the triangle. Start applying beads up to the first corner.

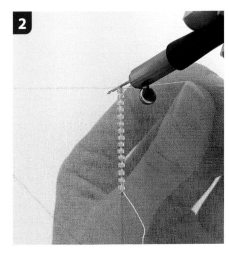

When you reach the corner, apply a bead so that the centre of the bead meets the next line of the triangle.

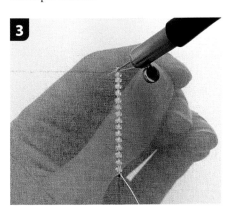

Make a small locking stitch at the end of the line of beads.

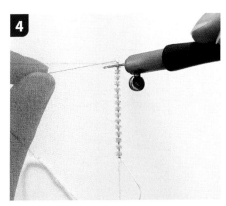

Insert the hook next to the centre of the last bead, quite close to the bead.

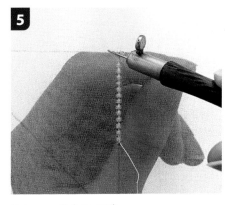

Make a small chain stitch.

Now working along the next line of the triangle, apply beads until you reach the next corner.

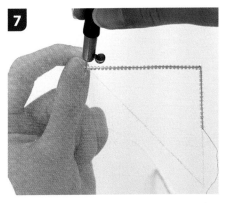

Even though this corner is sharper, it is worked in the same way as before: apply one more bead so that the centre of the bead meets the next line of the triangle.

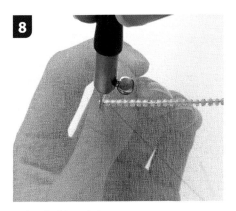

Make a locking stitch.

**9**

Then make a small chain stitch close to the centre of the last bead you applied.

**10**

Continue applying beads. When you reach the next corner of the triangle, repeat Steps 7 to 9, then continue applying beads.

**11**

When you have nearly reached the point where you began applying beads, apply one or two more beads to meet the starting point. Make sure you keep the spacing of these beads as even as possible so that the end of the line blends seamlessly into the beginning.

**12**

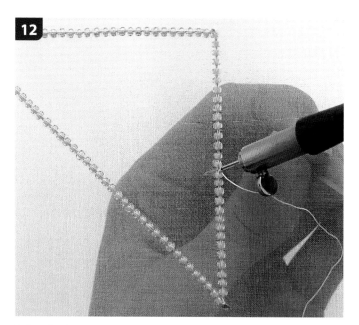

Make a finishing stitch into the same hole as the starting stitch and finish the thread ends.

**13**

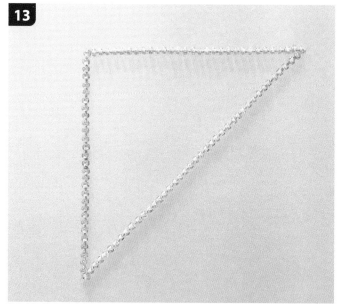

You should now have a completed beaded triangle with the beads forming neatly defined corners.

---

## Adjusting the Spacing of Beads

When you have a shape where the start and end points meet, and you have nearly reached the end of the shape, you must assess how much space you have left to determine how many beads you can apply to finish the shape. To neatly space the beads at the end of the shape you may need to undo a couple of your previous chain stitches and then shorten or lengthen them slightly to make more or less room for the last beads.

## Filling a Shape with Concentric Shapes

A simple way of filling a shape is to begin at the outside edge of the shape and work inwards, creating gradually smaller shapes until the area is filled. This technique can be used with beads, sequins or thread. This filling technique is explained in the following tutorial, with the example of a shape with a point, such as a teardrop shape. Do not forget that when you remove the fabric from the frame or hoop, it will relax slightly, which will mean the space between the lines of beads filling the shape will move closer together. You can therefore leave a slight gap between the lines of beads.

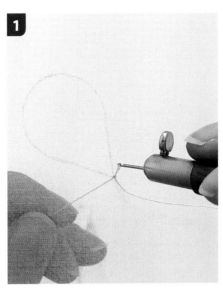

Trace a teardrop shape onto your fabric. Make a starting stitch just before the point of the shape. This means that the centre of the first bead you apply will sit adjacent to the line meeting it.

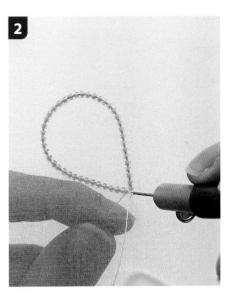

Apply beads around the edge of the shape until you reach the starting point; make a locking stitch at the end of the line of beads.

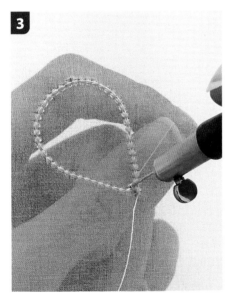

Make a small chain stitch to just above the centre of the last bead you applied.

Apply a bead, making sure it sits next to the previous row of beads without a large gap between them.

Then continue applying beads close to the previous line of beads, making sure the two lines of beads are spaced evenly apart around the whole of the shape.

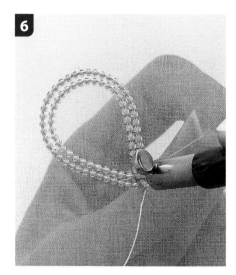

**6** Apply more beads until you reach the first bead you applied in this row; make a locking stitch at the end of the line beads.

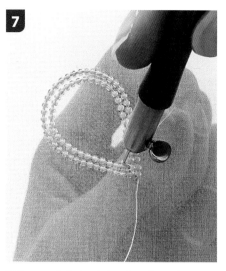

**7** Make a small chain stitch to just above the centre of the last bead you applied.

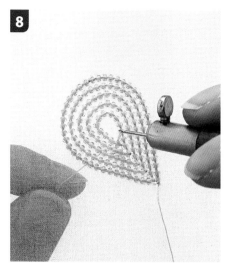

**8** Repeat Steps 4 to 7 to apply more lines of beads to gradually fill the shape.

**9** When you have only a very small space left in the centre of the shape, you will only need to apply a few more beads to fill the space.

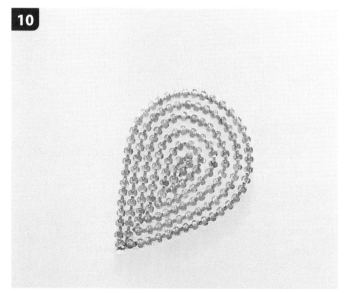

**10** Finish by making a locking stitch and finishing the thread ends. The shape should now be completely filled with beads.

## The Spacing of the Lines of Beads When Filling Shapes

When applying beads inside a curve, you may need to make your chain stitches slightly longer and closer to the previous line of beads. This is because as you progress around the curve, the stitches can slightly pull away from the previous line of beads and therefore get pushed closer together. Remember that the fabric will relax when you remove it from tension, which will push your lines of beads closer together, reducing the gap between the beads.

# FILLING A CIRCLE SHAPE

When filling a shape that does not have a point, such as a circle, you need to use small chain stitches at slightly different angles to get the thread to the right position to start the next line of beads.

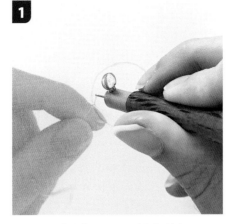
Trace a small circle onto your fabric. Make a starting stitch at the edge of the circle.

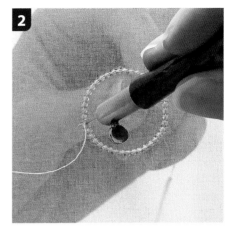
Apply beads all around the circle until you reach the first bead. Apply the last bead so that it meets the first bead with a small gap between them.

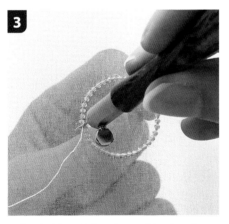
Make a locking stitch at the outside edge of the circle.

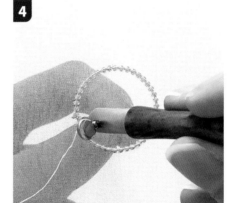
Make a small chain stitch across into the circle. Make this long enough to leave a gap for the next row of beads to be applied.

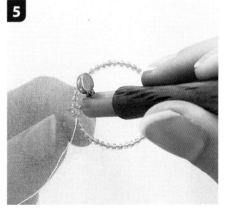
Push the hook into the fabric to make a chain stitch upwards to apply a bead.

Apply the bead, making sure it sits alongside the previous beads without a gap between them.

Apply more beads, making sure you retain the same spacing between the two rows of beads as you progress around the circle.

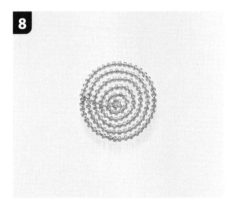
Repeat Steps 2 to 7 to fill the shape with beads, working each line of beads in a complete circle before starting the next line.

# PRACTICE DESIGN – SPRING FLOWERS PART 2

## BEADED BLUEBELL

This design featuring bluebells demonstrates how beads on their own can be used to embroider a complete design. There are several different shapes included in this design, which gives ample opportunity for practising techniques such as making corners with beads and filling shapes. Embroidering this design should also help you to begin to understand the order of how you should embroider a beaded design. This design features shapes that are outlined and filled in different shades and sections that overlap, such as the stem and leaf; these need to be embroidered in a particular order. It also shows how colour can be used in a design to denote separate details and add variety to a design. For example, different shades of beads have been used for the outlines and to fill the petals, and two different shades of green have been used to embroider the leaf and stem.

## Materials
White silk organza
Toho dark green silver-lined beads 15
Toho mid-green silver-lined beads 15
Toho light purple beads 15
Toho mid-purple beads 15
Cotton threads in colours to match the beads

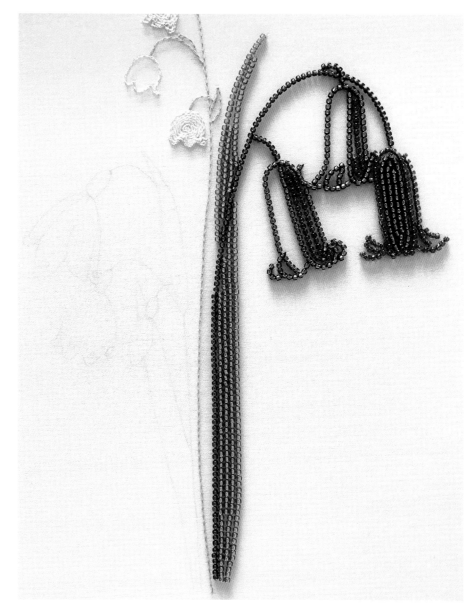

The finished practice design part 2. Featuring a bluebell embroidered entirely in beads, this practice design builds on what you have learned in this chapter and shows you how to approach applying these techniques to a design.

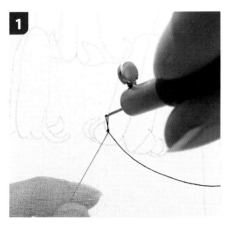

**1** Transfer the mid-purple beads to matching thread. On the flower closest to the stem, make a starting stitch at the end of the line where the petal is turned up.

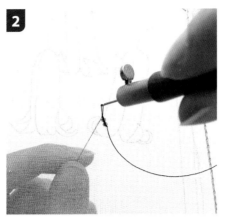

**2** Apply beads up to the point of the petal. Make a locking stitch after the last bead.

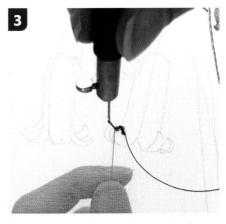

**3** To form a corner at the tip of the petal, make a small chain stitch downwards, close to the last bead. Then apply a bead along the next line of the petal.

**4** Apply beads along the curve at the bottom of the petal and up the line in the centre of the petal, stopping just before the top outline of the flower. Make two small chain stitches to the outline.

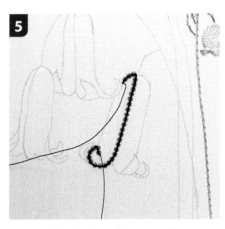

**5** Then apply beads along the curve at the top of the flower, stopping when you meet the overlapping petal. Make a finishing stitch at the end of the beads.

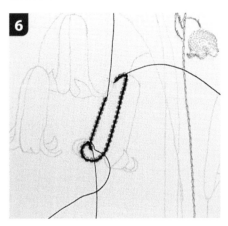

**6** Starting underneath the overlapping petal, apply beads down the line on the left of the flower.

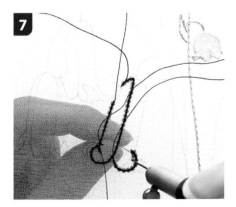

**7** Starting next to the central line on the flower, apply beads along the curve of the petal on the right. Make a locking stitch when you reach the tip of the petal, then a small chain stitch downwards, close to the bead.

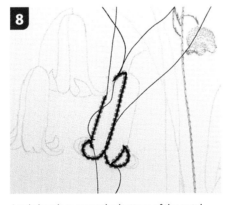

**8** Apply beads to meet the bottom of the petal.

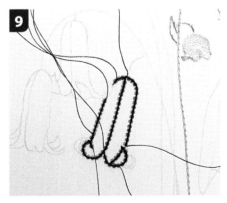

**9** Starting above the tip of the right petal, apply beads along the outline on the right of the flower. Make sure the beads meet at the top of the curve so that it looks like a continuous line.

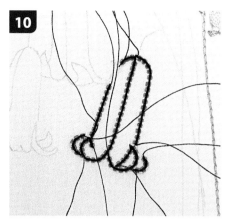

**10**

Starting at the tips of the petals, apply a line of beads to the small petals on either side of the flower.

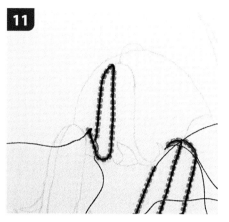

**11**

Starting from the tip of the petal, apply the mid-purple beads around the outline of the petal on the left of the middle flower.

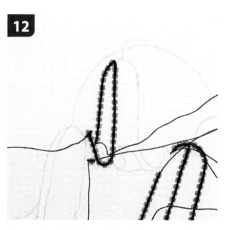

**12**

Apply a bead to the outline at the base of the left petal.

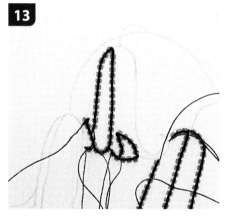

**13**

Starting next to the central line of beads, apply beads around the petal at the base of the flower.

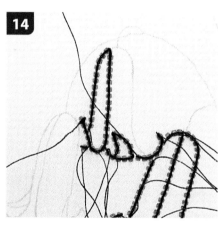

**14**

Starting next to the outline of the last petal you applied beads to, apply a line of beads along the petal on the right of the flower.

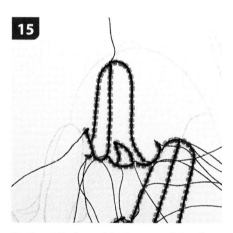

**15**

Starting at the base of the flower, apply beads along the outline on the right of the flower.

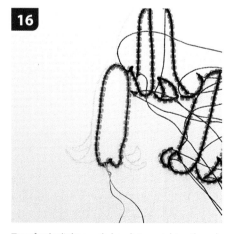

**16**

Transfer the light purple beads to matching thread. Starting from the point at the base of the central petal, apply beads around the petal. Make sure the beads form a point at the base of the petal.

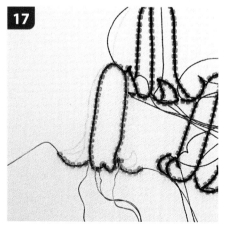

**17**

Starting at the tip of the petals on both sides of the flower, apply a line of beads.

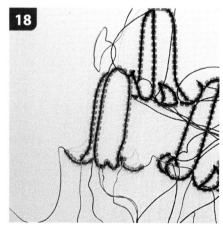

**18**

Starting at the bottom of the flower, apply a line of beads to the outline of the petal on the left.

*continued on the following page…*

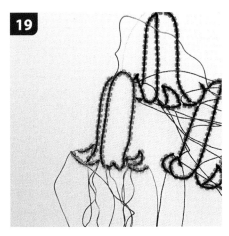

Starting at the base of the petal, apply beads around the petal on the right of the flower. Then, starting at the tip of the petal, apply a line of beads to the petal on the left.

Finish the thread ends to complete the outlines of the flowers.

On the flower closest to the stem, starting inside the tip of the petal, apply a line of the light purple beads along the inside of the petal.

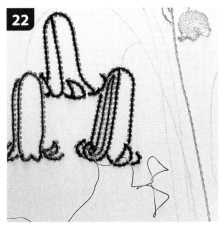

Form a point with a locking stitch followed by a small chain stitch downwards. Then apply a line of beads to fill the rest of the petal.

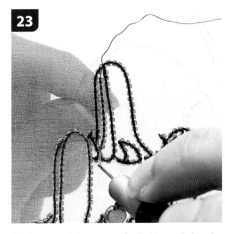

On the central flower, use the light purple beads to apply a line of beads inside the petal, starting at the base of the petal. Make a locking stitch after the last bead.

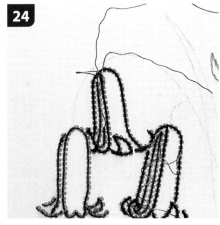

Make a small chain stitch close to the beads at the base of the petal. Then make a locking stitch and apply beads as far up as they will fit to fill the rest of the petal.

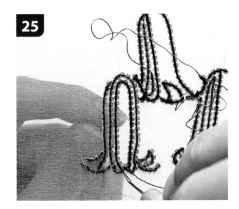

On the last flower, starting at the base of the petal, apply a line of the mid-purple beads around the inside of the petal. Finish with a locking stitch at the base of the petal.

Then make a small chain stitch close to the beads at the base of the petal. Make a locking stitch, then apply beads up the petal. Form a point with a locking stitch and small chain stitch downwards, then apply beads downwards to fill the rest of the petal.

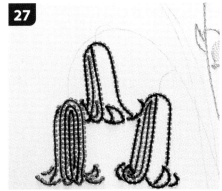

Finish the thread ends to complete the bluebell flowers.

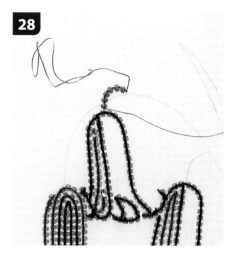

**28**

Starting above the top of the central bluebell, apply the dark green beads to the small curved stem.

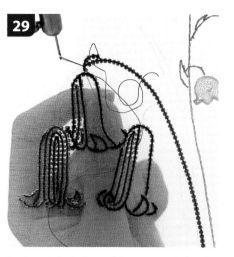

**29**

Starting at the bottom of the stem, apply beads up the stem. When you reach the small curved stem that intersects the line, make a chain stitch between the beads to the other side of the stem.

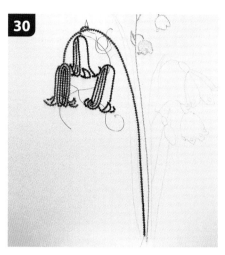

**30**

Then continue applying beads along the left-hand stem.

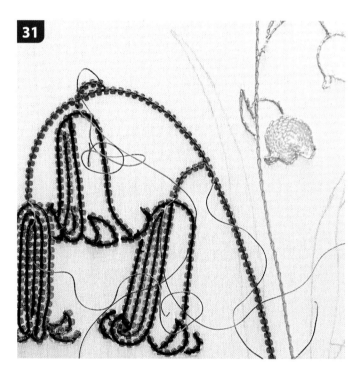

**31**

Starting above the right-hand flower, apply beads to the stem.

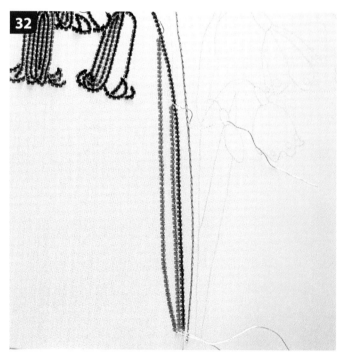

**32**

Starting at the base of the leaf, apply two lines of the mid-green beads to both sides of the outline of the bottom section of the leaf. Finish the lines when you reach the stem.

*continued on the following page…*

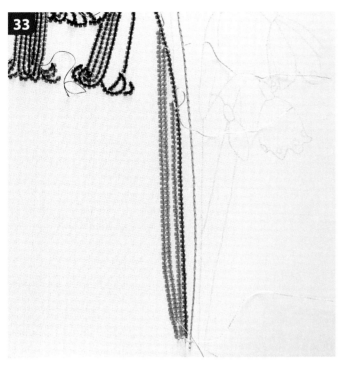

Starting at the base of the leaf, apply a line of beads inside the leaf.

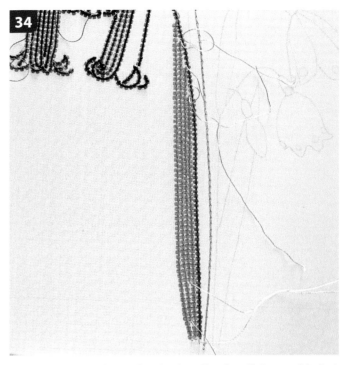

Starting at the base of the leaf, apply a line of beads to fill the rest of the leaf.

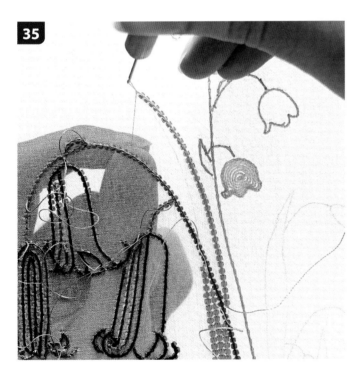

Starting above the stem, apply the beads to the outline on the right of the leaf. Make a locking stitch at the tip of the leaf.

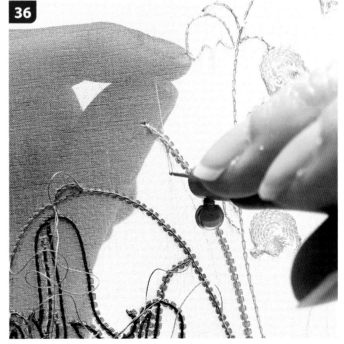

Make several chain stitches downwards close to the beads, then make a small chain stitch diagonally outwards when you reach the point where you will begin the next line of beads.

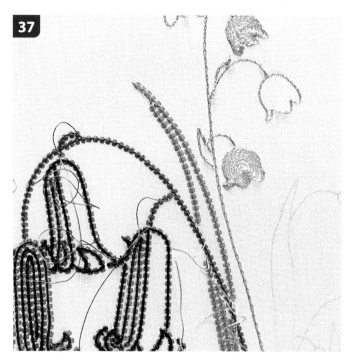

**37**

Apply beads downwards along the outline on the left of the leaf until you reach the stem.

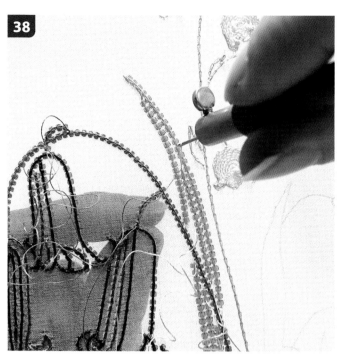

**38**

Starting above the stem, apply a line of beads inside the outline of the leaf. Apply the beads as far up the leaf as they will fit. Then make a locking stitch after the last bead.

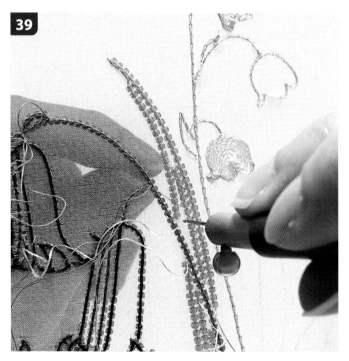

**39**

Repeat Step 36 to reach the point where you will begin applying the next line of beads.

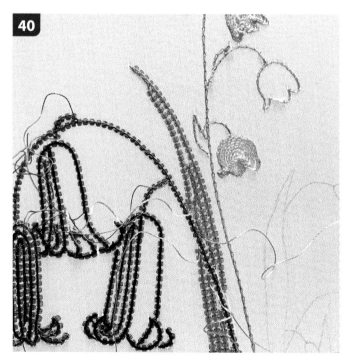

**40**

Apply a line of beads to fill the rest of the leaf. Then finish all the thread ends.

# CHAPTER 6

# APPLYING SEQUINS

Sequins are applied with a chain stitch in the same way as beads. However, there are different considerations with spacing when working with sequins and attention must be paid to whether the sequins have a right and wrong side when stringing them onto the working thread. It is also slightly harder to apply sequins than beads because they do not separate as easily as beads. This means it is easier to accidentally apply more than one sequin at a time.

Once you are confident with applying sequins, you can use the two different types of sequin, flat and cup, to create different effects within your embroidery. Cup sequins will create a more textural effect and flat sequins will create a smoother block of colour.

In the Appendix, you can find patterns for the shapes used to demonstrate the techniques in this chapter, and for the spring flower design at the end of this chapter.

## STRINGING SEQUINS ONTO THE WORKING THREAD

To apply sequins with the tambour hook, you first need to transfer the strung sequins to the thread you will be using to attach the sequins to the fabric. The process is the same as transferring strung beads to the thread, which is detailed in Chapter 5: Applying Beads. Be careful as you slide the sequins over the knot, as it is easy to pull the threads apart and end up with lots of loose sequins on the floor. Some sequins have a right side, for example cup sequins or iridescent sequins where the iridescent finish is only applied to one side of the sequin. You need to make sure that you string the sequins onto the thread the correct way so that the right side is facing up when the sequins have been applied to the fabric. When transferring sequins that have a right side to the thread, the sequin should be transferred right side first.

# HOW TO APPLY SEQUINS WITH THE TAMBOUR HOOK

**1**

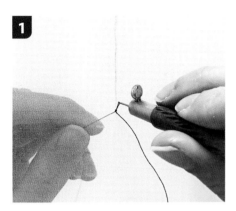

Draw a straight line onto your fabric and make a starting stitch where you want the line of sequins to begin.

**2**

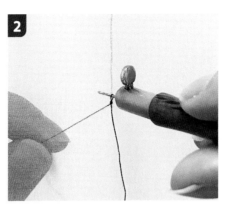

Push the hook into the fabric at a distance of about half the length of a sequin away from the starting point.

**3**

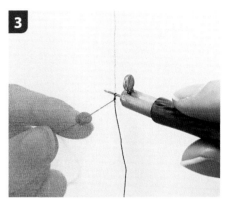

Underneath the fabric, with the hand that is controlling the thread, slide several sequins up the thread, leaving a small gap of thread between the sequins and the fabric surface.

**4**

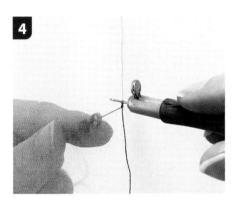

You should hold these sequins in your hand as you work and slide more sequins up the thread as needed.

**5**

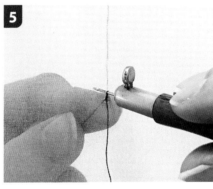

With your thumb and forefinger, separate the top sequin from the bunch and slide it up the thread to meet the fabric surface. Each time you pick up a sequin, you can run your thumbnail down the bunch of sequins, which will help to separate them.

**6**

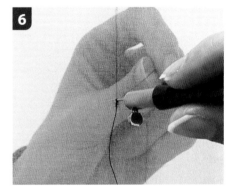

Holding the sequin in place, wrap the thread around the hook in an anticlockwise direction and turn the hook in an anticlockwise direction so the screw is pointing towards you.

**7**

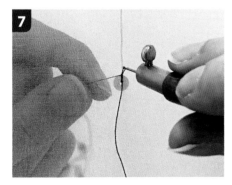

Pull the hook up through the fabric to make a chain stitch. There should now be one sequin secured in place by the chain stitch.

**8**

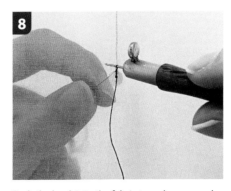

Push the hook into the fabric to make a second chain stitch which is an equal length to the first.

**9**

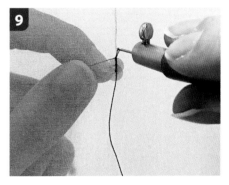

Make sure you have made the chain stitches the right length so that the hole in the previous sequin is covered by the second sequin.

**10**

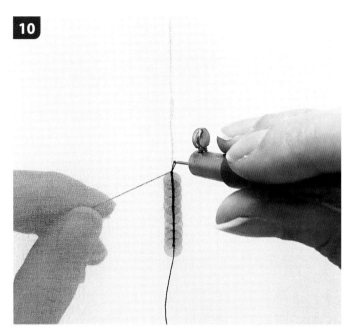

Repeat Steps 5 to 7 to apply more sequins, making sure you maintain the same length of chain stitch to ensure the sequins are perfectly spaced.

**11**

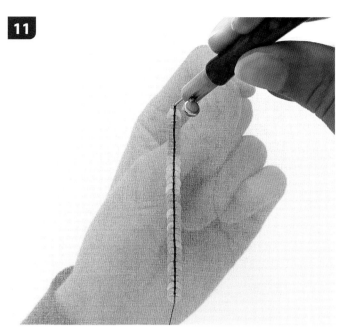

Continue applying sequins until you have reached the end of the line. Then make a finishing stitch after the last sequin.

**12**

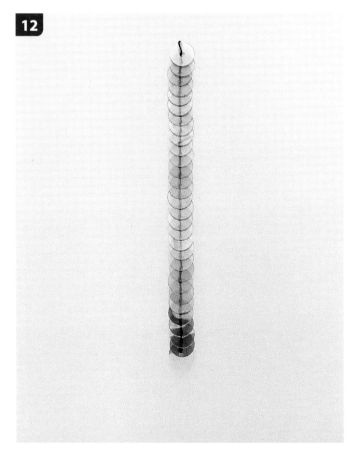

On the right side of your fabric you should now have a line of sequins neatly applied with even spacing.

### Separating Sequins

Sequins can stick together, and separating one sequin from the bunch can be hard at first – it is common to accidentally pick up two sequins at once. As you gain more experience with applying sequins, you will learn how to recognize the feel of a single sequin by its thickness and will be able to tell when you have picked up more than one sequin. You will also become more adept at separating the sequins in a quick action with your thumbnail.

## Perfecting the Spacing of Sequins

When applying sequins to fabric, you should aim for the chain stitch securing each sequin to be the right length so that each sequin covers the hole in the previous sequin. This creates a solid block of colour and creates a neater finish. To ensure the sequins overlap to cover the holes in the sequins, you will need to make the chain stitch about half the diameter of the sequin.

## How to Remove a Damaged Sequin

Sometimes you may come across an imperfect or damaged sequin as you are in the process of applying them. Instead of having to finish the thread to slide the sequin off in the middle of a line, and therefore breaking up a line, you can instead simply cut the sequin to remove it. To do this, cut directly through the sequin, making sure you cut through the hole in the sequin a little but being careful to not cut through the thread. The sequin will then easily come off the thread and you can continue applying more sequins as normal.

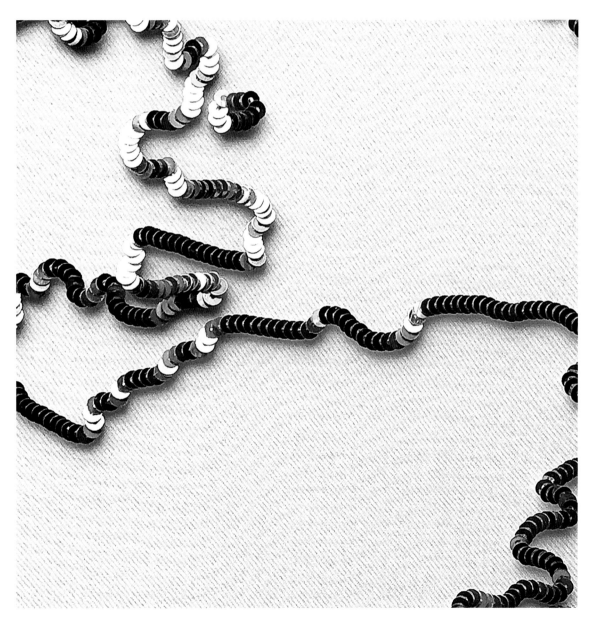

As you practise the techniques in this chapter, remember to keep the spacing of your sequins correct. The sequins should be spaced so the hole in each sequin is covered. This is relevant to the standard application of sequins in a continuous line. You will need to alter the length of your chain stitches depending on the size of sequin you are using.

# HOW TO APPLY SEQUINS TO A CORNER

Applying sequins to a corner is more simple than applying beads to a corner. This is because they overlap each other rather than sitting next to each other as beads do. When applied to a corner, sequins will not create as sharp a corner as chain stitch or beads due to their width and rounded shape.

# APPLYING SEQUINS TO A TRIANGLE SHAPE

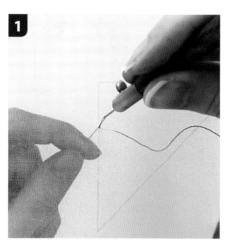

Trace a triangle onto your fabric and make a starting stitch at one of the corners of the triangle.

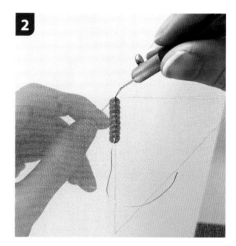

Apply sequins until you reach the next corner.

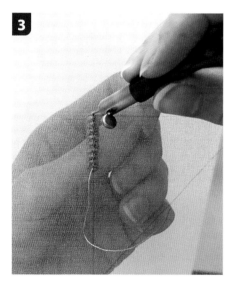

Make a locking stitch.

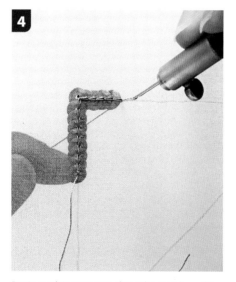

Begin applying sequins along the next line of the triangle.

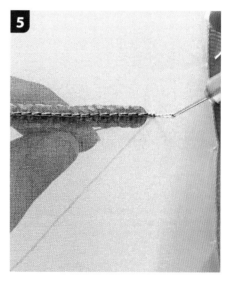

When you have almost reached the next corner, finish the line of sequins a short distance before the corner. Then make two small chain stitches up to the corner. This corner has to be approached differently to the previous corner because it is a sharper corner.

*continued on the following page…*

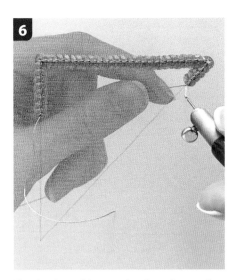

Then begin applying sequins along the next line.

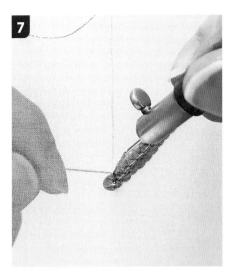

Repeat Step 5 when you reach the next corner.

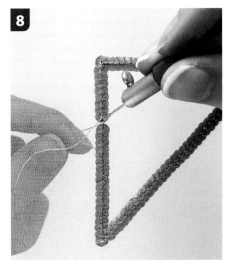

Continue applying sequins until you reach the point where you started applying the sequins.

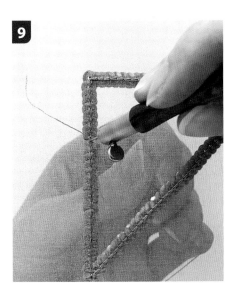

You may need to apply the last sequin underneath the first sequin so that there is not a noticeable break in the line. To do this, slightly push the first sequin out of the way so that the sequin you are applying sits underneath it.

Make a finishing stitch and finish the thread ends.

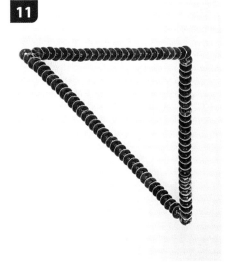

Your triangle should now be completely embroidered with sequins.

# FILLING A SHAPE WITH SEQUINS

Filling a shape with sequins is done in the same way as filling a shape with beads. However, there are some differences. First, you will need to apply each line of sequins slightly further apart to account for the width of the sequins. Second, when you start applying the sequins, you do not do this directly on the outline of the shape, as you would with beads; this is because the width of the sequins will make the shape larger if you do this. Instead, you should begin applying the sequins just inside the outline so the edges of the sequins overlap the outline only by a little. Finally, when filling a shape with sequins, you must make sure that there are no gaps between the sequins but also that the edges of the sequins do not overlap too much.

You can see an example of how sequins are used to fill shapes in the practice design for sequins and practise this yourself by embroidering the design.

This example of a shape filled with sequins shows a leaf that has had matt green sequins applied to fill it. This is approached in much the same way as beads – the main difference is that when filling a shape with sequins, attention must be paid to the spacing between the lines of sequins due to their width.

# PRACTICE DESIGN – SPRING FLOWERS PART 3

## SEQUINNED SPRING SNOWFLAKE

The final part of this practice design features a spring snowflake flower that is completely embroidered with sequins. Embroidering this design allows you to practise using sequins to outline and fill shapes and form corners. You will notice when working this design that you need to pay attention to the direction in which you apply sequins in order to apply sequins effectively. It will also help you to understand the order that you should embroider a design – generally, any shapes that are intended to be in the foreground or that overlap other shapes should be embroidered last.

### Materials
White silk organza
Porcelain white flat sequins 3mm
Iridescent clear flat sequins 3mm
Porcelain very light green flat sequins 3mm
Iridescent mid-green flat sequins 3mm
Matt dark green flat sequins 3mm
Cotton threads in colours to match the sequins

This sequinned spring snowflake concludes the three-part practice design. Featuring techniques such as outlining and filling shapes with sequins, it should help you to practise your skills with applying sequins. As you embroider this design, try to perfect the separating of the sequins with your hand underneath the fabric.

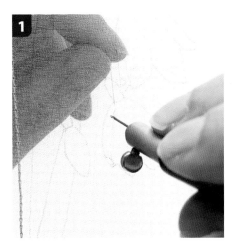

Transfer the white sequins to matching thread. Make a starting stitch just inside the outline of the middle flower.

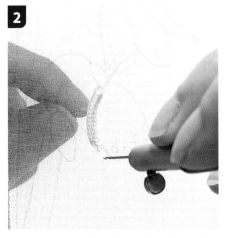

Apply the sequins along the inside of the outline so the sequins just overlap the outline. Make a locking stitch when you reach just before the point at the bottom of the petal.

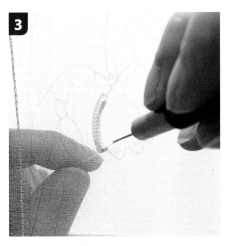

Apply a sequin sideways to form a corner. Then make a locking stitch.

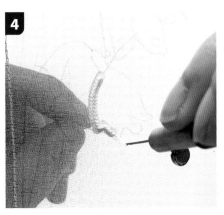

Apply sequins downwards to form another corner. Make a locking stitch just before the bottom of the petal.

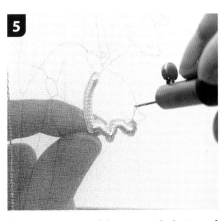

Apply sequins around the curve at the bottom of the petal. Then make a locking stitch.

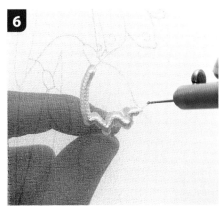

Apply sequins along the edge of the last point in the flower. Then make a locking stitch.

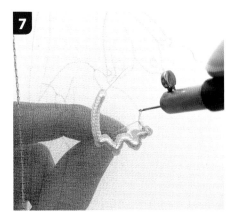

Apply two sequins up the side of the flower, until you reach the spot on the flower. Then make two chain stitches to a point a little bit beyond the spot.

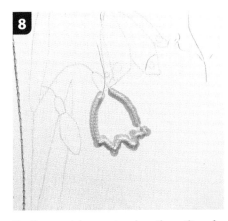

Continue applying sequins along the outline of the petal, until you reach the top of the flower.

Transfer the iridescent clear sequins to matching thread. On the largest flower, make a starting stitch at the base of the petal just inside the outline.

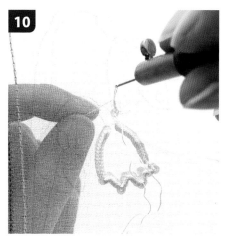

**10** Apply one sequin then make two chain stitches to a point a little distance beyond the spot on the petal.

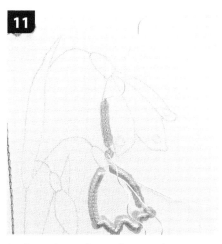

**11** Apply sequins up the petal, just inside the outline, to fill the petal.

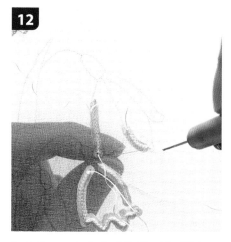

**12** Apply the sequins to the left side of the third petal. Stop just before the tip of the petal and make a locking stitch.

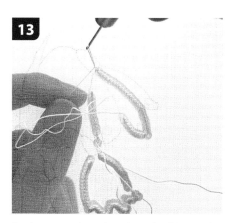

**13** Apply sequins along the other side of the petal, until you reach the top of the petal. Make a locking stitch.

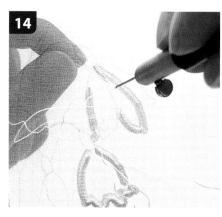

**14** Then make several chain stitches downwards, behind the sequins. Make a chain stitch and locking stitch diagonally outwards to reach the point where you will begin applying sequins again.

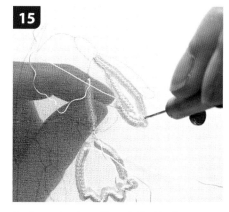

**15** Apply sequins down the petal inside the sequinned outline. When you are close to the spot on the petal, make a locking stitch just before it.

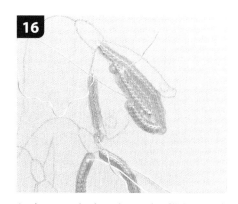

**16** Apply sequins back up the petal to fill the rest of the petal.

**17** Switch to the white sequins and apply a line of them down the left side of the petal. Make a locking stitch just before the point of the petal.

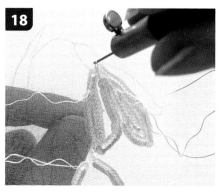

**18** Apply sequins just inside the outline, stopping just before you meet the start of the sequins at the top of the petal. Make a locking stitch.

*continued on the following page…*

**19**

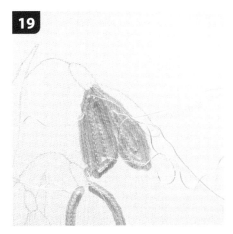

Apply sequins back down the petal to fill the rest of the petal. Stop the sequins at the top of the spot on the petal.

**20**

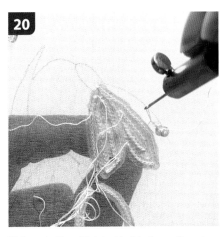

Make a starting stitch just inside the outline at the tip of the petal on the right of the flower. Apply two sequins then make two chain stitches to just beyond the spot on the petal.

**21**

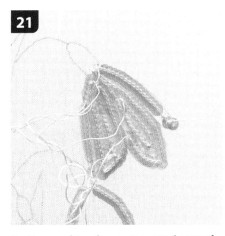

Continue applying the sequins up to the top of the petal.

**22**

Finish the thread ends.

**23**

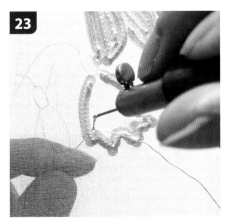

Transfer the very light green sequins to matching thread. Make a starting stitch at the bottom of one of the spots on the flower.

**24**

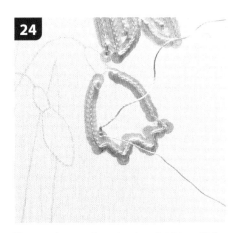

Then apply a sequin and make a finishing stitch.

**25**

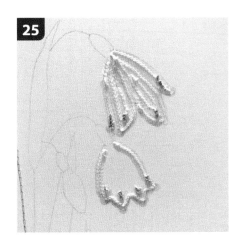

Repeat Steps 23 and 24 to apply sequins to all of the spots on the flowers.

**26**

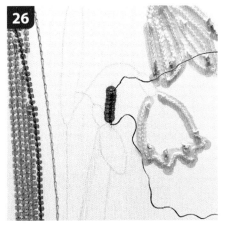

Starting at the tip of the leaf, apply the dark green sequins down to where the leaf meets the flower bud.

**27**

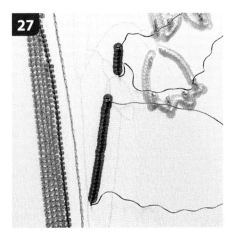

Starting underneath the flower bud, apply sequins to the outline of the leaf.

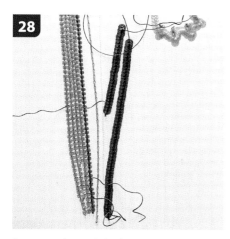

Starting underneath the flower bud, apply sequins to the other side of the leaf outline.

Apply the iridescent clear sequins just inside the outline of one side of the flower bud. Make a locking stitch just before the tip of the bud.

Apply sequins up the other side of the flower bud. Make a locking stitch at the top of the bud.

Make several chain stitches downwards to reach the point where you will begin applying the next sequins.

Apply a line of sequins down the centre of the bud to fill the bud.

Starting at the top of the stem, apply the mid-green sequins to the stem.

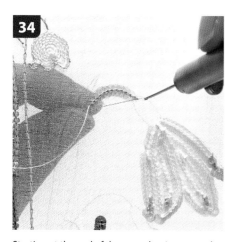

Starting at the end of the stem that is next to the leaf, apply the sequins to the stem for the largest flower. Make a locking stitch when you reach the top of the section where the stem widens.

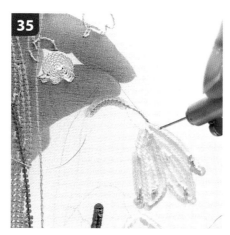

Make chain stitches down one side of the outline, just inside the outline. Then make a locking stitch just before the top of the flower.

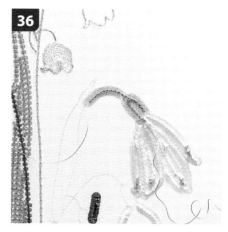

Beginning by working upwards over the chain stitches you just made, apply the sequins in a curve just inside the outline.

*continued on the following page…*

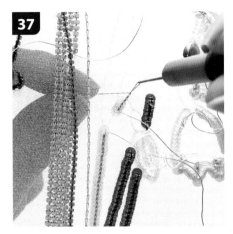

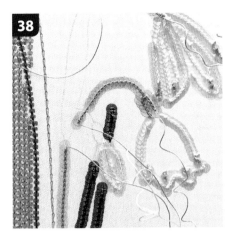

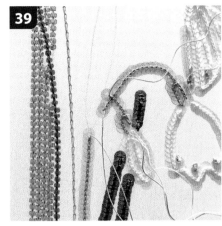

Starting at the end of the stem that is closest to the leaf, begin applying sequins. When you cross over the stem of the bud, make two chain stitches to leave a gap in the stem.

Continue applying sequins along the stem. Then repeat Steps 35 and 36 to apply sequins to the section of stem above the flower.

Starting next to the leaf, apply sequins along the stem then repeat Steps 35 and 36.

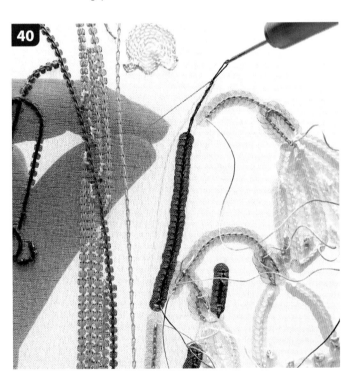

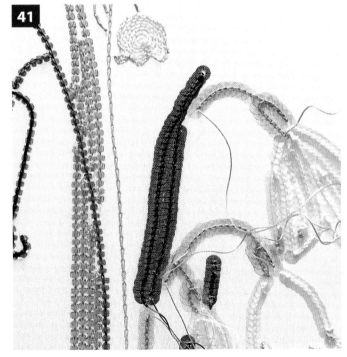

Starting at the bottom of the leaf, apply sequins just inside the outline. Finish the sequins part way up the leaf, then make chain stitches towards the tip of the leaf. Make a locking stitch just below the tip of the leaf.

Apply sequins back down the leaf. Then finish the thread ends.

The completed three-part practice design, which features a chain stitch lily of the valley, a beaded blue-bell and a sequinned spring snowflake flower. Embroidering all three parts of this design will allow you to practise the three main tambour skills before you move on to the advanced techniques in the next chapter.

CHAPTER 7

# ADVANCED TAMBOUR TECHNIQUES

When you are confident with using the tambour hook to make a chain stitch and apply beads and sequins, you can try these more advanced tambour techniques. These techniques will allow you to add different textures, raised elements and intricate patterns to your tambour designs.

In the Appendix, you can find patterns for the shapes used to demonstrate the techniques in this chapter.

## TAMBOUR CUTWORK

Cutwork is an embroidery technique in which several pieces of fabric are layered on top of each other. Usually the fabrics will be in a variety of different colours or textures. Stitching is then applied through all the layers of fabric to create a continuous shape where the end point matches the start. Then one or more layers of fabric are cut away from the inside of the shape to expose the different fabrics beneath. There is a special combination of stitches that are worked on top of each other that can be used to make cutwork with the tambour hook.

For tambour cutwork, the best fabric to use is organza. This is because you can layer up several pieces of organza and the combination of the layers does not become bulky. Also, you can still insert the hook

into the fabric easily. You can experiment with how many layers of organza you use but the more layers you use the harder it will become to insert the hook into the fabric. For this reason, about five layers of fabric is the maximum number you can use with the tambour hook.

When layering pieces of organza on top of each other, the colour of each piece of fabric will be altered by the colour of the piece of fabric underneath it. For example, if you layered magenta-coloured organza over blue-coloured organza, the magenta organza would appear to be purple. A dark-coloured organza will darken the organza you layer over it and a light-coloured fabric will lighten the colour of the organza on top of it. In the example featured in the following instructions, three layers of organza in different shades of blue have been used. This technique is worked on the right side of the fabric.

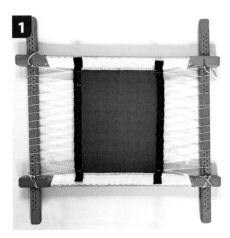

Begin by layering a few pieces of fabrics together and tensioning them using your preferred method. If using a slate frame, you will need to either pin or tack the fabric layers together around the edges to make it easy to tension all the fabric layers at the same time.

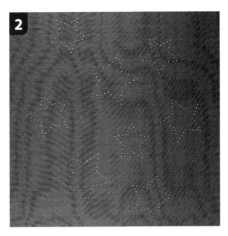

Trace a design onto your fabric or use the prick and pounce method if you cannot see through your fabric to trace the design.

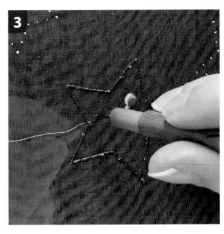

Make a starting stitch and make a chain stitch as normal all around the shape until you reach the starting point.

Make a locking stitch to anchor the end of the line of chain stitch close to the starting point.

Now begin making a chain stitch around the shape again, this time in the opposite direction to the previous line of chain stitch. You should make each chain stitch by pushing the hook into the centre of the previous chain stitches.

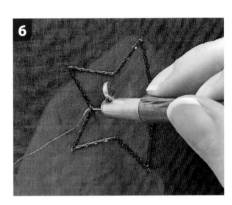

When you have once again reached the starting point, make another locking stitch.

Now working in the same direction, make a small diagonal chain stitch over the two lines of chain stitch. Make the chain stitch just long enough to reach over the chain stitch lines.

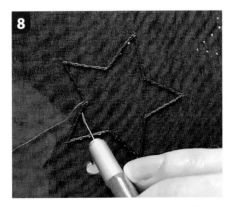

Make another chain stitch diagonally over the line to the opposite side of the line. Make this chain stitch the same length as the previous diagonal chain stitch.

Repeat Steps 7 and 8 to create a zig-zag line of chain stitches until you reach the starting point.

Make a locking stitch and cut the thread.

Bring the thread ends to the wrong side of the fabric and finish them as normal. Remove the fabric from the frame or hoop.

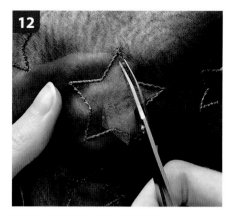

With the right side of the fabric facing you, use a pair of small, sharp, pointed embroidery scissors to carefully cut away one layer of fabric at a time to expose the layer of fabric underneath. Make sure you cut the fabric close to the stitching.

The cutwork is now complete.

## Which Type of Scissors to Use

A pair of curved-blade embroidery scissors are really useful for cutting away layers of fabric when using the cutwork technique. If you do not have a pair of these scissors, a regular pair of embroidery scissors will suffice but it is important that they are very sharp so that you are able to achieve a neat finish. It is also helpful if the scissors have a fine tip, as this will make it easier to cut away the layers of fabric close to the stitching.

Including several areas of cutwork in a design allows you to vary how many layers of fabric you cut away to expose different colours of fabric. In this example, three layers of organza have been used and the stars have had either one or two layers of fabric cut out. A feature can be made of the thread colours; here, three shades of blue thread add interest to the stitching.

A finished cutwork design, featuring stars of several sizes. Three layers of organza in different shades of blue were framed up for this sample. Once the stitching with the tambour hook was completed, one or more layers of fabric were cut away in the centre of the stars to expose the different shades of fabric underneath.

# Bricking Stitch

This technique features lines of bugle beads applied alongside each other in a brick pattern. Although it is not a particularly complicated technique, careful attention needs to be paid to the spacing of the beads to keep the brick pattern straight and even. It may help to draw lines along the fabric in the area where you will be applying the bugle beads to create a guide as to where to apply the beads. This technique is worked on the wrong side of the fabric.

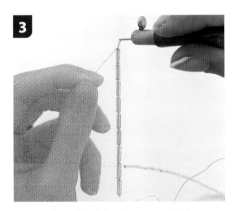

Draw a straight line on your fabric to use as a guide for applying the first line of bugle beads. Make a starting stitch at the beginning of the line.

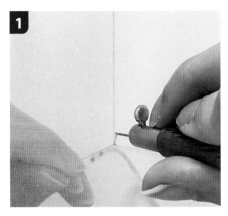

Push a bugle bead up to the fabric and apply it with a chain stitch that is slightly longer than the length of the bugle bead.

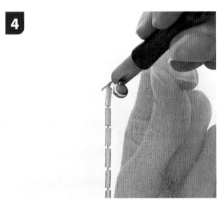

Keep applying bugle beads in a straight line until you reach the end of the area that you want to fill.

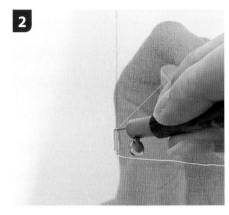

Make a locking stitch to anchor the end of the line of beads.

Working in the opposite direction, make a chain stitch without a bead; place this right next to the chain stitch that applied the last bugle bead, just before the point that is halfway along the bead. Make a locking stitch.

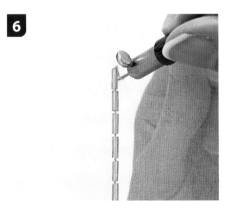

Make a small chain stitch across, to a point a short distance away from the line of bugle beads. This chain stitch determines the position of the next line of beads, so make sure to leave enough room for the bead to sit next to the previous line of beads.

Push a bead up to the fabric. Push the hook down into the fabric at a point halfway along the length of the adjacent bugle bead, leaving a small gap between the lines of chain stitches to allow space for the beads to sit neatly alongside each other.

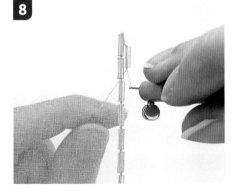

Apply the bead with a chain stitch.

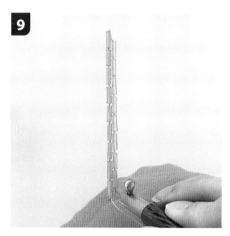

**9**

Apply more bugle beads until you reach the end of the previous line of beads. Make a locking stitch.

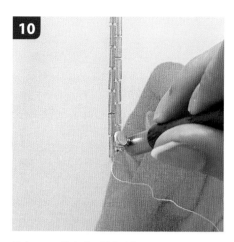

**10**

Make a small chain stitch sideways.

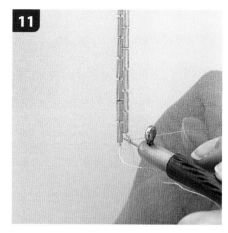

**11**

Make a chain stitch downwards, just before the point where you want to begin applying the next line of beads.

**12**

Make a locking stitch. Make sure this brings your thread level with the start of the bead in the first line of beads you applied.

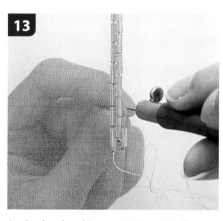

**13**

Apply a bead, making sure it sits next to the previous line of beads without a gap.

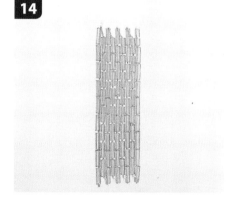

**14**

Repeat Steps 3 to 13 to apply more lines of bugle beads alongside each other, maintaining the brick pattern by applying each bugle bead halfway along the length of the adjacent bead.

You should now have your bugle beads neatly applied to your fabric in a brick pattern.

**15**

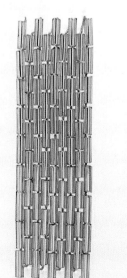
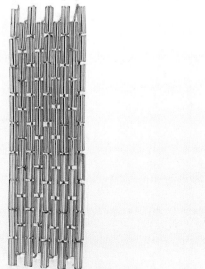

## VARIATIONS

You can work two lines of bugle beads applied at the same points alongside each other to create an enhanced brick pattern.

The gaps left at the end of the lines between the bugle beads can be filled with a bugle bead half the length of the others. The easiest way to do this is to use a needle and thread to sew the half-length bugle beads into the gaps once all the longer bugle beads have been applied with the tambour hook.

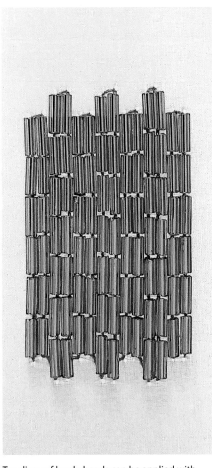

Two lines of bugle beads can be applied with the same spacing next to each other to create a more obvious brick pattern. Bugle beads of different sizes could be used for this to achieve even more variations on the technique.

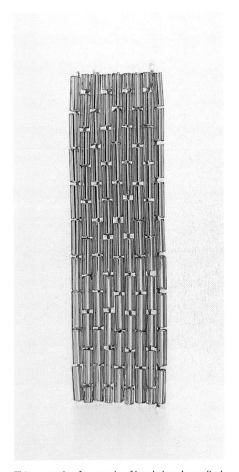

This example of a sample of bugle beads applied with the bricking stitch shows how the ends of the technique can be neatened with smaller bugle beads. These bugle beads must be half the size of the beads you used for the main part of the technique in order for them to fill the ends properly.

## VERMICELLI

Vermicelli is a technique used to apply beads and sequins in a wavy pattern. Each stitch is made in a different direction to the last to create this pattern. This is a technique commonly used to fill a large area of fabric and many examples can be seen used on garments in vintage and modern haute couture embroidery. Vermicelli can densely or sparsely fill an area depending on how close or spaced apart the wavy pattern is worked.

A pattern can be drawn on the wrong side of the fabric to follow when embroidering or it can be worked randomly with the pattern being made up as the embroidery progresses. It can be especially helpful to create a pattern for the vermicelli if you are working it within a particular shape. This means you can work out the best arrangement for the vermicelli pattern to fill the shape on paper.

The density of the embroidery can also be varied with the use of beads and sequins. For a dense pattern, a bead or sequin can be applied with every stitch, or for a sparser pattern, several plain chain stitches can be made between the bead or sequin. These variations of density can also be used in combination to create a graded effect by beginning with a dense pattern of beads or sequins then gradually decreasing the number of beads or sequins and increasing the number of plain chain stitches. This technique is worked on the wrong side of the fabric.

# VERMICELLI WITH A BEAD APPLIED WITH EVERY OTHER CHAIN STITCH

**1**

Trace a pattern onto the fabric or work the vermicelli freehand. Begin by making a starting stitch. Push a bead up to the fabric and apply it by making a chain stitch. Remember to make the chain stitch slightly larger than the bead.

**2**

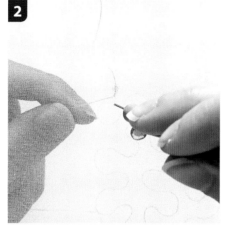

Make a chain stitch in a slightly different direction to the previous chain stitch. Make this chain stitch the same length as the previous chain stitch that you used to apply the bead.

**3**

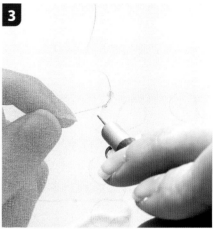

Push a bead up to the fabric and make a chain stitch in a different direction to the previous chain stitch to secure it.

**4**

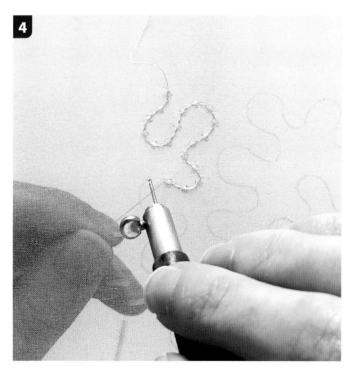

Keep applying beads and making chain stitches alternately, remembering to change the direction of each stitch to create the wavy, looping pattern of vermicelli.

**5**

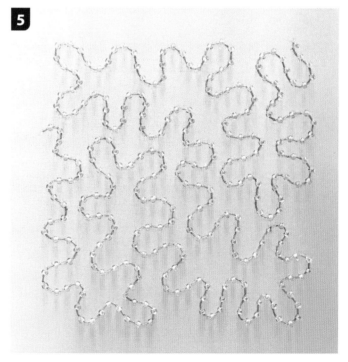

Continue working the vermicelli pattern to completely fill a shape or area of fabric. Make a finishing stitch after the last bead or chain stitch and finish the thread ends.

## What to Do if You Run Out of Beads or Sequins Before Finishing the Vermicelli

Ideally, vermicelli is embroidered with one single line with thread. However, when it is worked over a large area of fabric, vermicelli requires a great number of beads or sequins. If you have not strung enough beads or sequins onto your thread and have run out, with more fabric left to cover with the vermicelli, you can finish your thread so that you can string more beads or sequins onto it. You need to finish the thread and start a new one carefully so that no break in the line of stitching is visible.

You should finish and start your thread ends behind a bead or sequin. In this example, the beads are being applied with every other chain stitch, so two chain stitches have been made after the last bead to allow the next bead to cover the last chain stitch and finishing stitch.

## Variations

You can experiment with using sequins instead of beads, and by varying the density of the beads or sequins and the density of the pattern, to create different effects as shown in these examples.

In this example, the density of the beads is varied throughout the sample. In the top third of the sample, a bead is applied with every chain stitch. In the middle third, a bead is applied with every other chain stitch. In the bottom third, a bead is applied with every third chain stitch.

After applying a bead, make two chain stitches and then a finishing stitch.

Apply a bead. This bead should sit over the top of the last chain stitch.

String more beads onto the thread and make a starting stitch close to the beginning of the last chain stitch.

Continue the pattern of making chain stitches and applying beads to finish the vermicelli pattern. On the right side of the embroidery, the start and finish of the threads should be barely visible.

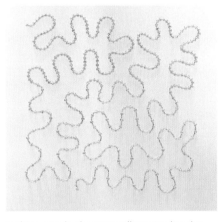

In this example, the vermicelli pattern has the same spacing but the beads have been applied in an ombré effect from the top to the bottom of the sample. This looks incredibly effective over a large area of fabric.

This sample uses the same technique of gradually decreasing the density of the beads, but the vermicelli is worked in a denser pattern in a smaller scale.

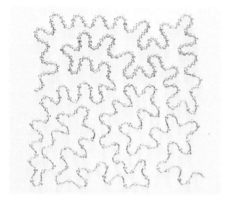

Vermicelli is such a versatile technique that can be used in a myriad of ways to achieve different effects. In this example, the same ombré effect is used as in the previous example but the vermicelli pattern is more densely arranged to create a closer application of the beads.

Vermicelli also looks really effective with sequins. In this sample, the sequins have been applied with three chain stitches between them to space them out.

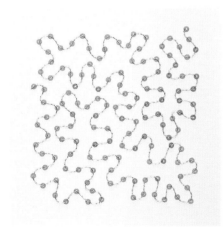

Vermicelli is widely used in the fashion industry for its effectiveness at filling an area relatively quickly. This sample shows how the technique looks with sequins, which, depending on the size of sequin used, can create the appearance of the area being more densely filled.

## SHORTENING STITCH LENGTHS – SCRUNCHED SEQUIN TEXTURE AND SEQUIN FLOWERS

Varying the stitch length of chain stitch when applying beads and sequins can be used to create different effects. For example, using a very short stitch when applying sequins will make the sequins stand up from the fabric, creating a three-dimensional effect that can be used for scrunched sequin texture or to create small sequin flowers.

Make a starting stitch. Then push a sequin up to the fabric and apply it with a very small chain stitch of about 1mm in length.

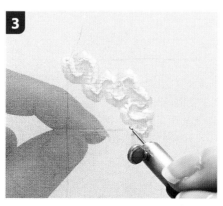

Continue applying sequins, changing the stitch direction each time to create wavy looping lines.

## SCRUNCHED SEQUIN TEXTURE

Scrunched sequin texture uses very small chain stitches to apply the sequins in a vermicelli pattern. Applying the sequins in a vermicelli pattern means that each sequin is applied in a different direction to the last, which results in a very textural and interesting effect. This technique works best with cup sequins, which, with their slightly curved shape, stand up from the fabric more effectively than flat sequins. This technique is worked on the wrong side of the fabric.

Apply another sequin with a chain stitch in a different direction to the previous chain stitch.

To create a dense texture, make the pattern quite compact so there are no gaps between the sequins. On the right side, your sequins should create a three-dimensional, textural effect.

## SEQUIN FLOWERS

Small sequin flowers can be made by applying sequins with very short chain stitches in a small circle. This also works best with cup sequins. This technique is worked on the wrong side of the fabric.

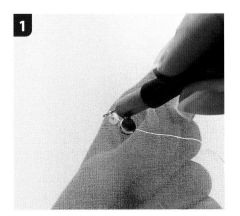

Make a starting stitch, then apply a sequin with a very small chain stitch of about 1mm in length.

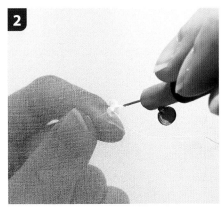

Changing the direction to begin creating a small circle, apply another sequin with a chain stitch of about 1mm in length.

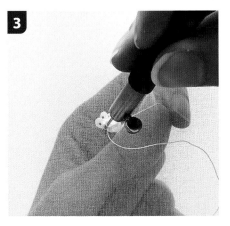

Continue applying sequins, changing the direction of the chain stitch each time to make a small circle.

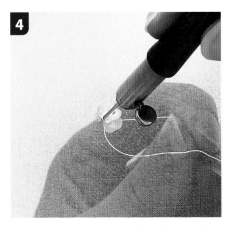

The last sequin applied should be done so with a chain stitch through the same hole as the point at which you started.

## VARIATION

You can also apply the sequins around a larger circle so there is a space left in the middle that can be filled with beads.

This example of a larger sequin flower uses the same technique for applying the sequins with short stitches to make them stand on their sides, but the centre of the circle has been opened up to allow detail to be added with beads.

Make a small locking stitch to the side of the first chain stitch and finish the thread tails through the back of the chain stitches as usual.

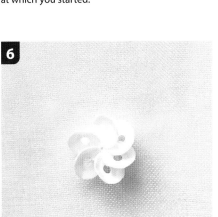

On the right side you should have a small circle of sequins that interlock with one another to create a flower shape.

# Making Appliqués from Tambour

Small motifs can be embroidered with the tambour hook that can then be cut out and sewn onto a different fabric. This technique can be used to apply tambour beading to garments, accessories or fabrics that are difficult or not possible to tambour bead onto. The motif needs to be embroidered onto a sheer fabric, such as organza, and then cut from the fabric, leaving a small border that can be turned under to hide and protect the raw edges. The motif is then carefully stitched onto another fabric, garment or object.

When making an appliqué from tambour beading, there are some consider-ations to bear in mind as to what kind of motif is appropriate for an appliqué. For example, you need to completely fill the motif with beads, sequins or chain stitch. If there are areas of fabric left exposed, you will be able to see the raw edges of the fabric and the stitches that have been made to secure the edges to the back of the motif through the fabric. You also need to make sure that there are no areas of the design that are too thin because it will be very difficult to turn under and stitch down the raw edges in these areas. If you do want to feature single lines of beads or sequins in an appliqué motif, it is best to split up your motif and create the main section of it on organza with the tambour hook, and then hand stitch fine details straight onto the fabric to which you are applying your appliqué with a needle and thread. For example, if your motif is a flower, you could embroider the flower head, apply it as an appliqué and then add a line of beads to create a flower stalk with a needle and thread. You should also avoid motifs with very sharp inward curves as this can make it difficult to turn the raw edges under.

This technique can be used in various ways to apply single motifs. Alternatively, individual pieces of a pattern can be embroidered and then assembled and stitched to another fabric to create the pattern.

This technique is worked on the right and wrong side of the fabric depending on the techniques used.

Embroider a motif with the tambour hook.

Carefully cut around the motif, leaving a border of organza of at least 5mm.

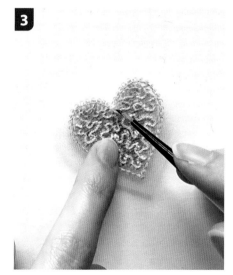

At sharp inward points you will need to make a cut into the fabric border to allow the fabric to be stitched down flat to the back of the motif. First, apply a small amount of PVA glue next to the stitching at the point you are going to cut to.

*continued on the following page…*

**4**

Then make a cut into the fabric border.

**5**

Thread a needle with a single strand of sewing thread and secure the thread to the wrong side of the motif by making three small stitches over each other.

**6**

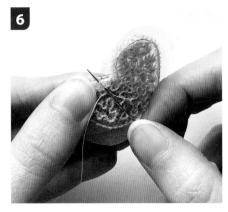

Begin to turn the organza border to the wrong side of the motif and bring the needle through the fabric border.

**7**

Then make a small stitch through the organza at the back of the embroidery. Then bring the needle up through the fabric border.

**8**

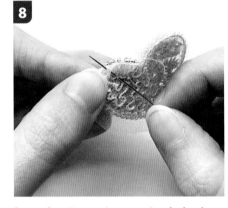

Repeat Step 7 to continue securing the border to the wrong side, folding the border over to the back as you go.

**9**

At any corners, you can fold one side of the border over the other side.

**10**

When all of the border has been stitched down, finish the thread with three small stitches over each other and cut the thread end off close to the fabric.

**11**

Lay your motif onto the item to which it will be sewn and pin it in position.

**12**

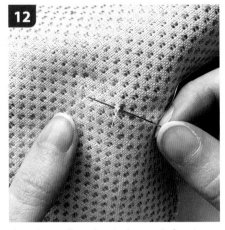

Thread a needle with a single strand of sewing thread in a colour that matches the fabric of the item to which you are applying the motif. Secure the thread end to the back of the base fabric with three small stitches over each other.

**13**

Bring the needle up through the base fabric to a point next to the outline of the appliqué motif.

**14**

Slide the needle through the organza at the edge of the motif to make a small stitch along the edge.

**15**

Bring the needle down through the base fabric and back up through the fabric a short distance away.

**16**

Repeat Steps 14 and 15 to sew the appliqué motif to the base fabric, progressing around the outline of the motif with each stitch you make.

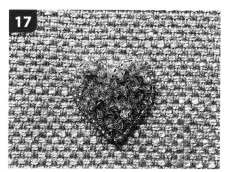

**17**

When you reach the point where you started sewing the motif to the base fabric, secure the thread on the back of the base fabric by making three small stitches over each other and cut the excess thread off. Your appliqué motif should now be securely applied to your base fabric.

## Point Tiré/Pulled Stitch

Point tiré or pulled stitch uses the tambour chain stitch to fill a small area. Point tire mimics satin stitch in its appearance, as it features flat stitches worked closely together to cover an area of fabric. The stitches can also be worked further apart to sparsely fill an area. This technique can be worked on the wrong or right side of the fabric.

## Long and Short Stitch With Point Tiré

**1**

Make a starting stitch and then a long chain stitch away from yourself.

**2**

Pull your hook back and pull the thread away from you to draw the stitch towards you.

*continued on the following page…*

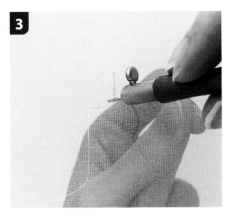

**3**

Make a chain stitch into the same hole as your starting stitch.

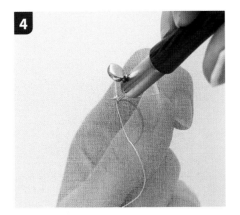

**4**

Make a very small chain stitch sideways.

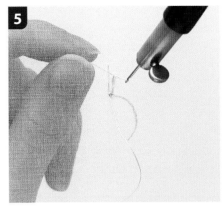

**5**

Make a chain stitch away from yourself, about half the length of the first long chain stitch you made.

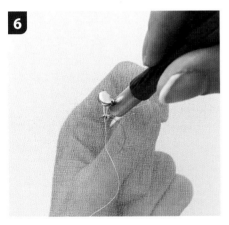

**6**

Pull your hook back and pull the thread to tighten the stitch. Make a chain stitch into the same hole as the start of the long chain stitch you just made. Then make a small stitch sideways.

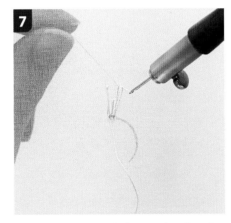

**7**

Make a long chain stitch, the same length as the first chain stitch you made.

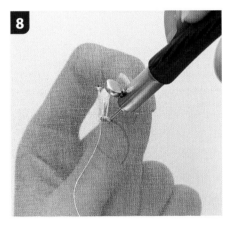

**8**

Pull the stitch back then make a chain stitch into the same hole as the long chain stitch. Then make a chain stitch sideways.

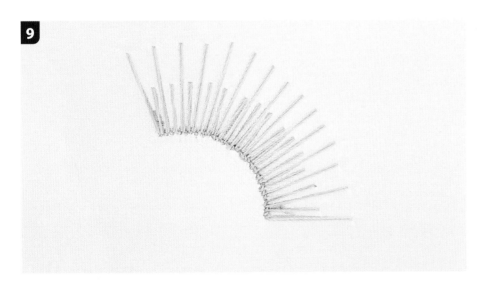

**9**

Repeat Steps 5 to 8 to create alternating long and short stitches. Then make a finishing stitch at the base of the last chain stitch.

# Variations on Applying Lines of Sequins

The standard way to apply sequins with the tambour hook is to attach a sequin with every chain stitch so the sequins overlap one another. There are various other ways you can space your sequin lines by combining them with different combinations of chain stitches.

## English Style

In English style, sequins are applied with every other chain stitch, which leaves an empty chain stitch between them. This allows the whole sequin to be seen. This technique requires careful spacing to ensure that the sequins do not overlap at all but also that they do not have large gaps between them. This technique is worked on the wrong side of the fabric.

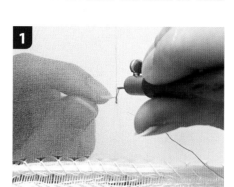

Make a starting stitch and then a chain stitch that is half the length of a sequin.

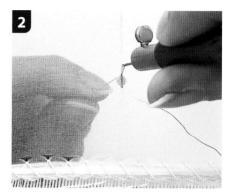

Then apply a sequin.

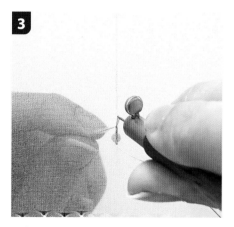

Make a chain stitch half the length of a sequin.

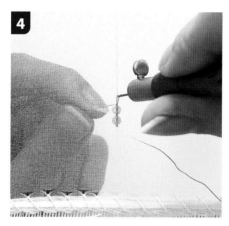

Apply another sequin. There should be a small gap between the sequins of no more than 1mm length.

Repeat Steps 3 to 4 to continue the line of sequins, ensuring the spacing is correct so that the sequins do not overlap.

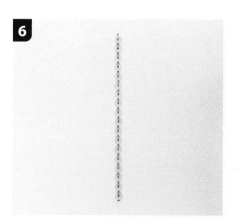

On the right side, the sequins should be attached on one side but not overlapping at all.

# Sequins Applied on Both Sides

This technique creates a line of sequins with a similar appearance to the English method. However, in this method the sequins are attached with stitches on both sides, unlike the English method in which sequins are only attached on one side. This technique is worked on the wrong side of the fabric.

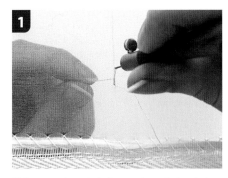

Make a starting stitch then make a chain stitch that is half the length of a sequin.

Pull the chain stitch back to create a pulled stitch.

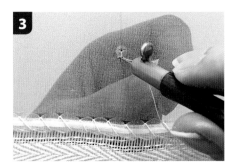

Apply a sequin by making a chain stitch into the same hole as the beginning of the starting stitch.

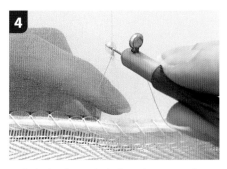

Push the hook into the hole in the centre of the sequin.

Make a chain stitch.

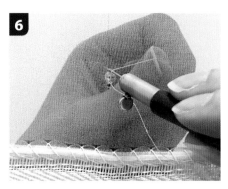

Push the hook into the fabric at the edge of the sequin and make a chain stitch forwards.

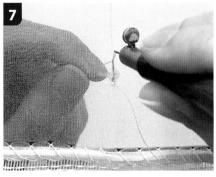

Make a chain stitch about half the length of a sequin.

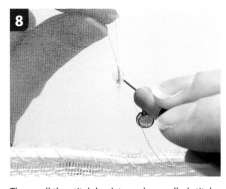

Then pull the stitch back to make a pulled stitch.

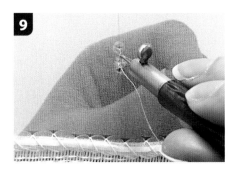

Apply a sequin by making a chain stitch close to the edge of the previous sequin.

Push the hook into the centre of the sequin and make a chain stitch.

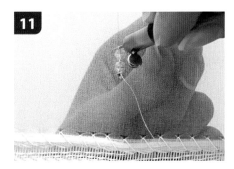

Make a chain stitch forwards to reach the edge of the sequin.

Repeat Steps 7 to 11 to apply more sequins.

On the right side you can see how the sequins are applied with stitches over both sides.

## FILLING SHAPES

Filling a shape in a design can be approached in several ways. The technique of filling a shape with concentric shapes is detailed in Chapter 5: Applying Beads. You can also fill shapes using diagonal lines, which is especially useful for filling a leaf, and by using a fan pattern. How you fill a shape is dependent on the type of shape; for example, filling a shape with a fan pattern will work best for a shape with a curved edge.

## DIAGONAL SEQUIN LINES FILLING FOR LEAVES

This filling technique uses sequins worked in lines alongside each other to fill a leaf shape. The lines are first worked on one side of the leaf from the outside edge to the centre, and then the reverse is worked from the opposite outside edge to the centre. The lines of sequins are slanted to create a 'v' shape. A line of beads can be worked down the centre of the leaf between the sequins to create a leaf vein. This technique is worked on the wrong side of the fabric.

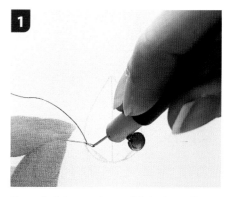

**1**

Trace a leaf shape onto your fabric, draw a line down the centre and draw two lines at an angle on either side of the leaf, just inside the bottom of the leaf. Make a starting stitch at the edge of the bottom of the leaf.

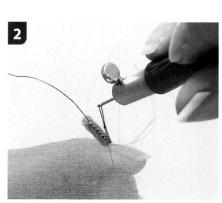

**2**

Following the angled line at the bottom of the leaf, apply a line of sequins to the other edge of the leaf and make a locking stitch. Make a chain stitch diagonally upwards.

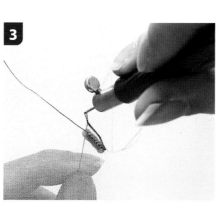

**3**

Then make a long chain stitch back to just before the edge of the leaf and make a locking stitch to meet the edge of the leaf.

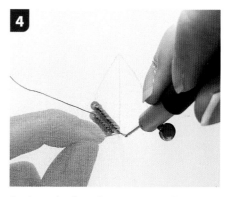

**4**

Apply another line of sequins next to the previous one up to the centre of the leaf. Make sure you have left enough space between the lines of sequins so they do not overlap too much but do not have a gap between them.

*continued on the following page…*

**5** Make a locking stitch at the end of the sequins. Then make a chain stitch diagonally upwards and a long chain stitch and locking stitch to meet the edge of the leaf.

**6** Apply a line of sequins until you reach the centre of the leaf.

**7** Repeat Steps 5 and 6 to apply more lines of sequins to completely fill half of the leaf. Make sure you retain the sloping angle with each line of sequins.

**8** Repeat Steps 2 to 7 to fill the other half of the leaf with sequins.

**9** Finish the thread ends. Your sequins should be applied to either side of the leaf at a diagonal angle.

**10** Apply a line of beads to fill the gaps in the centre of the leaf, inserting the hook in between the sequins on either side of the leaf. The line of beads adds a neat finishing touch to the leaf.

## FILLING AN AREA WITH SEQUINS IN A FAN SHAPE

This is a great technique for filling shapes with sequins by creating a fan shape with the lines of sequins. This works best with flat sequins because they can be overlapped and still lie flat. Cup sequins do not work so well for this technique because of their slightly three-dimensional quality, which causes the sequins to stand up at an angle from the fabric when they are overlapped. This technique has been demonstrated in a semi-circle shape. This technique is worked on the wrong side of the fabric.

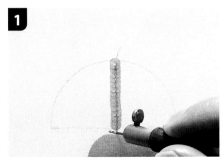

**1** Trace a semi-circle onto your fabric. Start at the top edge of the semi-circle in the centre of the shape and apply a line of sequins straight down the centre to the bottom of the shape. Make a locking stitch at the end of the line of sequins.

**2** Then make several long chain stitches in a diagonal angle back up to the top edge and make a locking stitch.

**3** Apply a sequin, making sure the positioning is correct so there is no gap between the sequins; the sequins should also not overlap too much.

**4**

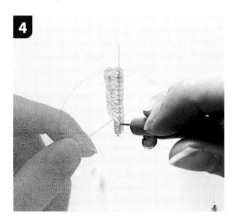

Apply more sequins in a diagonal direction. Finish the line of sequins before you reach the bottom edge of the shape and make a locking stitch.

**5**

Make a chain stitch at a diagonal angle upwards so that it does not overlap the last sequin you applied. Then make some long chain stitches back up to the top of the shape and make a locking stitch.

**6**

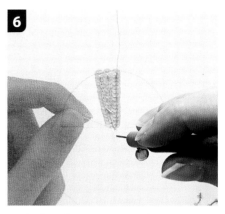

Apply a line of sequins down to the bottom of the shape. The sequins should overlap the previous lines of sequins as you approach the bottom of the shape. Make a locking stitch at the end of the line of sequins.

**7**

Repeat Steps 3 to 6 to apply more sequins, alternating partial and full rows of sequins.

**8**

Apply a few more sequins to fill the small space left and make a finishing stitch after the last sequin.

**9**

Make a starting stitch at the top edge of the semi-circle and begin applying sequins.

**10**

Repeat Steps 4 to 8 to fill the other side of the semi-circle with sequins.

**11**

On the right side of your fabric your sequins should be neatly applied to form a fan shape that fills the semi-circle.

This filling technique can also be used to fill other shapes, not just semi-circles or circles. When filling irregular shapes, it is often necessary to adapt the technique a little by applying two shorter lines of sequins between the longer lines to change the angle of the lines more quickly. You will notice it has been used in this way to fill certain areas of some of the designs in Chapter 9: Projects.

# CHAPTER 8

# DESIGNING FOR TAMBOUR

When creating designs for tambour beading, it is important to keep the design fairly simple. This is because lots of intricate details do not translate well into tambour beading. Tambour beading often suits quite a graphic style of design that features smooth lines and blocks of colour. Rather than focusing on creating lots of details in a design, with complicated shapes and lines, you should instead think about creating interest with the beads, sequins and threads you use and how you apply them to the fabric.

To take an example, if you were creating a design of a flower, you may create lines that are slightly wavy as in a real flower to portray the organic shape of the petals. However, unless the scale of your design is very large, a lot of these subtle details become lost as lines of beads or sequins are too thick to impart these details. This is especially the case with a line of sequins, as these can make a quite chunky line, meaning that lines of sequins that are subtly uneven may translate as an error in applying the sequins rather than a design feature.

This image shows the paper design for an embroidery next to the finished sample. It also features a plan for another embroidery that indicates the type of bead or sequin and its size and finish in more detail. This can be a great way to plan an embroidery before you begin applying the materials.

# DRAWING A DESIGN

A design always begins with a drawing. Drawings can be made from observing the subject matter in person or from a photograph. Many separate drawings can be made for one design, which can be combined in a particular arrangement to create the design. A useful way to plan a design is to make small sketches of the design. This can be useful to decide on the layout of the design and which drawings you want to include.

You may need to simplify a drawing to make it suitable to use with tambour beading. It is best to draw in your natural style and adapt your drawings for the designs rather than trying to draw in a way that will be suitable, because this can be a difficult and unnatural way to draw.

A good way to create designs from drawings is to use a vector-based design program such as Adobe Illustrator. This makes creating a design quicker and more efficient. You can scan your drawings to get them onto a computer and then the lines of the drawings can be traced over to turn them into vector format. Using this method means you can alter the drawing as many times as you like with the freedom to quickly undo steps if you feel the design is not working. You can create multiple variations of a design with minimal effort and adjust the design in many ways until you are happy. Using a vector-based program also means that you can easily scale your designs as large as you want without the lines becoming pixelated and blurry. You can then print your designs onto paper.

When printing designs, make sure that they are printed at the correct size and not sized to fit a paper size. If you want to print large designs and only have access to an A4 printer, you can use the tile option when printing, which means the printer will split the design over several pieces of paper. The printer will print each section of the design so that it slightly overlaps with the next section of the design. There is usually an option to input how wide you want the overlap sections to be. Always make sure you set the overlap to at least 3cm (1in) because having a generous overlap will make it easier to accurately fit the design together. Once all the sections of the design have been printed, you can then carefully line up the design lines where they overlap and tape the pieces of paper together to join up the design.

Although using a vector-based design program can help to simplify the design process, it is not the only option. For some, these programs can be prohibitively expensive, especially if they are only being used occasionally. Designs for tambour can also be created with a pencil and paper and a photocopier/scanner. Making quick, small sketches of design ideas is a useful way to work out the layout and compo-

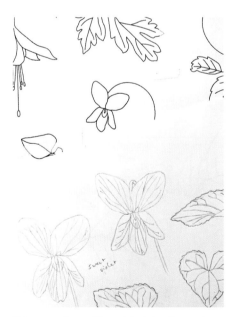

This comparison of the original drawing next to the final design shows how the drawing has been simplified to make it suitable for tambour beading. Any small details, such as the lines on the petals, and any fiddly shapes have been removed. This makes a design that can be effectively used for tambour beading.

The final paper design and the original drawing are placed side by side here. The original drawing was quite simple so it did not need to be altered too much to create the design. However, some of the geese were removed and the lines on the wings were reduced. This was done digitally using Adobe Illustrator to trace and then alter the drawing.

nents of a design. Once a design idea has been decided on, you can make larger, more detailed drawings of what you wish to include in the design. These drawings can then be traced using tracing paper or a light pad, and the drawings can be cut out and assembled on top of a piece of paper into a design. Once the desired arrangement of the drawings has been achieved, you can stick the drawings onto the piece of paper. You can change the scale of the design by scanning it and enlarging or reducing the size using a photocopier.

If you are not confident with drawing, this should not discourage you from creating your own designs. You can use your camera as your drawing tool; you can collect many photographs of your desired subject matter and trace areas of an image either by hand with tracing paper or a light pad, or using a vector-based design program. The traced motifs from many separate images can then be arranged into a design, using the same technique explained in the previous paragraph.

Always keep all your drawings and paper versions of your designs because they can be a useful reference for future designs. You may want to rework an existing design or use sections from a design to easily create a new one. It can be helpful to keep drawings and designs together in the same file, organized by subject matter. For example, all drawings and designs containing flowers can be grouped together.

Before you transfer your finished design to the fabric, you may need to reflect your design. If you are embroidering your design with beads or sequins, you will need to transfer your design to the wrong side of the fabric. This means your design must be reflected so that on the right side of the fabric the design is the correct orientation. If you have a design that features beads and sequins, and also has sections of just chain stitch, the chain stitch sections can be transferred to the wrong side of the fabric alongside the areas that will be embroidered with beads and sequins. When using a sheer fabric, the lines drawn on the wrong side to show the areas where the chain stitch is to be applied should be visible through the fabric when the chain stitch is being embroidered on the right side.

## SCALE

The scale of your design and the size of the beads or sequins you are using will affect how detailed your design can be. The larger the scale of your design the more detail you can include. How small you can make a design is limited by the size of the beads or sequins you will be using. The smaller the beads or sequins you are using the more detailed the design can be. The smallest designs and details can be created using only decorative chain stitch because it creates a very fine line.

You will need to take the size of your materials into account when scaling a design. Your design may influence your material choices. For example, you might have to use smaller beads or sequins, or your material choices may influence your design. If you want to embroider your design with sequins, for example, you may need to make it a bit larger because of the width of the sequins. If you are not sure whether the sizes of your chosen materials will work with the scale of your design, you can embroider a test version of a section of your design to see if the scale works in practice.

If you have created your design on a computer, it can be hard to envisage the scale of the design from a computer screen. It is a good idea to print out your design to check if you are happy with the size and make any adjustments to the scale of your digital design if you feel it is needed.

In this tambour-beaded cosmos you can see how a larger scale has allowed more detail to be added to the petals. This has been done using interesting applications of the materials and using more than one material to fill the petals. You can adjust the scale of your design to add more or less detail.

## HOW WILL YOU EMBROIDER THE DESIGN?

When making a design for tambour beading, you need to decide how you are actually going to embroider the design. Will your design be embroidered with chain stitch, beads or sequins, or a mixture of the three? Which of these you use to embroider your design will affect the scale of your design.

You also need to consider the application of your materials. This includes deciding which techniques you will use to embroider each section of your design. Perhaps there is a particular technique you would like to include or certain techniques that best suit specific areas of your design. You can think about how you could use a variety of techniques to create more interest in your design. You can *refer* to the advanced techniques in Chapter 7: Advanced Techniques to select some of these techniques to use.

The advanced techniques will help you to add really interesting details through the way you apply your materials.

Because tambour beading is worked with one single length of thread, it is best to think about ways in which you can work a design so that you can embroider sections with a continuous length of thread. Do not make a design with lots of very small details for which you would only need to apply one bead or sequin to cover the area. Instead, it is better to eliminate some details so you have larger areas to embroider. This will mean that you have less thread ends to finish, which means your design will be less labour intensive.

Before starting to embroider a design, you also need to consider the order in which you will embroider the design. If your design includes shapes that overlap or intersect, you need to decide which part to embroider first. Usually the shapes that you want to appear to be in the foreground or on top of other shapes should be embroidered last.

## WHAT WILL YOU BE MAKING YOUR TAMBOUR BEADING INTO?

A tambour embroidery can be made into many different finished items, such as a framed picture or a cushion, or used to decorate garments or interior decorations. Although it can be used to make embroideries that appear quite delicate, tambour is very durable, which means it is well suited to be used as embellishment on a wide variety of items. You may choose to make something from scratch out of the fabric to which you have applied your tambour embroidery, or you could apply your embroidery to an existing item by making appliqués from your tambour embroidery. The projects contained in Chapter 9 include many ideas for items on which your tambour embroidery could feature.

You will need to decide what you are going to make your tambour embroidery into when you are creating a design because this will influence certain aspects of your design. For example, some items will require you to create your design to fit within certain dimensions or shapes, such as if you are creating a framed embroidery or cushion. Alternatively, if you are making embroidery that is going to be cut out from the fabric onto which it is embroidered, such as when creating an appliqué embellishment or seasonal decorations, you may need to alter your design to make it suitable. For example, you must not include too many thin areas or single lines of chain stitch, beads or sequins that would be too fiddly to finish neatly.

If tambour beading is to be made into a garment, bag or other sewn item, it is most easily applied to the fabric before

Considering the placement of the materials and the techniques you are going to use to embroider a design will result in a more effective finished embroidery. In this design, the sequins have been applied using the fan-filling technique for the wings, and the rest of the design uses a simple application of filling techniques.

it is constructed into the finished item. Flat pattern pieces are drawn onto fabric and the design is embroidered within the pattern piece outline. Once the embroidery is complete, the pattern pieces are cut out and constructed. When there are seams to be sewn up, you will need to leave a space around the edge of the pattern pieces to allow room for the sewing machine's presser foot to pass over the seams. Once the item is constructed, you can then hand sew beads in the gaps left at the seams.

## SELECTING BEAD AND SEQUIN FINISHES

When choosing sequins and beads to use in a design, you will need to think about which finishes you choose. For example, do you want to use opaque or semi-transparent beads? When selecting sequins, there are even more finishes to choose from; you will need to think about whether you want the sequins to be a metallic or matt finish and whether you want the sequins to reflect multiple colours by using an iridescent finish. The finish of beads and sequins you use will alter the appearance of your design. For example, if you use mostly metallic or glossy sequins and beads, your design will reflect the light more and appear more sparkly. If you use opaque and matt-finish sequins and beads, however, the colours will appear more solid, as they do not reflect the light as much. You can experiment with using a mix of matt and shiny sequins and beads in different areas of a design to create contrast.

There are many different sizes and finishes of beads and sequins. Using a variety of these in your designs will help you to create contrast and interest. For example, in this fairly simple grid design, a mix of finishes and types of beads and sequins in a selection of complementary shades of blue and green have been used.

# Choosing Colours

Colours can be chosen based on the subject matter of the embroidery. For example, if you are embroidering a design featuring particular flowers, you may wish to embroider the flowers in the same colour as they naturally are. Colours can also bear no relation to the subject matter. For example, you could embroider a floral design entirely in metallic tones of gold and silver. By using a variety of shades or finishes of gold and silver, you would be able to define the separate features of the flowers.

A single colour can be used in a design to great effect. Whitework embroidery is a technique that uses only white threads embroidered onto a white fabric. In this style of embroidery, the focus moves to the textures of the embroidery rather than the colour. Similar to whitework, you can create varied textures in a design by using a combination of different beads and sequins and techniques.

Colour selection is often instinctive, so when choosing colours, think about what appeals to you and which colour combinations you prefer. You might have a favourite colour that you want to include in a design or perhaps you have found the perfect colour of sequin that you really want to use. In this case, you can start with one colour as the basis of your colour selection and choose the rest of your colours to suit.

When a design features a lot of the same colour, for example if your design features a lot of leaves that you intend to embroider in green, it is usually better to use several different shades of the colour to add variety. Embroidering all the leaves in the same shade of green could make the leaves appear rather flat as there is nothing to distinguish one leaf from another.

The colour of the fabric you use will also affect the appearance of your embroidery. A sheer white fabric will almost become invisible, which can create the illusion of your design floating. This means the background fabric colour does not detract from the embroidery. If, however, you choose a coloured sheer fabric in a dark colour, such as black, this will add impact to your embroidery and can make the colours of the beads and sequins appear more vibrant. This is because the colours of the embroidery are in strong contrast to the background colour. It is worth experimenting with different background fabric colours as this can add extra interest to a design.

You can plan and test the colours you will use by colouring a printed version of your design with coloured pens, pencils or paint. This will help you to envision how the colours will appear so you can decide if the colours you have chosen will work together.

There is a cost element to choosing colours because the more colours you include in a design the more materials you will need. Using many colours in one design will mean that you will need to purchase a greater quantity of beads, sequins or threads. This may not be such a concern if you plan to use the same colours in other designs as well, but the initial outlay can be expensive.

You will probably find that you will be purchasing most of your materials online.

This design features many leaves and stems that are all green. In a single design like this, with a lot of the same colour, it would be very uninteresting to embroider all of these sections in the same shade. Instead, several shades of the same colour that complement each other can be used to create variety and indicate different areas of a design.

It is important to remember that colours can appear different on a screen, so you may not be viewing an accurate colour representation of the material. Many companies selling fabric online offer a sample service that allows you to see a small swatch of fabric in person. This is a really useful way to decide on fabric colours. However, it is not usually possible to view samples of sequins or beads in person before purchasing a greater quantity, which means that you will need to choose the colours of your beads and sequins based on the photos online. This is a perfectly suitable way of selecting bead and sequin colours but may prove to be more challenging if you require a very specific shade of a colour.

This sample, which features a black background created with several layers of organza, helps the colours used in the embroidery on top to stand out. Using different coloured background fabrics will give a very difference appearance to your embroidery. Pick out background colours that appeal to you and experiment with them to see how they affect the embroidery.

Printing out your finished designs onto paper and colouring them in with pencils or paints is a good way to plan the colours of your embroidery before you begin. This has been done in these two examples of designs. The beads, sequins and threads that were used in the embroidery were selected based on these plans.

# CHAPTER 9

# PROJECTS

The following collection of projects includes a variety of the techniques featured throughout this book. To demonstrate how tambour embroidery can be used to decorate many different items, each design has been made into a finished item such as a cushion, framed embroidery or a bag.

When embroidering these projects, remember to apply the skills you have learnt from the previous chapters in this book. Remember to make locking stitches to form corners, and make plain chain stitches when applying beads or sequins to reach the right point for applying the next line of beads or sequins without starting a new line of thread. These projects use a variety of the essential tambour skills and some of the advanced tambour techniques. You can refer back to the technique chapters as a reference to embroider these designs.

Details of the materials that have been used in each project have been provided. You can use this as a guide when selecting beads, sequins and threads for these projects. Do not worry if you cannot find beads and sequins in the exact colour or size as is specified; you can use beads or sequins in the closest size you can find, and when it

comes to colour, you can of course make your own adaptations.

All of the patterns for each embroidery project can be found in the Appendix.

## LEAF CLUTCH BAG

This clutch bag features a simple design of cutwork leaves that expose the exquisite silk satin underneath the organza. The vermicelli that fills the space around the leaves is one single line of embroidery. Clear bugle beads are applied to the vermicelli with every third chain stitch to create a subtle glittering effect over the surface of the fabric.

The first project in this chapter is this clutch bag featuring an all-over vermicelli application of short bugle beads and leaves embroidered with the cutwork stitch. The magenta silk organza and silk satin used to make the bag create a beautiful backdrop to the embroidery, which has been kept to a very limited palette of colours.

## MATERIALS

Magenta silk organza, about 38cm × 50cm (15in × 20in)
Magenta silk satin fabric, two pieces for the front and back of the bag and two pieces for the lining
White silk organza, two pieces
Bag stabilizer, fusible or non-fusible
Clear bugle beads 2mm
Magenta cotton thread
Metal bag clasp, 20cm (8in) wide
Tacky fabric glue, such as Gütermann HT2

## MAKING THE EMBROIDERY

When embroidering the vermicelli in this design, you need to leave some space without beads at the edges of the embroidery for the seams of the clutch bag to be sewn together. This is because if you apply beads right up to the edges of the design, the presser foot of the sewing machine will not be able to pass over the beads. You should leave a space of about 1cm (1/3in) from the edge of the bag where you do not apply any beads and instead make empty chain stitches. Make sure that you count the stitches so you know where the beads would have been applied, to allow you to continue the pattern of applying beads in the correct order. After you have sewn the bag together, you can apply some beads over the chain stitch with a needle and thread. However, if you are sewing the bag together by hand, you can continue applying the beads at the edges of the design.

The vermicelli is embroidered in one single line. This means you need to make sure you transfer a large quantity of beads to the thread before you begin so you do not run out of beads before you complete the long line of vermicelli.

Due to the fact that the embroidered organza will shrink slightly when removed from the tension of the slate frame or hoop, you may need to trim your other pattern pieces down slightly to match the embroidered pieces of the bag.

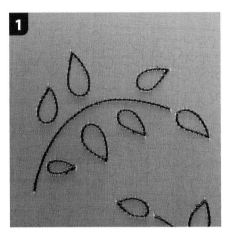

Transfer the design to the magenta organza and, starting at the tip of the leaves, embroider the leaves with the cutwork stitch. Use the cutwork stitch to embroider the stems as well.

Start to embroider the vermicelli pattern using the magenta thread and the clear bugle beads. Make two empty chain stitches between each bead you apply. When you approach the edges of the design, do not apply any beads to the vermicelli within about 1cm (⅓in) from the edge of the bag.

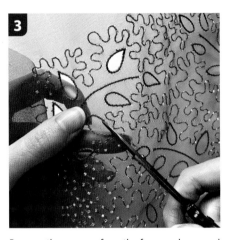

Remove the organza from the frame or hoop and use a small pair of scissors to carefully cut the fabric away from the inside of the leaves.

## Making the Bag

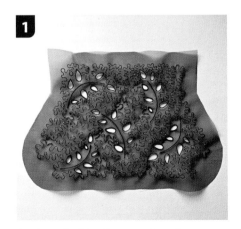

Cut the embroidered organza along the outer seam allowance lines to make the two outer pieces of the bag.

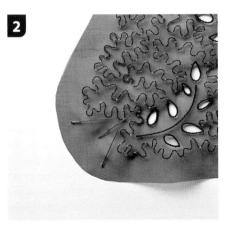

On the right side of the fabric, place a pin at the three points of each dart.

Lay the pieces of magenta silk satin right-side up on a flat surface and place the pieces of embroidery on top, right sides up. Line up all the edges and pin together. Trim the silk satin to match the size of the organza pieces if necessary.

**4**

Sew around both of the pinned pieces of fabric, about 1cm (⅓in) from the edge, to secure the organza and the silk satin pieces together. Then sew a zig-zag stitch around the edges. This will prevent the fabric from fraying.

**5**

Cut out two pieces of the magenta silk satin for the lining using the bag pattern piece. Line these two pieces up against the front pieces of the bag and trim them down to the same size if necessary. Sew a zig-zag stitch around the edges of both of the lining pieces.

**6**

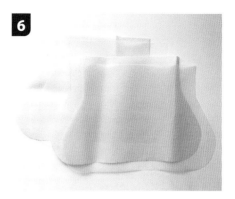

Cut out two pieces of organza and two pieces of stabilizer using the bag pattern piece. Line these four pieces up against one of the front pieces of the bag and trim them down to the same size if necessary.

**7**

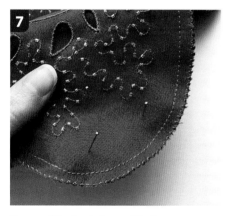

On one of the front pieces of the bag, remove the end of the pins from the fabric that are marking a dart so that the pins are left stuck into the fabric where they were pushed in at the three points of the dart.

**8**

With the wrong side of the fabric facing you, pull out a pin. There will be a small hole visible that is left in the fabric where the pin was inserted. Mark this point with a white pencil. Repeat with the other two pins.

**9**

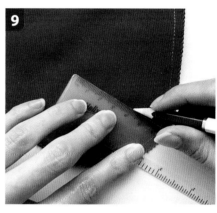

Draw a line between the dots to mark the dart onto the back of the fabric. Draw these two lines right to the edge of the fabric.

**10**

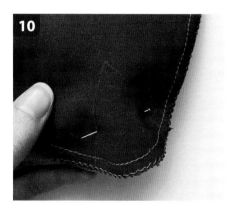

Place a pin through the two points that were marked with dots in Step 8.

**11**

Then fold the dart in half and push the pin in to attach the two sides of the dart together. Make sure you line up both sides of the dart when pushing this pin in.

**12**

Thread a needle with a single length of thread in a contrasting colour to the fabric. Push the needle into the fabric a little bit below the point of the dart; make sure you push the needle through both sides of the dart.

*continued on the following page…*

Make running stitches all the way along the dart, making sure the two sides of the dart are lined up as you go.

Starting from the edge of the fabric, sew along the dart. Instead of making a reverse stitch at the point of the dart, stitch forwards all the way to the point and pull the fabric from the machine, leaving the thread tails long.

Remove the tacking stitches from the dart and then tie the thread tails at the point of the dart into a knot. Cut off the thread tails close to the knot.

Press the darts flat with an iron; on one side of the bag, press the darts upwards and on the other side press the darts downwards. This will spread the fabric bulk along the seam instead of having it all in one place. Place the two pieces of the bag right sides together, line up the edges and pin them together.

Measure 7.5cm (3in) down from the top of the bag and mark this point onto the fabric. Sew around the bottom section of the bag between the two marked points, about 1.5cm (½in) away from the edge, to secure the pieces of the bag together. Leave the top of the bag unstitched.

Cut a few small triangles out of the seam allowance along the curved corners to reduce bulk in the corners of the bag. Turn the bag the right way round and press the seams with an iron.

If your bag stabilizer is fusible, iron the white organza onto the stabilizer. Lay the stabilizer glue-side up and place the organza on top. Place an inexpensive piece of fabric over the top to prevent the glue from melting onto your iron. Sew the darts and then sew the two pieces of the stabilizer together in the same way as the front pieces of the bag.

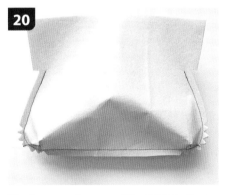

Trim the seam allowance of the stabilizer down to about 1cm (⅓in) wide; leave the top side seams untrimmed. Cut triangles out of the seam allowance at the curves. Then turn the stabilizer the right way round and press the seams with an iron.

Place the stabilizer inside the front pieces of the bag, line up the top edges and pin together.

**22** Sew along the top of the bag on both sides and stitch as far down the side seams as you can.

**23** Mark lines onto the top and sides of the bag 1cm (⅓in) away from the edge. Then mark a 1cm (⅓in) diagonal line at each corner.

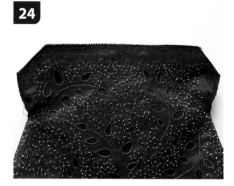

**24** Fold the fabric over at the diagonal lines on the corners and stitch the corners down close to the folds.

**25** Fold 1cm (⅓in) of fabric over at the top and sides of the bag and stitch down close to the folds.

**26** On the lining pieces, sew the darts and seams in the same way as the front pieces of the bag. On the wrong side of the fabric, repeat Step 23 and then fold the fabric over at the diagonal lines and along the top and sides by 1cm (1/3 in). Pin the folded edge in place.

**27** Place the lining inside the bag and line up the top edges. Pin the lining and the bag fabric together along the top and sides.

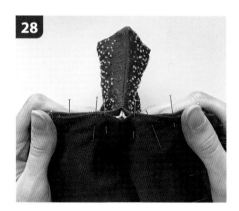

**28** You will need to cut a slit into the seam allowances of the stabilizer to allow the layers of the bag to be pinned together down to the end of the stitched seam.

**29** Thread a needle with a single strand of magenta thread and secure it to the seam allowance of the outer layer of the bag. Bring the needle out through the folded edge then make a stitch through the folded edge of the lining.

**30** Then make a stitch through the edge of the outer layer of the bag.

*continued on the following page…*

**31**

Make a stitch through the edge of the lining.

**32**

Then repeat Steps 30 and 31 to make stitches through the outer layer and lining alternately to secure the layers of the bag together.

**33**

Run the fabric glue along the inside of one side of the bag frame. Do not apply too much glue so that when you push the bag in, the glue does not seep out onto the fabric.

**34**

Push one side of the bag into the frame. Make sure to push the bag firmly into the frame so the top of the bag is positioned at the top of the inside of the frame. Leave to dry.

**35**

Glue the other side of the bag into the frame by repeating Steps 33 and 34. Once dry, check that the bag is firmly glued into the frame by pulling the fabric just below the frame.

**36**

Thread a needle with a single strand of the magenta thread and secure it with three small stitches over a chain stitch to which you will apply a bead. Make sure you only stitch through the organza layer.

**37**

Thread a bead onto the needle. Then bring the needle down at the other end of the chain stitch and back up at the end of the chain stitch to apply the bead.

**38**

Bring the needle underneath two chain stitches to reach the next chain stitch over which you will apply a bead.

**39**

When you need to secure the thread end, do this by making three small stitches underneath a bead. Continue sewing beads on top of every third chain stitch around the edges of the bag until you have filled the space that was left without beads.

Due to the shrinkage of the embroidered fabric after it has been removed from the frame, the darts may have slightly moved position. For marking the darts onto the other pieces of the bag that are not embroidered, you can use the darts that you marked onto your embroidered pattern pieces as a guide. After cutting the pieces down to match the size of the embroidered pieces, lay the embroidered pieces on top, push pins in at the three points of the dart and mark the points on the lining or stabilizer. Then join the dots.

# FLOCK OF GEESE

This small framed design makes use of the sheer quality of the organza by layering up three pieces of fabric that each feature a different embroidery. When layered up, each piece of the embroidery works as one to create a design that has perspective. The cloud layer, which is the bottom layer, appears subtle. The middle layer is embroidered with only one type of bead to create a sil- houette of geese that sits underneath the detailed top layer. The top layer features the most detail and the largest mixture of beads and sequins.

## MATERIALS

White silk organza, three pieces measuring about 33cm × 26cm (13in × 10in)
Cotton threads in colours that match the beads and sequins

**For the Three Geese Layer**
Metallic matt gold flat sequins 3mm
Glossy white round beads 13
Toho milky white silver-lined beads 15
Toho lustred mid-brown beads 15
Clear crystal bugle beads 2mm length

**For the Skein of Geese Layer**
Toho lustred mid-brown beads 15

**For the Cloud Layer**
Metallic iridescent flat sequins 3mm

The finished 'Flock of Geese' project has been framed in a simple grey frame to highlight the colours in the embroidery. The design uses advanced techniques, such as applying sequins in a fan arrangement, to create a stunning application of sequins on the geese featured in the top layer of this project.

# THREE GEESE LAYER

**1**

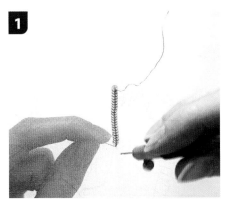

On the largest of the three geese, starting at the top edge of the wing, apply a line of metallic matt gold sequins to roughly halfway down the wing so they slightly overlap the outline. Then make a locking stitch.

**2**

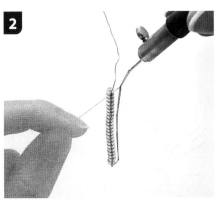

Make a chain stitch diagonally sideways then make several long chain stitches back up to the top of the wing. Then make a locking stitch.

**3**

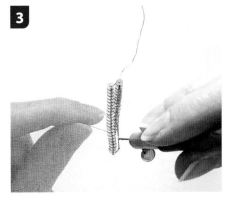

Apply another line of sequins in a diagonal angle so that, at the end of the line, the sequins overlap the previous line of sequins. Make a locking stitch.

**4**

Repeat Step 2 to bring the thread to the top of the wing and then apply sequins at a diagonal angle to finish just before the end of the first line of sequins you applied. Make a locking stitch.

**5**

Repeat Step 2. Then apply sequins, starting at a more diagonal angle to fill the top of the feather, then changing the angle. Finish the line of sequins a short distance before the end of the previous line of sequins.

**6**

Repeat Step 2. Then apply a line of sequins up to the outline of the wing, making sure the end of the line of sequins overlaps the previous lines of sequins.

**7**

Keep repeating Step 2 and alternating the short and full length lines of sequins to alter the angle of the sequins with each line you apply.

**8**

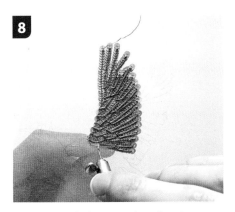

When you reach the point where the wing bends into the goose body, you need to apply two short lines of sequins between full lines of sequins to change the angle of the sequin lines more quickly.

**9**

Extend the sequin lines to fill the body and bottom foot of the goose.

**10**

Then make a few full lines of sequins to fill the rest of the goose body and apply a short line of sequins to finish filling the bottom foot.

**11**

You should now have completely filled the largest goose's wing and body with sequins.

**12**

Using the same process, fill the upper section of the top wing and the bottom wing of the smallest goose with sequins.

**13**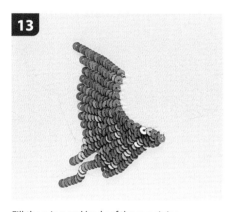

Fill the wing and body of the remaining goose with sequins.

**14**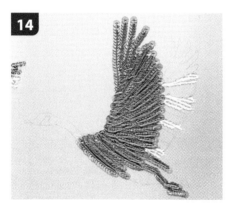

Begin filling the other wing of the largest goose with lines of beads. Start with one type of bead and apply the beads so they fill separate sections of the wing. Use the glossy white, mid-brown, white silver-lined and clear bugle beads for this.

**15**

To account for the change in angle of the sections of the wing, you will need to apply some shorter lines of beads to some of the sections. For example, on this section, work two lines of beads next to each other with the second line ending just before the previous line.

**16**

Make a locking stitch and one or two chain stitches to move the thread to where you want to apply the next line of beads.

**17**

Then apply a line of beads next to the outline at the top of this section.

**18**

Make a locking stitch and then a small chain stitch in the opposite direction, and apply a line of beads underneath the previous line to finish filling the section.

*continued on the following page…*

Fill the remaining sections of the wing with beads.

Then outline the mark on the face with mid-brown beads and apply one bead to fill the centre of the shape.

Using the glossy white beads, apply a line of beads between the lines of sequins. Then create a corner in the line; apply a short line of beads to the edge of the outline and then down to the point of the foot and make a locking stitch.

Apply beads underneath the previous line then make a chain stitch to cross the thread over the previous line of beads. Apply beads along the outline up to the edge of a sequin.

Then apply beads to fill the space left between the beads.

Starting at the bottom of the goose body, begin outlining the shape with the glossy white beads.

Fill the rest of the shape with beads.

To fill the goose head with the glossy white beads, apply the beads along the top outline, starting next to the sequins. Make a locking stitch at the end of the line of beads.

Make two chain stitches in the opposite direction close to the beads. Apply beads to meet the brown beads. Then make a locking stitch, apply one bead and then make a corner and apply beads up to the sequins, underneath the beads applied to the outline, and make a locking stitch.

**28**

Make a small chain stitch sideways and apply beads along the bottom outline of the goose head. Finish by applying one or two beads in the opposite direction to fill the small space left next to the brown beads.

**29**

The largest goose should now be completely embroidered with beads and sequins. Use the same process to fill the rest of the other geese with beads.

The top layer of the 'Flock of Geese' design features three geese in flight. The geese are completely filled with beads and sequins in a variety of shades of white and soft brown with metallic accents. The fan-filling technique is used to apply metallic matt sequins to the wings of the geese. The soft sheen of these sequins beautifully highlights the wings.

## SKEIN OF GEESE LAYER

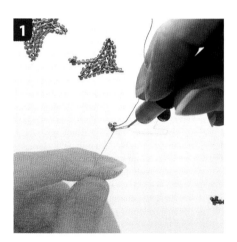

**1**

Using the mid-brown beads, apply three beads around the head of a goose; apply each bead in a different direction.

**2**

Then apply beads around the outline of the goose.

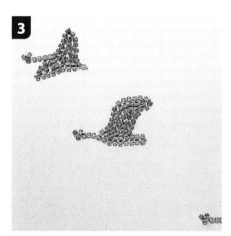

**3**

Then fill the outlined goose with beads.

*continued on the following page…*

Fill all of the other geese with the mid-brown beads, using the same process of beginning with filling the head with three beads, then outlining the goose and filling it with beads.

The middle layer features a skein of geese. Each goose is small and is filled with beads. The lustred finish of the mid-brown beads applied to each goose gives them a subtle sheen. These beads are also used in the top layer of the 'Flock of Geese' design, which helps to create a harmonious link between the separate embroideries.

## CLOUD LAYER

Once you have completed each embroidered layer, follow the instructions in the next section to mount the embroidery to prepare it for framing.

Trace the design onto your fabric. Apply the silver iridescent sequins over all the lines of the clouds and finish the thread ends.

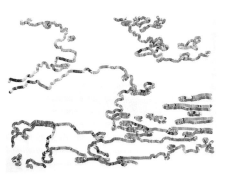

The bottom layer of the design features clouds that are simply embroidered with lines of sequins. This depiction of a winter sky forms the perfect backdrop to the embroidered geese. The iridescent finish of the silver sequins makes the clouds catch the eye even when placed underneath the two other layers of embroidery that make up the 'Flock of Geese' design.

## MOUNTING EMBROIDERY FOR FRAMING

Once the embroidery is finished and the fabric has been removed from the frame or hoop, it needs to be prepared for framing. This is done by mounting the embroidery on stiff board. Your mounted embroidery can then be placed in a frame or taken to a framer who will make a frame to fit the mounted embroidery.

When preparing an embroidery for framing, the board that you mount the embroidery onto should always be either acid-free mount board or unbuffered cotton rag mount board, which is naturally acid free. Unbuffered cotton rag mount board is the preferable type to use for mounting fabric derived from animal fibres such as silk. This is because, unlike acid-free mount board, it does not have to be treated with chemicals to make it acid free that can damage the silk fabric over time. However, it can be hard to source unbuffered cotton rag mount board; the best way to get some is to ask a framer if they can obtain some for you. If your only option is to use acid-free mount board, before mounting the embroidery, you can cover the mount board with a layer of fabric. This additional layer of fabric underneath your embroidery can act as a barrier between the embroidery and the mount board.

To ensure you have a stable base to apply your embroidery to, you should use either a thick mount board or two layers of around 2mm thick mount board glued together. It is best to use conservation PVA glue for this because its pH is neutral, which means it does not give off acidic gases that could damage the fabric and embroidery over time.

Mount board is usually only available in white, black or a very limited range of colours. It is unlikely that you will be able to match the colour of the mount board to the colour of the fabric you have made your embroidery on. If you have created your embroidery on a sheer fabric, such as silk organza, you will be able to see the mount board through your fabric. To hide the mount board and create a solid colour behind your embroidery that matches the colour of the fabric you have created your embroidery on, you can cover the mount board with an opaque fabric before mounting the embroidery.

When choosing a frame to display your embroidery in, you should pick a box frame. This type of frame has a gap between the glass and the contents of the frame. This is very important when displaying an embroidery because the space means that the embroidery is not flattened by the glass. Although many people are often tempted to frame embroidery without glass to allow the fine work of an embroidery to be viewed without any barrier, it is advisable to include glass when framing. This is because glass creates a protective environment for the embroidery that does not allow dust or impurities to settle on the embroidery. To avoid the problem of reflections on the glass blocking the view of the embroidery, you can use specialist types of glass such as art glass. Art glass appears to be almost invisible in the frame because it does not reflect light, which means the embroidery can be viewed clearly through the glass.

If you engage the services of a framer to make a frame for your embroidery, make sure that the framer does not use any glue to secure the embroidery into the frame because this can yellow over time and emit acidic gases that can damage the fabric.

# HOW TO MOUNT EMBROIDERY FOR FRAMING

The instructions below give directions for mounting the embroidery for the 'Flock of Geese' project. These instructions can be followed for mounting any embroidery because the process is the same. The geese project includes three layers of embroidery that are mounted individually onto the same piece of mount board. The method for this is included in the instructions here but if you are only mounting one layer of embroidery you can ignore the steps that include how to mount the further two layers of embroidery. The first layer applied in the instructions is a plain piece of fabric. This is added to hide the mount board. If you created your embroidery on an opaque fabric, you do not need to include this extra layer of fabric.

The positioning of your embroidery in the frame needs to be considered for each piece of embroidery that you mount for framing. For example, if you want your embroidery to be centred in the middle of your frame, you need to position it in the centre of the mount board. This means the top and bottom and both sides of the longest and widest points of your embroidery should be an equal distance away from the edges of the mount board.

## Positioning of Each Layer of the 'Flock of Geese' Project

Follow this guidance when pinning each layer of embroidery to the mount board to determine the position of the embroidery in the frame.

- Three geese layer: the embroidery should be centred in the middle of the mount board.
- Skein of geese layer: the embroidery should be centred in the middle of the mount board.
- Cloud layer: the edges of the embroidery should line up with the edges of the mount board.

## Materials and Equipment

Mount board (acid free or unbuffered cotton rag mount board), one thick piece of mount board or two pieces cut to 148mm × 210mm (6in × 8in) for the geese project

Strong thread, such as buttonhole thread

General sewing needle

Silk twill or other opaque fabric, 8cm (3in) wider on each side than the piece of mount board on which you will be mounting the embroidery

Bobble-headed pins

Conservation PVA glue

If you are using mount board of around 2mm thick, you need to glue two pieces of mount board together with some PVA glue and leave to dry under a heavy book. Lay the silk twill on a flat surface right-side down. Place the mount board on top in the centre of the fabric.

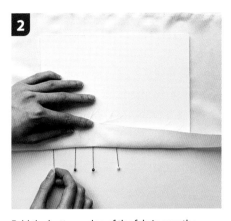

Fold the bottom edge of the fabric over the mount board and, starting from the centre and working outwards in one direction, place pins through the fabric and the edge of the mount board.

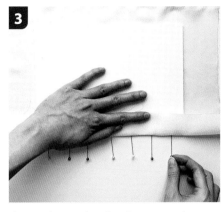

Then working in the other direction, apply pins to secure the fabric along the edge of the mount board.

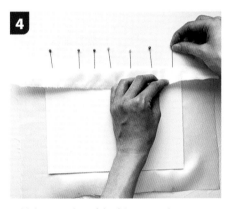

Fold the top edge of the fabric over the mount board and, pulling the fabric slightly so that it is taught against the mount board, secure the fabric with pins, starting from the centre.

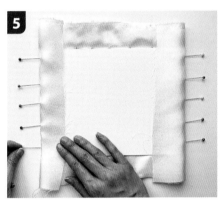

Fold the fabric over one of the sides of the mount board and secure with pins in the same way as before. Then fold the other side of the fabric over and secure with pins, making sure the fabric is taut across the board.

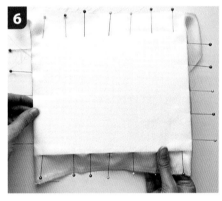

Turn the board over to check the fabric is flat against the board and that there are no bumps or ripples in the fabric. Make adjustments by removing a pin and pulling the fabric slightly to tighten the tension then replace the pin.

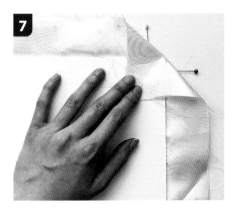

Turn the board back to the wrong side. Fold one of the corners of the fabric over to make a diagonal fold at the corner.

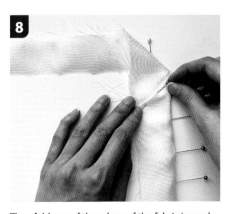

Then fold one of the edges of the fabric inwards and pin it in place at the corner.

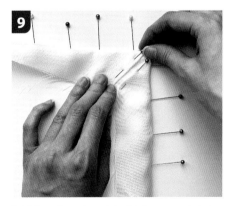

Fold the other edge of the fabric over and pin in the same way as before to create a mitred corner.

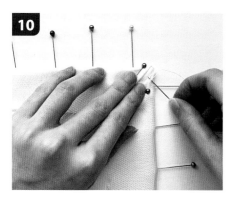

Thread your needle with a single length of buttonhole thread and secure it with three small stitches through the fabric.

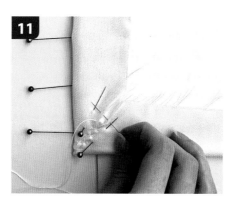

Stitch the two folds of fabric that form the mitred corner together, working from the edge of the board towards the centre.

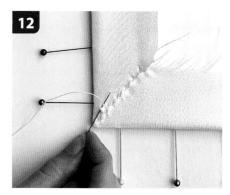

Then working in the opposite direction, make stitches over your previous stitches to form cross stitches. Secure the thread with three small stitches through the fabric and cut the thread, leaving a short length of thread.

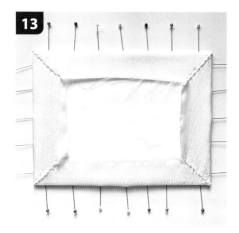

Repeat Steps 7 to 12 to mitre and stitch the other corners of the fabric.

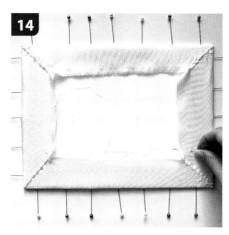

Thread the needle with a long double length of thread and secure the thread at the edge of the fabric next to the corner with three small stitches. Bring the needle down through the opposite edge of the fabric 1.5cm (1/2in) away from the raw edge.

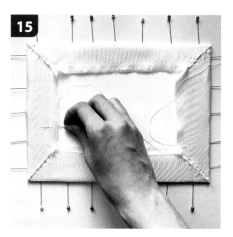

Then bring the needle up through the other edge of the fabric 1.5cm (1/2in) away from the edge, about 2cm (¾in) away from the last stitch you made on this side of the fabric.

Keep making stitches through each edge of the fabric. Then, starting with the first stitch you made, pull each stitch tight to tension the fabric.

Keeping the tension of the thread, make three small stitches to secure the thread to the fabric and cut off the thread tail.

continued on the following page…

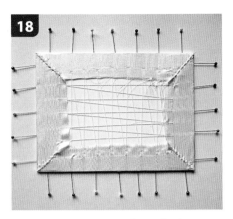

Repeat Steps 14 to 17 to make stitches between the other edges of the fabric over the top of the stitches you have just made. The fabric should now be neatly covering the mount board. Remove all the pins at the edges of the board.

Now you can move on to mounting the embroidery. Take the cloud layer and place it on top of the mount board, lining up the edges of the embroidery and the mount board. Place a pin in the centre of each edge of the mount board to hold the fabric in place on the mount board.

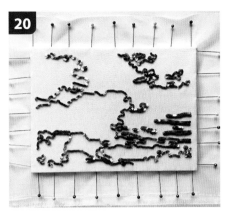

Pin the top and bottom edges of the fabric to the mount board, working outwards from the central pin in both directions. Then pin both sides of the fabric to the mount board in the same way.

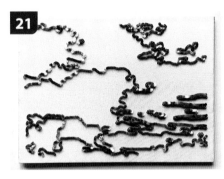

Check that the embroidery is properly lined up with the edges of the mount board and is well tensioned. Then mitre the corners of the fabric and make stitches to tension the fabric along the top and bottom and sides of the fabric as before.

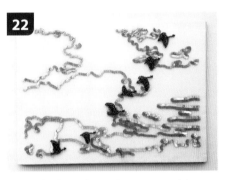

Mount the skein of geese layer on top of the cloud layer in the same way as you mounted the cloud layer.

Mount the three geese layer in the same way. The mounting of the embroidery is now complete and it is ready to be framed.

## SPRING FLOWERS SCULPTURE

This sculptural tambour embroidery is created by individually embroidering each petal with the tambour hook and then joining them together to create three-dimensional flowers. The five flowers that represent the essence of spring are embroidered with sequins and decorative chain stitch. Once assembled, the flowers are arranged together and displayed under a glass dome.

This sculptural embroidery pushes the boundaries of tambour beading, taking it from a flat piece of fabric and turning it into three-dimensional flowers. It features instantly recognizable flowers that are the epitome of spring. Only sequins and chain stitch have been used to embroider the petals and leaves in this project in order to keep them as thin as possible.

## MATERIALS

White silk organza, one piece large enough for all the front and back templates, or split into several pieces in a hoop or frame

Mid- and dark green organza

Cotton threads in colours that match the beads and sequins

Wire 28 gauge and 18 gauge

Air-dry clay

Acid-free tissue paper torn into strips

Loose silver leaf

Conservation PVA glue

Paper flower stamens, small and medium size

Small piece of yellow felt

Glass dome with wooden base 27cm height

### For the Tulip
Porcelain light pink flat sequins 3mm
Porcelain white flat sequins 3mm
Iridescent light green flat sequins 3mm

### For the Daffodil
Glossy porcelain mid-yellow flat sequins 4mm
Mid-yellow variegated stranded cotton embroidery thread
Dark green stranded cotton embroidery thread

### For the Bluebell
Mid-purple stranded cotton embroidery thread
Dark purple stranded cotton embroidery thread
Matt dark green flat sequins 3mm

### For the Primrose
Porcelain pale yellow flat sequins 3mm
Porcelain mid yellow flat sequins 3mm
Mid-green stranded cotton embroidery thread
Dark green stranded cotton embroidery thread
Glossy mid yellow bead 10

### For the Crocus
Glossy crystal mid-purple flat sequins 3mm
Mid-green stranded cotton embroidery thread

## PREPARATION

Start by transferring the designs for all the petals and leaves to the fabric. Make sure you leave at least 3cm (1in) of space between the shapes to allow room for a fabric border around the petals and leaves when cutting them out once the embroidery is completed. It is helpful to write a number next to each petal and leaf on the fabric so you can easily match up the front and back pieces of each petal and leaf when you cut them out.

## EMBROIDERING THE PETALS AND LEAVES

The front and back pieces of the petals and leaves are embroidered separately and then sewn together to create double-sided petals and leaves.

**Bluebell: Front of the Petals**

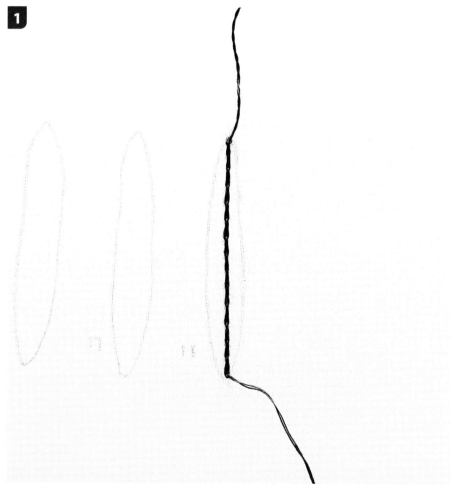

**1**

With a single strand of the dark purple stranded cotton embroidery thread, make a line of chain stitch down the centre of the petal, from the top of the petal to the bottom.

*continued on the following page…*

**2**

Starting at the top of the petal in the same hole as the start of the chain stitch line, make a chain stitch along the edge of the petal using a single strand of the mid-purple embroidery thread. Make a locking stitch at the bottom of the petal and then make chain stitches next to the dark purple chain stitch line. At the top of the petal, make a locking stitch

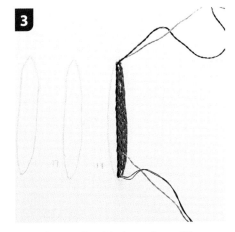

**3**

Make chain stitch inside the outline to fill the shape.

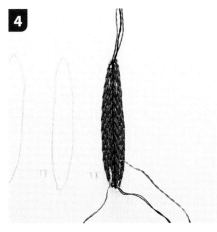

**4**

Repeat Steps 2 to 3 to fill the other side of the petal with chain stitch. Finish the thread tails with a needle using the method described in the 'Finishing the Thread Tails' instructions later in this project.

## Bluebell: Back of the Petals

**1**

Using a single strand of the medium purple stranded cotton embroidery thread, make a chain stitch around the edge of the petal, starting at the top of the petal and finishing with a locking stitch into the same hole as the starting stitch.

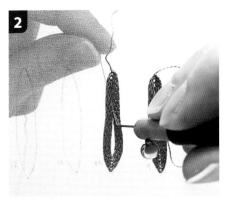

**2**

Start filling the petal with chain stitch inside the outline. When the space left to fill becomes a point, you can fill this with a pulled stitch.

**3**

Continue making chain stitch inside the previous line to fill the shape. Finish the thread tails with a needle using the method described in the 'Finishing the Thread Tails' instructions.

### Separating Strands of Embroidery Thread

Stranded cotton embroidery thread is comprised of a number of strands of threads that are loosely twisted together. This makes it possible to separate a single strand of thread, but this must be done correctly to avoid tangling the thread. To do this, separate a single strand at the top of the thread and hold it apart from the rest of the threads in one hand. With your other hand, place your finger in the gap and then run your finger down the length of the thread. The thread will untwist to separate the single strand.

## Finishing the Thread Tails

When using embroidery thread, the thread tails need to be finished differently because the thread is more fragile. If the normal method is used, there is a risk of catching the thread in the hook, which could easily break the thread.

## Bluebell: Front and Back of the Leaf

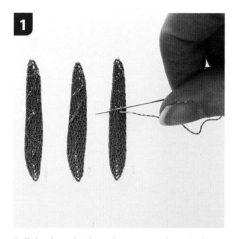

**1**

Pull the thread tails to the wrong side with the hook. Thread one of the thread tails into a needle and slide the needle through the back of several stitches. You can also thread two thread tails into the needle at the same time if the thread tails are close to each other.

**2**

Then slide the needle through the back of several stitches in the opposite direction to last time and cut the thread close to the back of the embroidery.

Chain stitch around the outline of the leaf. Then, starting at the top of the leaf, apply a line of the dark green sequins to one edge of the leaf. Then, starting at the top again, apply a line of sequins to the other edge of the leaf. Then, starting from the top each time, fill the rest of the leaf with lines of sequins.

## Daffodil: Front and Back of the Petals

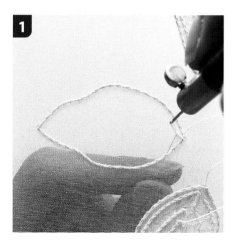

**1**

Make a chain stitch all the way around the outline of the petal and then make a chain stitch to bring the thread to where you want to apply the first sequin.

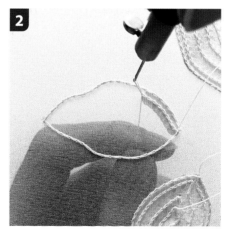

**2**

Start applying the mid-yellow sequins around the edge of the petal, just inside the outline so that the edges of the sequin cover the chain stitch around the edge of the petal.

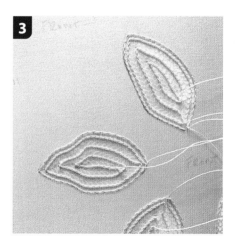

**3**

Continue applying sequins around the edge of the petal until you reach the point where you started. Then make a chain stitch to bring the thread to where you want to start applying the next sequin. Then fill the petal with the sequins. Repeat Steps 1 to 3 to fill all the petals with sequins.

# Daffodil: Outside and Inside of the Trumpet

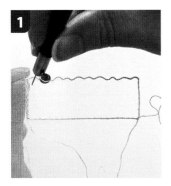

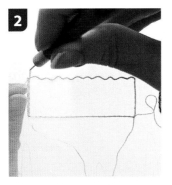

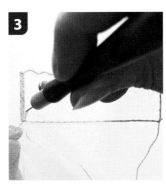

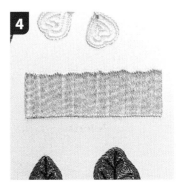

**1** Use a single strand of the mid-yellow embroidery thread to outline the trumpet with chain stitch, starting in one of the bottom corners. When you reach the point where you started, make a chain stitch next to the first line you made and then make a small pulled stitch over the top line of chain stitch.

**2** Make a small chain stitch downwards next to the previous line of chain stitch, underneath the chain stitch line at the top of the trumpet. Then make a small chain stitch straight up over the top line of chain stitch and pull this stitch back to make a pulled stitch.

**3** Make a line of chain stitch down to the base of the trumpet. Make a small chain stitch down over the bottom line of chain stitch and then make a small chain stitch diagonally up over the line of chain stitch.

**4** Make a line of chain stitch up to the top of the trumpet and then make a small pulled stitch over the top line of chain stitch. Then repeat Steps 2 to 3 to continue making lines of chain stitch until the trumpet is filled.

# Daffodil: Front and Back of the Leaves

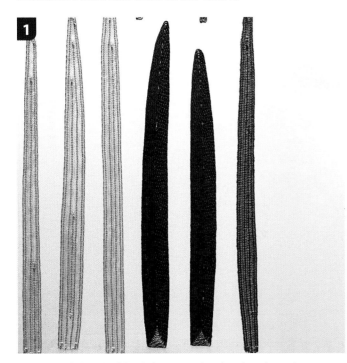

**1** Using a single length of the dark green embroidery thread, start by making a chain stitch around the edge of the leaf and then fill the leaf with chain stitch.

**2** When you have nearly used up a length of the embroidery thread, finish the thread as usual and then start a new thread in the centre of the last chain stitch. This will create a seamless break in the chain stitch.

## Tulip: Front of the Outer Petals

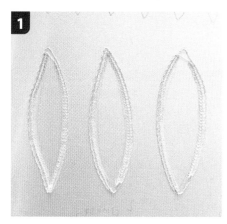

Make a chain stitch all the way around the outline of the petal. Then apply white sequins around the edge, leaving gaps at either the top or bottom of the petal. Make the white edging of each petal slightly different.

Fill the area left with the light pink sequins.

## Tulip: Back of the Outer Petals

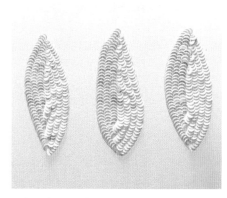

Make a chain stitch around the outline of the petals and then fill the petals with white sequins.

## Tulip: Front and Back of the Smaller Inner Petals

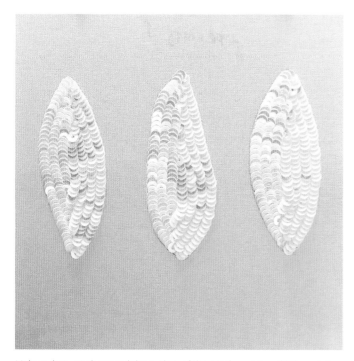

Make a chain stitch around the outline of the petals and then fill the petals with white sequins.

## Tulip: Front and Back of the Leaves

Make a chain stitch around the outline of the leaves and then, starting from the top of the leaf, apply a line of the iridescent green sequins down one side of the leaf. Starting at the top again, apply a line of sequins to the other edge of the leaf. Then fill the rest of the leaf with lines of sequins, starting from the top each time.

## Primrose: Front of the Petals

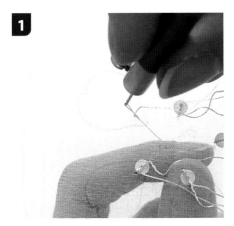

Make a starting stitch about half a sequin's diameter from the point at the base of the petal.

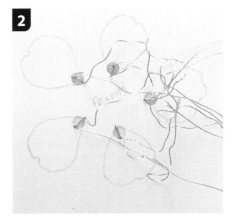

Then make a chain stitch forwards and use the technique of attaching sequins on both sides to apply a mid-yellow sequin to the petal.

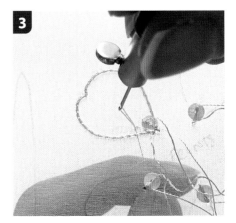

Make a chain stitch around the outline of the petal. Then make a chain stitch into the petal where you want to start applying the sequins.

## Primrose: Back of the Petals

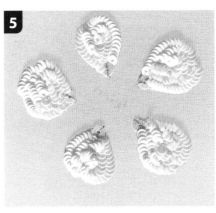

Fill the petal with the light yellow sequins.

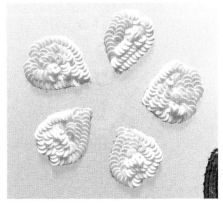

Make sure you do not overlap the mid-yellow sequin when filling the petal.

Chain stitch around the outline of the petals and then fill the petals with the light yellow sequins.

## Primrose: Front of the Leaves

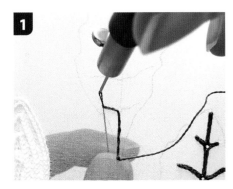

Starting at the base of the leaf, make a chain stitch up the central leaf vein and then along the first horizontal leaf vein with a single strand of the dark green embroidery thread. Make a locking stitch.

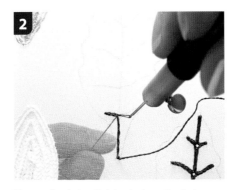

Then make chain stitch back along the first horizontal leaf vein, very close to your previous chain stitches. Then make a locking stitch.

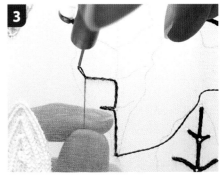

Continue making chain stitch up the central leaf vein, then along the next horizontal leaf vein.

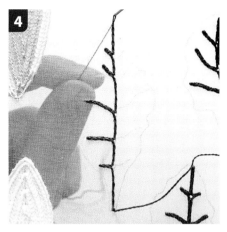

**4**

Continue making chain stitch over the leaf veins until you reach the top of the leaf vein. Make a locking stitch.

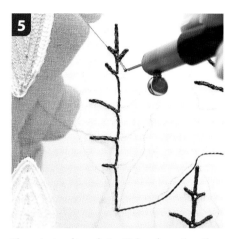

**5**

Then start making chain stitches down the other side of the leaf veins.

**6**

Continue making chain stitch over the leaf veins until you reach the bottom of the leaf.

**7**

With a single strand of the mid-green embroidery thread, outline the leaf with chain stitch.

**8**

Then make chain stitch around the leaf veins on one side of the leaf. Make sure this chain stitch is very close to the leaf vein chain stitch so that there is no gap between them. Make a locking stitch at the top of the leaf.

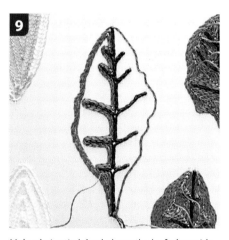

**9**

Make chain stitch back down the leaf, alongside the outline of the leaf. Then fill the section at the bottom of the leaf completely with chain stitch and finish the thread.

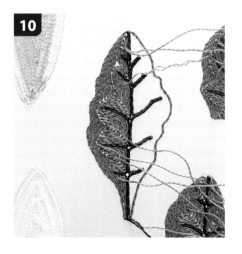

**10**

Continue making chain stitch to completely fill one side of the leaf, working a complete line of chain stitch around the inside of your previous chain stitches. Fill sections individually when there is no room to make a line of chain stitch between the sections of the leaf separated by the leaf veins.

Fill the other side of the leaf with chain stitch in the same way. Then finish the thread tails with a needle as described previously. Embroider the leaf veins and fill all the other leaves in the same way.

**11**

### Primrose: Back of the Leaves

Outline and then fill the leaves with chain stitch using a single strand of the mid-green embroidery thread.

### Crocus: Front and Back of the Petals

Chain stitch around the edge of the petal and then fill the petal with the mid-purple sequins.

### Crocus: Front and Back of the Leaves

Using a single strand of the mid-green embroidery thread, chain stitch around the outline of the leaf. Make chain stitch inside the outline to fill the shape.

## FINISHING THE EDGES OF THE PETALS AND LEAVES AND APPLYING WIRE

### Cutting Out the Petals and Leaves

When the embroidery of each petal and leaf has been completed, you can remove the fabric from the frame or hoop and cut around each of them. Make sure you leave a border of about 5mm of fabric around the petals and leaves. This border will later be stitched to the wrong side of the petal or leaf to hide it.

### Applying Wire to the Back Pieces of the Petals and Leaves Embroidered with Embroidery Thread

The first stage of finishing the petals and leaves that were embroidered with embroidery thread is to apply 28 gauge wire around the edges. All of the flowers and leaves in this project need to have wire applied to them to allow them to be manipulated into three-dimensional shapes. The front pieces of the petals and leaves do not need to have wire applied to them.

The process of applying the wire to the back of the petals and leaves embroidered with sequins is slightly different to applying wire to the petals and leaves embroidered with embroidery thread. The petals and leaves embroidered with sequins need to have their fabric borders stitched down before the wire is applied, so these instructions have been placed after the finishing of the fabric borders. Use the process detailed in the following instructions to apply the wire to the back pieces of all of the petals and leaves that are embroidered with embroidery thread.

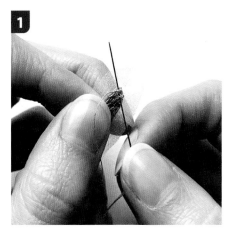

Cut a length of wire long enough to go around the edges of the petal with a short length left over. Fold one end of the wire over. Thread a needle with a single strand of sewing thread and secure it on the back of the petal. Make your stitches by sliding the needle through the back of the chain stitches. Position the folded-over end of the wire at the top of the petal and make two small stitches over the wire.

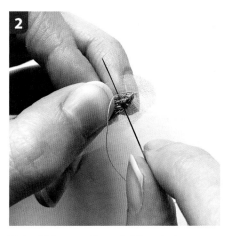

Make stitches over the end of the wire to secure it to the back of the petal.

**3**

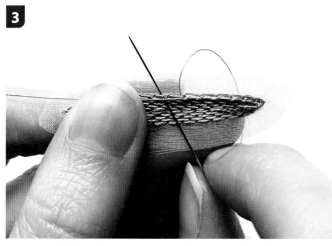

Then make small stitches over the wire and through the back of the chain stitches to secure the wire to the edges of the petal.

Bend the wire at the tip of the petal and around any curves in the petal to make the wire match the shape of the petal. Continue applying the wire to the petal until you reach the top of the petal; then make a few stitches over the wire at the top. Do not finish the thread because this can be used to stitch the fabric border down in the next step.

**4**

## Finishing the Edges of the Petals and Leaves

Once the wire has been applied, the fabric border around the petals and leaves that are embroidered with embroidery thread can be turned to the wrong side and stitched down. To do this, use the same technique that is explained in more detail in the appliqué instructions in Chapter 7: Advanced Techniques. You can finish the fabric borders of the petals embroidered with sequins now too because the wire is applied after this is done.

**1**

Before finishing the edges of the fabric, you can cut triangles out of the fabric border to reduce bulk at the tips of small petals such as the bluebell petals.

**2**

Fold the fabric border over and stitch it to the back of the petal by making your stitches through the back of the chain stitches. For the sequinned petals and leaves, fold the fabric over so the line of chain stitch on the outline is flipped over so it sits just inside the edge of the fabric border. This will pull the sequins together at the edges on both sides of the petal or leaf when you sew them together.

## Applying Wire to the Back Pieces of the Petals and Leaves Embroidered with Sequins

**1** Secure a single length of sewing thread to the back of the petal at the base of the petal. Bend a piece of 28 gauge wire in half that is long enough to go around the outlines of the petal with a short length left over.

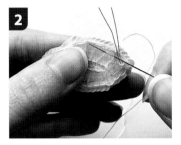

**2** Position the folded end of the wire at the base of the petal and make several small stitches over the fold with a single length of thread. Then slide the needle underneath the fabric border to move a short distance around the outline of the petal. Make a small stitch over the wire and then slide the needle under the fabric border again.

**3** Continue making small stitches over the wire while progressing around the outline of the petal, bending the wire into shape as you do so. You should be applying the wire just inside the edge of the petal.

**4** Continue applying the wire all around the outline of the petal and then make several stitches over the wire at the base of the petal. Leave the rest of the wire extending beyond the base of the petal.

## Sewing the Front and Back Pieces of the Petals and Leaves Together

After all the edges of the petals and leaves have been finished, the front and back pieces of each petal and leaf can be sewn together.

**1** Thread a needle with a single strand of thread in a colour that matches the main colour of the petal. Secure it to the back of the front piece of the petal and bring the thread to the base of the petal. Place the front and back pieces of the petal wrong sides together and make a small stitch through the edge of the back piece of the petal, at the bottom of the petal.

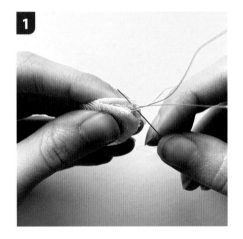

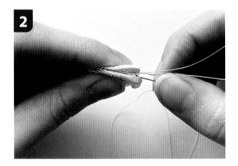

**2** Then make a small stitch through the edge of the front piece of the petal.

**3** Make a small stitch through the edge of the back piece of the petal.

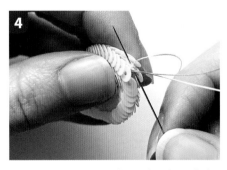

**4** Repeat Steps 2 to 3 to make stitches through the edges of both pieces of the petal alternately until you have stitched all the way around the petal. Make several small stitches through the edge of the petal to secure the thread end. Cut the thread tail close to the petal.

# CONSTRUCTING THE FLOWERS

## Making Flower Stamen Centres

Three of the flowers in this project feature stamens in their centres. This includes the daffodil, tulip and crocus flowers. These are made from paper flower stamens, which can be bought in several different sizes and colours from cake decorating or craft shops. Some stamens, generally the larger ones, are wired. It is useful to have wired stamens for the larger flowers in this project, but for the crocus flower you can use smaller unwired stamens. Plain white stamens can be dipped in paint to colour them.

Take several flower stamens and cut all of them except one down to the desired length. Apply a thin layer of glue to a small strip of tissue paper. Place the stamens on the tissue paper, lining up the bottom of the short stamens. Roll the tissue paper up around the stamens and let the glue dry. Then bend the stamens outwards a little to arrange them at different angles.

## Constructing the Daffodil

**1**

Curve the trumpet into a circle and secure a single length of yellow embroidery thread to the bottom corner of the trumpet. Then make a small stitch through the edge of the opposite end of the trumpet.

**2**

Continue making stitches as in Step 1 through each end of the trumpet alternately to join the two ends together.

**3**

Fold the wire over towards the centre of the trumpet and then roughly in the centre; fold the wire so that it forms a right angle.

**4**

Take two of the daffodil petals and twist the wires together to attach the petals to each other.

**5**

Attach the other petals to the flower one by one by twisting the wires around the wires of the other petals. Position the petals so that they are spaced slightly apart in the centre of the flower.

**6**

Insert the wire from the trumpet through the centre of the daffodil petals.

*continued on the following page…*

**7**

Twist the wire from the trumpet around the wire from the petals. Position the trumpet so that the join will be facing downwards when the stem is applied.

**8**

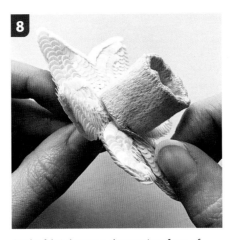

On the fabric between the sequins of one of the petals, secure a single strand of the same embroidery thread that you used to embroider the trumpet. Then make a stitch through the base of the trumpet. Then make a stitch down through the petal.

**9**

Bring the needle back up through the petal a short distance away. On the back side of the petal, this stitch should be hidden underneath the sequins. Then stitch around the whole of the trumpet to secure it to the petals.

**10**

Attach five pearlescent stamens together to form a bunch of stamens about 1.5cm (½in) long, not including the one stamen that is left long. Cut a 1.5cm (½in) diameter circle of yellow felt and sew the same mid-yellow sequins that you used to embroider the daffodil petals onto one side of the felt to cover it. Leave a small space in the centre without any sequins covering it.

**11**

Push the point of a sharp pair of scissors into the centre of the felt to make a small hole in the felt.

**12**

Insert the wire of the stamens through the hole in the felt.

**13**

Insert the long stamen through the trumpet and the centre of the petals. Pull the stamens down so that the sequinned circle is positioned at the base of the trumpet.

**14**

Bend the wire over at a right angle about 1cm (⅓in) away from the petals. This will form the top of the stem.

# Constructing the Tulip

**1** Twist the wires of the three inner petals together and shape them into a gentle curve at the base of the petals.

**2** Twist the wires of the three outer petals around the wires of the inner petals, positioning each outer petal over where the edges of the inner petals meet.

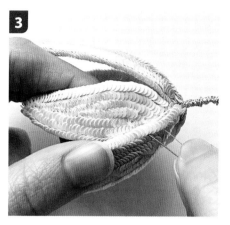

**3** Secure a single strand of sewing thread to the fabric of one of the outer petals between two lines of sequins near the edge of the petal. Then make a stitch down through the petal between the sequins and down through the inner petal.

**4** Bring the needle up through the inner petal and the outer petal.

**5** Then make another stitch down through the two petals.

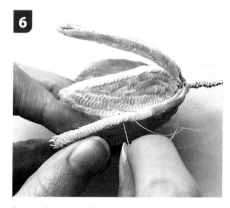

**6** Repeat Steps 4 and 5 until you have reached nearly halfway up the outer petal. Finish with a stitch down through the outer petal.

**7** Then bring the needle down between the layers of the inner petal and bring the needle up on the other side of the petal towards the bottom.

**8** Repeat Steps 3 to 7 to stitch both sides of the outer petals to the inner petals. This helps the tulip to hold its shape.

**9** Use three gold stamens to make a centre for the tulip. Then insert the long stamen through the centre of the flower.

## Constructing the Bluebell

**1** Finish the front and back of all the petals and sew them together. Then shape each petal by curling the bottom tip and bending the top of the petal slightly.

**2** Attach two petals together by twisting the wires together. Then secure a single strand of the light purple embroidery thread to the edge of one of the petals. Make a small stitch through the edge of other petal.

**3** Then make a small stitch through the edge of the first petal.

**4** Repeat the process of making a stitch through the edge of each petal alternately until you reach a point about three quarters of the way down the length of the petal. Then make a stitch upwards through the edge of a petal.

**5** Make another stitch through the edge of a petal to bring the thread towards the top of the petals; when you make this stitch, bring the needle out between the join in the petals. Then make an angled stitch through the two layers of a petal to bring the needle out at the edge of the petal.

**6** Add the other petals one by one, repeating Steps 2 to 5 to sew the edges of the petals together. Then use the same technique to join the first and the last petals together.

**7** To finish the thread, make a long stitch through the two layers of one of the petals and cut the thread close to the petal.

**8** Assemble all of the bluebell flowers by repeating Steps 1 to 7.

**9** Take two of the bluebell flowers and, starting 1cm (⅓in) up the wire of one of the bluebells, wrap it around the wire stem of the other bluebell, 2cm (¾in) away from the flower. The wire of the bluebell on the right will form the main stem. Bend the wire of the main stem into a slight curve.

**10**

Position another bluebell along the main stem 2cm (¾in) away from the second bluebell and, starting 1cm (⅓in) up the wire, wrap the wire of this bluebell around the main stem.

**11**

Take another bluebell and position it 1.5cm (½in) away from the third bluebell. Starting 1cm (⅓in) up the wire, twist it together with the main stem so that the wire of the bluebell you are applying elongates the main stem.

**12**

Position the last bluebell flower 1.5cm (½in) away from the fourth bluebell; starting 1cm (⅓in) up the wire, wrap it around the main stem.

## Constructing the Primrose

Twist the wires of the five primrose petals together and position the petals so that the edges of each petal meet but do not overlap. Make sure that the petals are positioned close together at the centre of the flower.

## Constructing the Crocus

Twist the wires of the five crocus petals together and curve them at the base to form a bowl-shaped flower. Then take five small flower stamens and attach them together. Thread the long stamen through the centre of the flower.

## Making the Flower Stems

Once the flowers have been constructed, they can be joined to the thicker wire that forms the base of the flower stems. The stems are then thickened with strips of tissue paper and glue, and finally wrapped with strips of bias-cut organza (*see* 'Cutting Fabric on the Bias' for more information).

## Attaching the Flowers to the Stems and Thickening the Stems

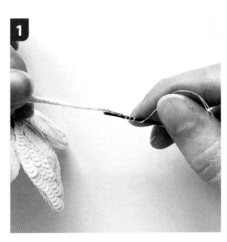

Take a flower and a piece of the 18 gauge wire, which will form the stem. Wrap the wire attached to the petals around the top of the thick wire.

Apply a thin layer of glue to a strip of tissue paper over the point where the thinner and thicker wires join and wrap it around the wires to secure the flower onto the stem. Put to one side to dry.

Now apply glue to more strips of tissue paper and wrap them around the wire stem. Do this down the whole length of the stem. Apply a few strips of tissue paper at one time and let the glue dry before adding more layers.

Continue applying strips of tissue paper to gradually build up the thickness of the stem and to smooth any bumps or dips in the stem until the desired thickness has been achieved. Bend the excess wire over at the end of the stem and shape it into a spiral.

### Stem Lengths

When finishing the stems of the flowers, use the measurements given here for the length of the stems:

- daffodil, 16cm (including the bend at the top of the stem)
- tulip, 17cm
- bluebell, 19.5cm (from where the stem meets the first flower to the end of the stem; it is easiest to measure the length of this stem before bending it)
- primrose, 7cm
- crocus, 7cm.

## Covering the Stems with Fabric

**1**

To make the fabric strips to cover the stems, cut 2.5cm (1in) wide strips of organza on the bias and then fold them in half and iron flat. Apply a small blob of glue to the top of the stem and then take the organza and place it, with the fold in the organza facing upwards towards the flower petals, on top of the glued area. Hold it in place for a few minutes until the glue has dried.

**2**

Then turning the stem as you go, begin to wrap the organza around the stem. Make sure you cover the glued area by wrapping the organza around the top of the stem a few times. Then hold the organza at a slight angle and turn the stem at the same time to wrap the organza down the length of the stem. Hold the organza tightly as you do this to retain the tension.

**3**

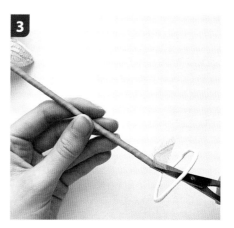

When you have almost reached the end of the stem, place a small blob of glue at the base, holding the organza tightly at the same time to stop it from unravelling. Then roll the organza over the glued area and hold it in place for a few minutes until the glue has dried. Cut the organza close to the stem.

**4**

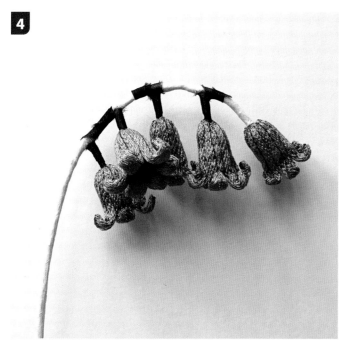

For the bluebell, wrap small lengths of organza around the short stems above the flowers first, then start from the top of the stem and apply a length of organza all the way down the stem.

### Cutting Fabric on the Bias

All woven fabric has a grain line. The straight grain is parallel to the selvedge. The selvedges are narrow bands on both sides of the fabric that are formed during the weaving process; the selvedge is a straight edge. Fabric is usually cut on the straight grain but can be cut diagonally, which is called cutting on the bias. To cut fabric on the bias, draw a line at a 45-degree angle from the selvedge. Cutting fabric on the bias means it is more unstable and therefore has some stretch, which is crucial to allow the organza strips to wrap smoothly around the flower stems.

### Colour of the Organza Strips

Two different shades of green organza are used to wrap the stems. The shade of fabric that you should use for each of the flowers is indicated here:

- daffodil, mid-green
- tulip, mid-green
- primrose, mid-green
- bluebell, dark green
- crocus, dark green.

## Attaching the Leaves

Once you have wrapped the stems with organza, you can attach the leaves to the stems.

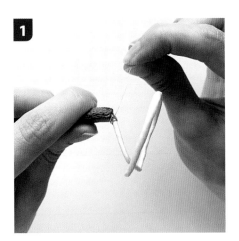

Position a leaf at the bottom of the stem. Wrap the wire at the bottom of the leaf around the stem, at the point just before the bend at the base of the stem.

Repeat Step 1 to attach more leaves to the stem. Follow Steps 1 and to 2 to attach the leaves to the daffodil, bluebell, tulip and crocus stems.

For the primrose, start by twisting the wire at the bottom of the leaves together to form a group of three leaves and another group of two leaves. Then wrap the first group of leaves around the base of the stem, followed by the second group of leaves, in the same way as described in Step 1.

## Stitching the Leaves Together at the Base

The bluebell, daffodil and tulip, which have long leaves, need to have the leaves stitched together at the base. This helps the leaves to stand up properly and stay in position.

For the daffodil, secure a single strand of thread in a matching colour to the base of one of the leaves. Then make stitches through the edge of each leaf alternately to attach them together.

Stop about 2cm (¾in) up the leaf and then repeat on the other side of the leaves.

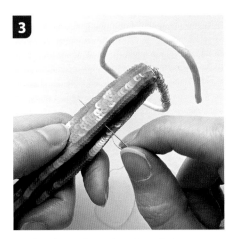

For the tulip, make stitches through the two layers of the leaves, inserting the needle on one side of the leaf and bringing it out on the other side. Stitch through all the leaves in this way to form a circle of thread that holds the three leaves together.

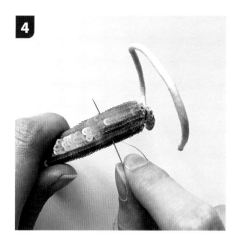

**4**

Repeat Step 3 a little further down the leaves.

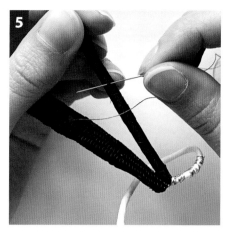

**5**

For the bluebell, secure the thread to the leaf about 3cm (1in) up from the base of the leaf. Bring the thread out through the centre of the leaf. Then make a small stitch through the organza on the stem.

**6**

Make a stitch back through the leaf. Then secure the thread through the leaf.

## Adding a Centre to the Primrose Flower

A small bead is added to the centre of the primrose flower to finish it. Because this bead is glued in place, it is easiest to do this once the stem has been formed, the leaves are added and the primrose can stand up on its own due to the circle of wire at the base of the stem.

## CONSTRUCTING THE FLORAL ARRANGEMENT

The flowers can now be combined into an arrangement and secured to the wooden base of the glass dome to complete the project.

Apply a small blob of glue to the centre of the flower and then thread a mid yellow bead onto a needle. Place the bead in the centre of the flower and then gently slide the needle out from the bead.

**1**

Take a small piece of air-dry clay and roll it into a ball. Place it onto a piece of plastic or other non-porous surface. Push the base of one of the flower stems into the clay and, as you do so, push the ball of clay down to flatten it. Prop the flower up for several hours until the clay is dry. Repeat this process at the base of all the flower stems.

**2**

Take the wooden base of the glass dome and position the tulip in the centre. Apply a thin layer of glue to a strip of tissue paper and stick it to the base of the stem and the wooden base. Apply several more strips of tissue paper to secure the stem to the wooden base.

*continued on the following page…*

Arrange the other flowers around the tulip and secure the stems to the wooden base in the same way.

Begin filling the space around the stems by pushing small pieces of clay into the gaps.

Continue building a mound of clay around the bottom of the stems until you have a smooth, rounded base of clay. Leave to dry for at least 48 hours.

Apply glue to strips of tissue paper and begin to cover the clay. Extend the tissue paper strips beyond the clay slightly so they are also attached to the wooden base. As the clay dries, it may have lifted up around the edges. If so, push it down at the edges to crack it a little so it touches the wooden base, before you apply the tissue paper over it.

Continue applying strips of tissue paper until you have completely covered the clay. Leave to dry for at least 24 hours.

Apply a thin layer of glue onto a small area of the tissue paper. Then place a piece of silver leaf on top of the glue. Try to wrinkle the silver leaf as you apply it.

Completely cover the tissue paper with silver leaf. Let the glue dry and then gently rub the edges of the silver leaf with a paintbrush to remove any that has not adhered to the base.

Take a sheet of silver leaf and rub a paintbrush over it to break it up into small pieces. Apply small blobs of glue to the silver leaf at the base of the stems and drop some of the broken-up silver leaf on top of the glue.

Continue applying pieces of the broken-up silver leaf to the base to create a rough texture. Extend the silver leaf beyond the clay base slightly and fade it out by applying individual pieces of silver leaf and leaving gaps between the pieces. Leave the glue to dry for 24 hours before placing the glass dome over the flowers.

# Appliqué Butterfly and Clover

This project is a good example of how tambour beading can be applied to any fabric by making tambour-beaded motifs into appliqués. A T-shirt would not be suitable for tambour beading because the fabric is stretchy, which means it cannot be properly tensioned. This butterfly, which is embroidered with sequins and beads, is embroidered onto organza first and then applied to the T-shirt.

The butterfly and clover design is embroidered with both flat and cup sequins in a variety of finishes to create contrast and varying textures within the design.

The finished appliqué butterfly and clover project. This project is an example of how tambour beading can first be applied to organza and then cut out and stitched to any type of fabric, regardless of whether it is suitable to be tambour-beaded onto. This plain white T-shirt has been embellished with the butterfly and clover design to add a lovely touch of detail.

## Materials

White silk organza, one piece of around 22cm × 22cm (9in × 9in)

Pearl mid-green flat sequins 3mm

Iridescent light orange cup sequins 3mm

Glossy porcelain white flat sequins 3mm

Porcelain light blue flat sequins 4mm

Nacrolaque medium blue flat sequins 3mm

Metallic dark blue cup sequins 3mm

Clear bugle beads 2mm

Glossy dark blue beads 10

Cotton threads in colours that match the beads and sequins

A T-shirt or other fabric item to sew the appliqué onto

## Making the Embroidery

**1**

Fill all of the clover leaves with lines of the mid-green sequins. Use the technique of filling leaves with sequins explained in Chapter 7: Advanced Techniques.

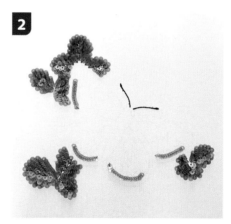

**2**

Apply the orange cup sequins in lines on the wings. On the top wings, start applying sequins from the top of each line. For the bottom wings, start applying the sequins from the end furthest away from the body of the butterfly.

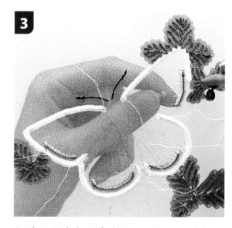

**3**

Apply a single line of white sequins around the edge of the wings, just inside the outline so that the edges of the sequins overlap the outline of the butterfly. On the bottom wings, start applying the sequins underneath the top wings, finishing next to the butterfly body. On the top wings, start applying the sequins next to the butterfly body.

*continued on the following page…*

**4**

Apply the pale blue sequins to the wings. To do this, start by working a line of sequins next to the white sequins. When you reach the start of the orange sequins, make a locking stitch and then make several chain stitches back to where you will begin applying the next line of sequins.

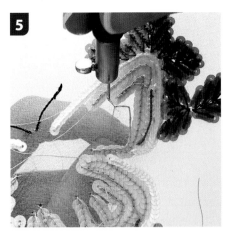

**5**

Then apply a line of sequins next to the previous blue sequins and the orange sequins. Make chain stitches back to just below where you started the line of sequins.

**6**

Apply another line of sequins and again make several chain stitches back.

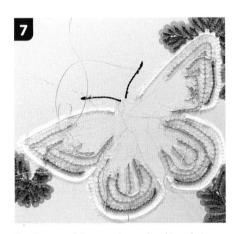

**7**

Continue applying sequins and making chain stitches to fill the shape. Try to avoid covering the marks on the wings, which will later be filled with other sequins.

**8**

On the right side, you can see how applying the blue sequins in this way means that the direction of the sequins is the same within each wing, and the direction is also mirrored on each side of the butterfly.

**9**

Using the fan-filling technique, fill the remaining space left in the wings with the mid-blue sequins. Make lines of chain stitches between the lines of sequins to apply each line of sequins in the same direction.

**10**

Fill all of the wings in the same way; you may have to make two shorter lines of sequins in between the longer lines.

Apply one of the dark blue sequins to the bottom of the butterfly body and make a locking stitch.

**11**

**12** Make a small chain stitch to the right, diagonally upwards, and apply a line of sequins up the side of the butterfly body, stopping at the line that divides the two sections of the body.

**13** Make a chain stitch sideways to the left and then make several chain stitches down the side of the body. Apply a line of sequins up the left side of the body; then make chain stitches back down to the bottom of the body.

**14** Finish filling the bottom section of the body by applying a line of sequins up the centre.

**15**

Outline the top section of the body with sequins and then fill the middle. Finish the thread ends.

Apply lines of the clear bugle beads in the centre of the clover leaves to complete the embroidery.

**16**

## Applying the Embroidery to the T-shirt

For more detailed instructions about how to make embroidery into an appliqué and apply it to an item, *see* Chapter 7: Advanced Techniques.

**1** Cut the fabric, leaving a border of at least 5mm around the embroidery. Finish the raw edges of the fabric by stitching them to the back of the embroidery.

**2** Position the appliqué onto the T-shirt and pin it in place.

*continued on the following page…*

Secure a single strand of cotton thread, in a colour that matches the T-shirt, to the T-shirt fabric at a point that will be covered by the appliqué.

Make stitches through the edge of the appliqué and the T-shirt alternately around the appliqué to apply it to the T-shirt, being careful not to pull the stitches too tight to avoid distorting the T-shirt fabric.

Lightly mark the antennae onto the T-shirt with a pencil.

Thread a fine needle with a double length of sewing thread in a colour that matches the beads, and secure it on the back of the T-shirt behind the butterfly. Bring the needle up at the top of butterfly body.

Thread a blue bead onto the needle and then bring the needle down to make a small stitch to secure the bead in place. Bring the needle up about the length of a bead away from the last bead.

Thread a bead onto the needle, then bring the needle down close to the last bead. Bring the needle up about the length of a bead away from the last bead.

Following the pencil marks, repeat Step 8 to apply more beads until you reach the end of the antenna.

Finish the thread with three small stitches behind the line of beads. Then repeat Steps 6 to 10 to apply beads to the other antenna.

# CHECK CUSHION

This cushion features a very simple design of a grid of straight lines that imitates a woven check fabric. Several different patterns of beads and sequins interspersed with empty chain stitches have been used to create variety in the application of the materials. This makes the simple design appear more interesting and complex. Due to the size of this cushion, the embroidery can only be worked in a slate frame.

The finished check cushion project. An example of how tambour beading can be used on items for interior decoration, this cushion features a design of interwoven lines. The sequins and beads in shades of blue and green are applied in different spacings of a bead or sequin followed by a number of chain stitches to create interesting lines.

## MATERIALS

Mint green silk organza, one piece measuring 45cm × 45cm (18in × 18in)

Blue-green silk dupion, one piece measuring 43cm × 43cm (17in × 17in), two pieces measuring 43 × 27cm (17in × 11in)

Green sewing thread to match the silk dupion fabric

Porcelain off-white cup sequins 4mm

Porcelain light blue flat sequins 4mm

Porcelain chartreuse flat sequins 3mm

Iridescent very light green cup sequins 4mm

Iridescent medium green cup sequins 4mm

Light blue with silver heart bugle beads 1 (2mm)

Opaque turquoise round beads 12

Glossy ivory round beads 10

Cotton threads in colours that match the beads and sequins

Three buttons 15mm diameter

Cushion pad 45cm × 45cm (18in × 18in)

When embroidering this design, you need to leave some space at the edges of the embroidery for the seams of the cushion to be sewn up. Instead of applying beads and sequins right from the start and right up to the edges of the design as you normally would, you must start and stop applying them about 1.5cm away from the edges. This means there are no beads or sequins obstructing the presser foot of the sewing machine when you sew the seams. Instead of finishing your thread at the point where you stop applying the beads and sequins you should make some plain chain stitches up to the edge of the design. When you have finished sewing the cushion together you can sew on some beads and sequins by hand to fill the gaps next to the seams.

This design is embroidered so that the lines appear to cross over and under each other. This is achieved by either continuing the pattern of applying beads or sequins so that the line appears to be over the line underneath it or by making several empty chain stitches so that the line which crosses it can pass over the top. Guidance has been given in the instructions below to show how to manage the intersections of the lines. However, this will depend on the spacing of your stitches and will vary between people because your stitches may be slightly shorter or longer which will affect the way the intersections are managed. For example, where in the instructions it may tell you to make three chain stitches to leave an empty space without a bead, this is because the spac-

ing means there would normally be a bead applied with the second empty chain stitch. This would not allow the intersecting line to cross over it so the pattern of the beads must be broken with the three empty chain stitches. But your spacing may mean that by continuing the pattern of beads and empty chain stitches normally you would have an empty chain stitch intersecting the line so you do not need to disrupt the pattern by making extra empty chain stitches.

On the pattern provided for this cushion in the patterns chapter, each horizontal and vertical line has been assigned a number. The number of the lines are referred to in the instructions below to identify which line is to be embroidered.

## PATTERNS OF APPLYING BEADS AND SEQUINS

In this design the beads and sequins are applied in four different patterns. These patterns are referred to in the instructions by the number they are assigned in the list below.

1. A bead or sequin applied with every chain stitch.
2. One bead or sequin, one empty chain stitch.
3. One bead, one empty chain stitch, two beads, one empty chain stitch.
4. One sequin, two empty chain stitches, two sequins, two empty chain stitches.

# Embroidering the Front of the Cushion

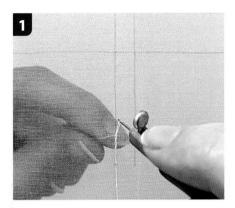

Trace the design onto the fabric. Turn the frame so the top of the design is closest to you. Then, starting on the vertical line number 11, with the glossy ivory beads and matching thread, make a starting stitch and several chain stitches to 1.5cm (½in) away from the start of the line.

Start applying the beads, in pattern number 2.

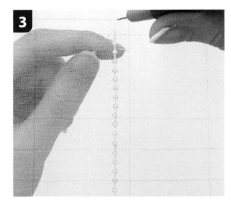

Continue applying beads, making sure that when you cross over the second horizontal line of the design this is done with a chain stitch. Make three chain stitches over the fourth horizontal line.

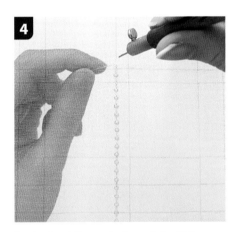

Apply a bead then make three chain stitches over the fifth horizontal line.

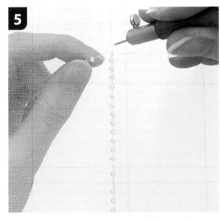

Continue applying the beads and then make two chain stitches over the seventh horizontal line.

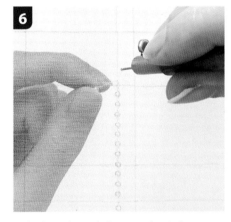

Make three chain stitches over the ninth horizontal line.

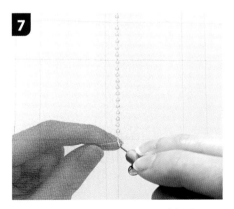

Turn the frame so that the bottom of the design is closest to you and then make three chain stitches over the eleventh horizontal line.

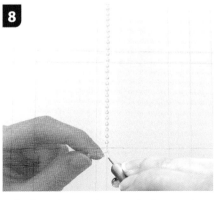

Make three chain stitches over the fourteenth horizontal line.

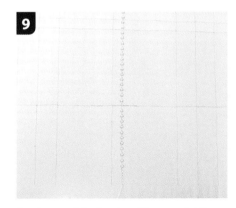

Continue applying beads until you reach 1.5cm (½in) away from the end of the line. Then make chain stitches up to the end of the line.

**10**

Turn the frame so that the top of the design is closest to you. Then on the vertical line number 10, start with 1.5cm (½in) of chain stitches. Then repeat Steps 2 to 9 to apply ivory beads to the line and finish with 1.5cm (½in) of chain stitches.

**11**

Starting from the top of the design, start applying the glossy ivory beads to the vertical line number 2 in pattern number 1. Make two chain stitches over the first horizontal line. Make two chain stitches over the third horizontal line. Make two chain stitches over the sixth horizontal line. Make two chain stitches over the eighth horizontal line.

**12**

Turn the frame so the bottom of the design is closest to you. Make two chain stitches over the tenth horizontal line. Make two chain stitches over the twelfth horizontal line. Apply one bead, then make two chain stitches over the thirteenth horizontal line. Continue until the end of the line.

**13**

With the bottom of the design closest to you and starting from the left of the design, begin applying the ivory beads to the horizontal line number 11 in pattern number 3. Finish the line when you meet the second vertical line.

**14**

Resume applying the beads on the other side of the vertical line of beads. Make four chain stitches over the fifth vertical line.

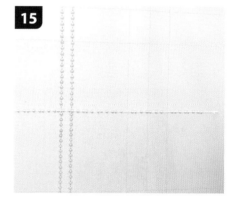

**15**

Make three chain stitches over the seventh vertical line. Make three chain stitches over the ninth vertical line. Make three chain stitches over the twelfth vertical line. Make three chain stitches over the fourteenth vertical line. Then continue until the end of the line.

**16**

Starting from the left, apply a line of the light blue flat sequins to the horizontal line number 12 in pattern number 1. Make two chain stitches over the first vertical line.

Make two chain stitches over the third vertical line. Make two chain stitches over the fourth vertical line and two chain stitches over the sixth vertical line. Make two chain stitches over the eighth vertical line and two chain stitches over the tenth vertical line. Make two chain stitches over the eleventh vertical line and then two chain stitches over the thirteenth vertical line. Continue until the end of the line.

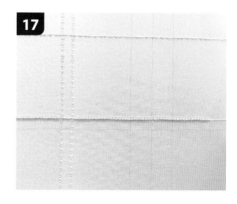

**17**

*continued on the following page…*

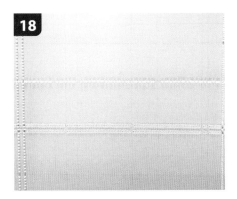

Repeat Steps 16 and 17 to apply a line of light blue flat sequins to the horizontal line number 13 in the same way.

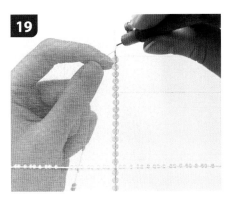

Starting from the bottom of the design, apply a line of light blue flat sequins to the vertical line number 6. Apply the sequins in pattern number 2. Make two chain stitches over the first vertical line. Make two chain stitches over the fourth horizontal line and two chain stitches over the sixth horizontal line.

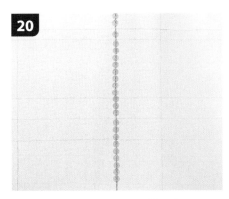

Turn the frame so that the top of the design is closest to you. Then make two chain stitches over the eighth horizontal line. Make two chain stitches over the tenth horizontal line and two chain stitches over the eleventh horizontal line. Make two chain stitches over the thirteenth horizontal line. Continue until the end of the line.

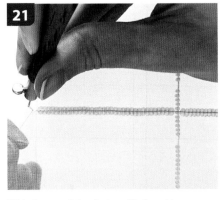

With the top of the design still closest to you, begin applying the iridescent very light green cup sequins to the horizontal line number 7, starting from the right. Apply the sequins in pattern number 1. Make one chain stitch over the second and fifth vertical lines.

Make one chain stitch over the seventh vertical line and one chain stitch over the ninth vertical line. Make one chain stitch over the twelfth vertical line and one chain stitch over the fourteenth vertical line. Continue until the end of the line.

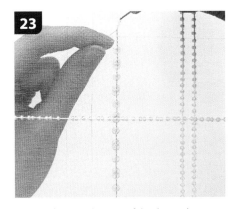

Starting from the bottom of the design, begin applying a line of the very light green cup sequins to the vertical line number 9 in pattern number 4. Apply the sequins up to the second horizontal line. Resume the sequins after the second horizontal line. Resume the line of sequins again after the third horizontal line. Make four chain stitches over the fifth horizontal line.

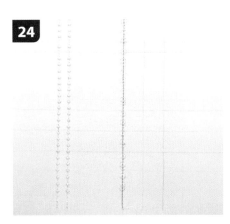

Turn the frame so the top of the design is closest to you. Then make two chain stitches over the seventh horizontal line and two chain stitches over the ninth horizontal line. Make three chain stitches over the twelfth horizontal line and three chain stitches over the fourteenth horizontal line. Continue until the end of the line.

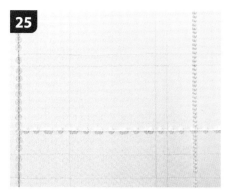

**25**

With the top of the design closest to you, begin applying the ivory cup sequins to the horizontal line number 3, starting from the right. Apply the sequins in pattern number 4. Make four chain stitches over the first vertical line and two chain stitches over the third vertical line. Make two chain stitches over the fourth vertical line. Continue applying the sequins up to the sixth vertical line.

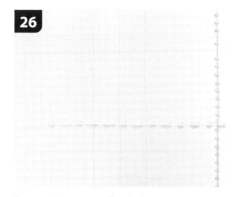

**26**

Resume the sequins after the line. Make three chain stitches over the eighth vertical line and four chain stitches over the tenth vertical line. Make two chain stitches over the eleventh vertical line and two chain stitches over the thirteenth vertical line. Continue until the end of the line.

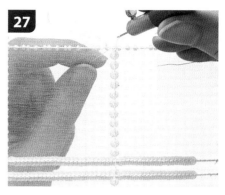

**27**

Starting from the bottom of the design, begin applying the ivory cup sequins to the vertical line number 13 in pattern number 2. Make one chain stitch over the first horizontal line. Continue applying the sequins up to the fourth horizontal line. Resume the sequins after the line.

**28**

Turn the frame so the top of the design is closest to you. Make two chain stitches over the sixth horizontal line. Continue applying the sequins up to the eighth horizontal line. Resume the sequins after the line.

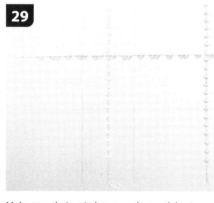

**29**

Make two chain stitches over the tenth horizontal line and two chain stitches over the eleventh horizontal line. Make two chain stitches over the thirteenth horizontal line. Continue until the end of the line.

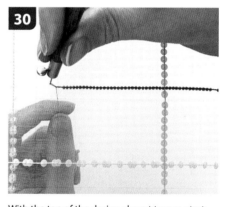

**30**

With the top of the design closest to you, start applying the turquoise beads to the horizontal line number 5. Apply the beads in pattern number 1, starting from the right. Make one chain stitch to cross between the beads on the second vertical line. Make two chain stitches over the fifth vertical line and two chain stitches over the seventh vertical line.

**31**

Apply beads up to the ninth vertical line of sequins, then resume the line of beads on the other side of the sequins. Make two chain stitches over the twelfth vertical line. Make two chain stitches over the fourteenth vertical line. Then continue to the end of the line.

*continued on the following page…*

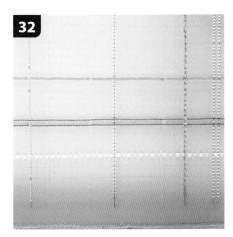

Repeat Steps 30 to 31 to apply another line of turquoise beads to the horizontal line number 4.

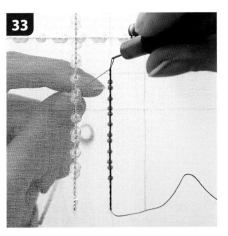

Starting at the top of the design, begin applying turquoise beads to the vertical line number 8. Apply the beads in pattern number 3. Make two chain stitches over the second horizontal line. Make two chain stitches to cross between the beads on the fourth horizontal line and two chain stitches over the fifth horizontal line. Apply beads up to the seventh horizontal line, then resume the beads after the line. Make three chain stitches over the ninth horizontal line.

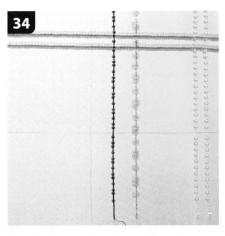

Turn the frame so the bottom of the design is closest to you. Make two stitches over the eleventh horizontal line. Make two chain stitches over the fourteenth horizontal line. Continue until the end of the line.

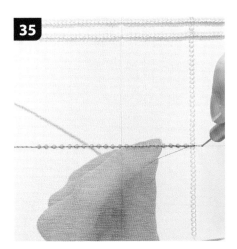

With the bottom of the design closest to you, starting from the left, begin applying the turquoise beads to the horizontal line number 14. Apply the beads in pattern number 2. Make two chain stitches over the second vertical line. Make two chain stitches over the fifth vertical line and three chain stitches over the seventh vertical line.

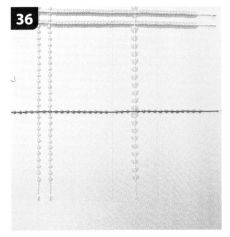

Continue applying the beads up to the ninth vertical line, then resume the beads after the line. Make three chain stitches over the twelfth vertical line and one chain stitch over the fourteenth vertical line. Continue until the end of the line.

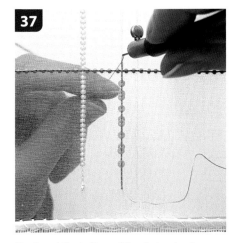

Starting at the bottom of the design, begin applying the chartreuse flat sequins to the vertical line number 3. Apply the sequins in pattern number 4. Make five chain stitches over the first horizontal line. Make three chain stitches over the fourth horizontal line and two chain stitches over the sixth horizontal line.

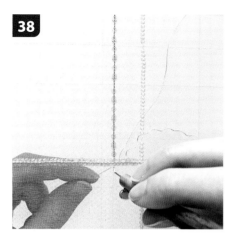

**38**

Turn the frame so the top of the design is closest to you. Continue applying sequins up to the eighth horizontal line, then resume the sequins after the line. Apply the sequins up to the tenth horizontal line, then resume the sequins after the line. Make one chain stitch and apply one sequin up to the eleventh horizontal line. Resume the sequins after the line, starting with two chain stitches. Make four chain stitches over the thirteenth horizontal line.

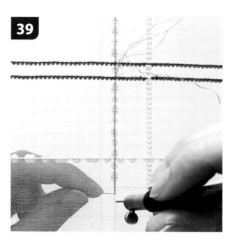

**39**

Continue until the end of the line. Then repeat Steps 37 to 38 to apply sequins to the vertical line number 4 in the same way.

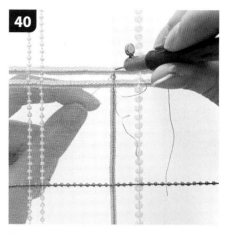

**40**

Starting from the bottom of the design, begin applying the chartreuse sequins to the vertical line number 12. Apply the sequins in pattern number 1 up to the second horizontal line then resume the sequins after the line by making one chain stitch and applying one sequin. Resume the sequins after the third horizontal line of blue sequins. Make two chain stitches over the fifth horizontal line.

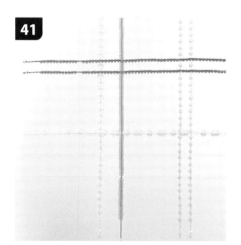

**41**

Turn the frame so the top of the design is closest to you. Make two chain stitches over the seventh horizontal line and two chain stitches over the ninth horizontal line. Make two chain stitches over the twelfth horizontal line and two chain stitches over the fourteenth horizontal line. Continue until the end of the line.

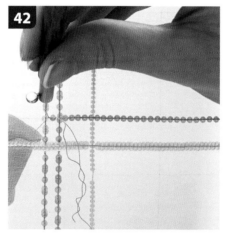

**42**

With the top of the design closest to you, starting from the right, begin applying the chartreuse sequins to the horizontal line number 8. Apply the sequins in pattern number 2 up to the third vertical line. Resume the sequins after the line. Make a chain stitch then apply one sequin.

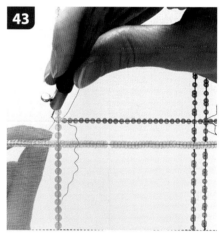

**43**

Resume the line of sequins after the fourth vertical line then apply sequins up to the sixth vertical line. Then resume the sequins after the line.

*continued on the following page…*

**44**

Make two chain stitches over the eighth vertical line. Apply the sequins up to the tenth vertical line, then resume the sequins after the line. Make one chain stitch and apply one sequin. Resume the line of sequins after the eleventh vertical line. Then make two chain stitches over the thirteenth vertical line. Continue until the end of the line.

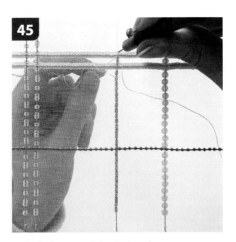

**45**

With the bottom of the design closest to you, begin applying the blue bugle beads to the vertical line number 5. Apply the beads in pattern number 1 up to the second horizontal line then apply one bead between the second and third horizontal lines. Resume the line of beads after the third horizontal line, then make two chain stitches over the fifth horizontal line.

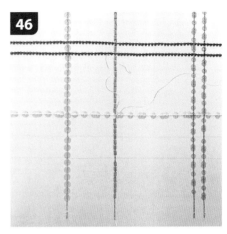

**46**

Turn the frame so the top of the design is closest to you. Then apply the beads up to the seventh horizontal line. Resume the beads after the line. Make two chain stitches over the ninth horizontal line. Apply the beads up to the twelfth horizontal line then resume the beads after the line. Make two chain stitches over the fourteenth horizontal line. Continue until the end of the line.

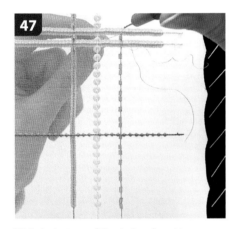

**47**

With the bottom of the design closest to you, start applying blue bugle beads to the vertical line number 14. Apply the beads in pattern number 3 up to the second horizontal line. Then apply one bead between the second and third horizontal lines. Make two chain stitches over the fifth horizontal line.

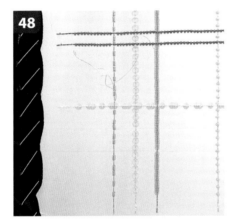

**48**

Turn the frame so the top of the design is closest to you. Apply beads up to the seventh horizontal line then resume the beads after the line. Make two chain stitches over the ninth horizontal line. Apply beads up to the twelfth horizontal line, then resume the beads after the line. Make two chain stitches over the fourteenth horizontal line. Continue until the end of the line.

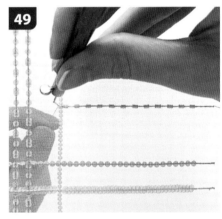

**49**

With the top of the design closest to you, starting from the right, begin applying blue bugle beads to the horizontal line number 9. Apply the beads in pattern number 2. Make one chain stitch over the second vertical line. Make one chain stitch over the fifth vertical line and two chain stitches over the seventh vertical line.

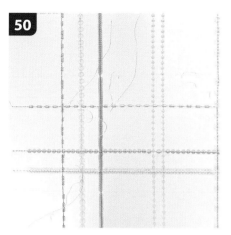

**50**

Apply beads up to the ninth vertical line then resume the beads after the line. Apply beads up to the twelfth vertical line then resume the beads after the line. Apply beads up to the fourteenth vertical line then resume the beads after the line. Continue until the end of the line.

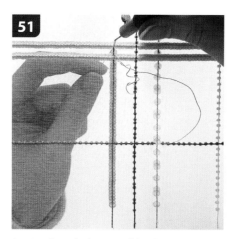

**51**

Starting from the bottom of the design, begin applying the mid-green cup sequins to the vertical line number 7. Apply the sequins in pattern number 1 up to the second horizontal line, then resume the sequins after the line. Make one chain stitch and apply one sequin. Resume the sequins after the third horizontal line. Make three chain stitches over the fifth horizontal line.

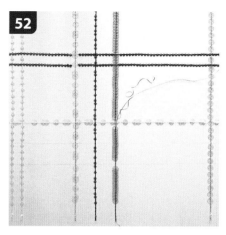

**52**

Turn the frame so the top of the design is closest to you. Make three chain stitches over the seventh horizontal line. Make three chain stitches over the ninth horizontal line. Apply the sequins up to the twelfth horizontal line, then resume the sequins after the line. Make three chain stitches over the fourteenth horizontal line. Continue until the end of the line.

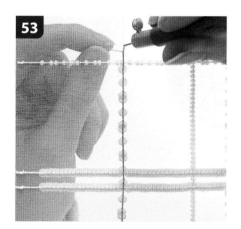

**53**

Starting from the bottom of the design, begin applying the mid-green sequins to the vertical line number 1. Apply the sequins in pattern number 4. Make three chain stitches over the fourth horizontal line.

**54**

Turn the frame so the top of the design is closest to you. Apply sequins up to the sixth horizontal line, resume the sequins after the line. Apply sequins up to the eighth horizontal line. Then resume the sequins after the line, starting with two chain stitches. Make four chain stitches over the tenth horizontal line. Make three chain stitches over the eleventh horizontal line and three chain stitches over the thirteenth horizontal line. Continue until the end of the line.

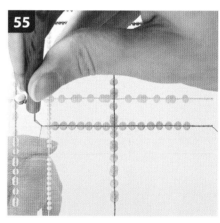

**55**

With the top of the design closest to you and starting from the right, begin applying the mid-green sequins to the horizontal line number 2. Apply the sequins in pattern number 2. Make two chain stitches over the second vertical line. Apply sequins up to the fifth vertical line, resume the sequins after the line.

*continued on the following page…*

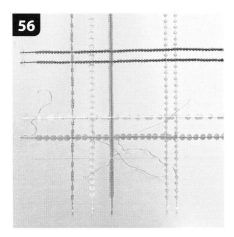

**56**

Apply sequins up to the seventh vertical line, then resume the sequins after the line. Make two chain stitches over the ninth vertical line. Apply sequins up to the twelfth vertical line, resume the sequins after the line. Apply sequins up to the fourteenth vertical line, resume the sequins after the line. Continue until the end of the line.

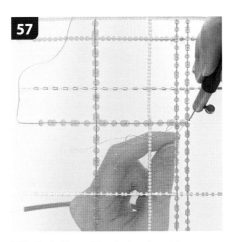

**57**

With the bottom of the design closest to you and starting from the left, begin applying the mid-green sequins to the horizontal line number 10. Apply the sequins in pattern number 4. Make four chain stitches over the first vertical line. Apply sequins up to the third vertical line, resume the sequins after the line. Make one chain stitch and apply one sequin up to the fourth vertical line.

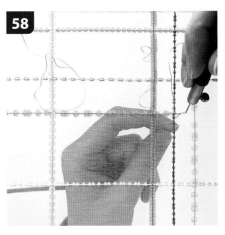

**58**

Resume the sequins after the fourth vertical line, starting with two chain stitches. Apply sequins up to the sixth vertical line, resume the sequins after the line. Apply sequins up to the eighth vertical line. Then resume the sequins after the line, starting with one chain stitch.

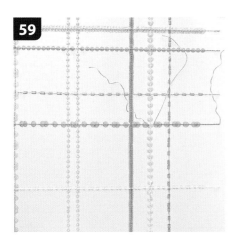

**59**

Make two chain stitches over the tenth vertical line and two chain stitches over the eleventh vertical line. Apply sequins up to the thirteenth vertical line. Resume the sequins after the line, starting with one chain stitch. Continue until the end of the line.

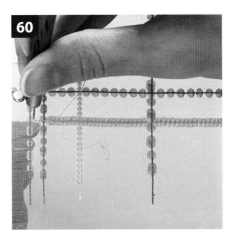

**60**

With the top of the design closest to you and starting from the right, begin applying the very light green cup sequins to the horizontal line number 1. Apply the sequins in pattern number 1. Make two chain stitches over the first vertical line. Apply sequins up to the third vertical line, resume the sequins after the line.

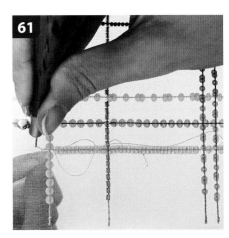

**61**

Make one chain stitch and apply one sequin up to the fourth vertical line. Resume the sequins after the line, starting with one chain stitch. Apply sequins up to the sixth vertical line. Resume the sequins after the line, starting with one chain stitch.

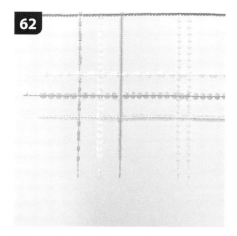

**62**

Make two chain stitches over the eighth vertical line and two chain stitches over the tenth vertical line. Make two chain stitches over the eleventh vertical line and two chain stitches over the thirteenth vertical line. Continue until the end of the line.

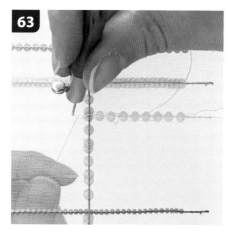

**63**

With the top of the design closest to you and starting from the right, begin applying the off-white cup sequins to the horizontal line number 6. Apply the sequins in pattern number 2 up to the first vertical line, resume the sequins after the line.

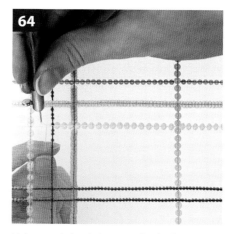

**64**

Make two chain stitches over the third vertical line and two chain stitches over the fourth vertical line. Make two chain stitches over the sixth vertical line and two chain stitches over the eighth vertical line.

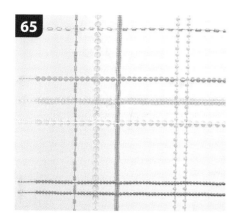

**65**

Make two chain stitches over the tenth vertical line and two chain stitches over the eleventh vertical line. Apply sequins up to the thirteenth vertical line. Resume the sequins after the line, starting with one chain stitch. Continue until the end of the line.

## MAKING THE CUSHION

When sewing buttonholes, it is best to test the length by sewing the buttonhole on a scrap piece of fabric before doing so on your actual pattern pieces. Doing this means you can check that the button fits through the buttonhole.

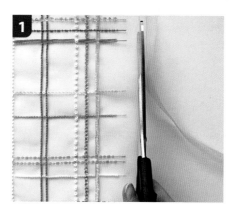

**1**

Once the embroidery is complete and the fabric is removed from the frame, mark out a distance of 1.5cm (½in) from the edges of the design and cut along these lines.

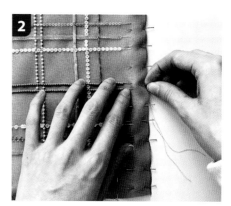

**2**

Place the 43cm × 43cm (17in × 17in) piece of silk dupion on a flat surface and lay the embroidered silk organza on top. Line up the edges and pin together.

*continued on the following page…*

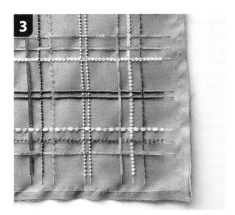

Sew around the fabric 1cm (⅓in) from the edge to secure the two pieces of fabric together.

To prevent the fabric from fraying, sew around the edges of all the pieces of fabric with a zig-zag stitch.

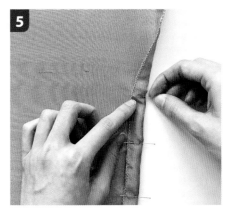

Take one of the 43 × 27cm (17in × 11in) pieces of silk dupion. Fold one of the longest edges over by 1.5cm (½in) and secure it with pins. Iron the fold in the fabric flat to form a sharp crease and remove the pins.

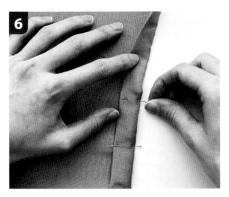

Fold the fabric over again on the same edge, this time by 2cm (¾in), and secure it with pins. Iron the fold flat and remove the pins.

Thread a needle with a single length of thread and bring the needle through the fold at the edge of the fabric. Do not pull the thread all the way through the fabric; leave a short tail of thread.

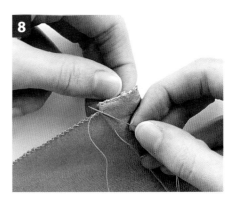

At the edge of the fabric, make a very small stitch.

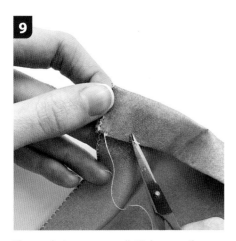

Then make two more small stitches over the previous one to secure the thread end. Cut the thread tail close to the fabric.

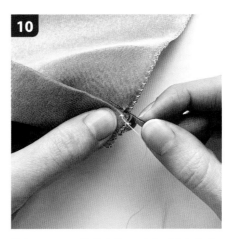

Make a very small stitch through the fabric, just below the fold.

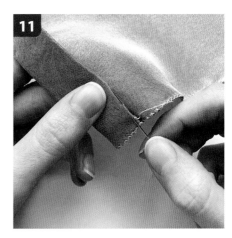

Make a stitch of about 1cm (⅓in) length through the bottom of the fold.

**12**

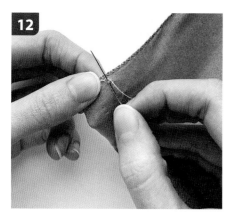

Repeat Steps 10 and 11 to sew the fold down. Finish with a small stitch through the bottom of the fold and make two more small stitches over the top.

**13**

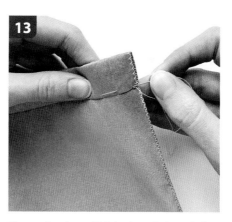

Then make a long stitch backwards through the fold and cut the thread close to the fabric.

**14**

Repeat Steps 5 to 13 with the other piece of silk dupion. On the right side of the fabric you should only be able to see very small stitches.

**15**

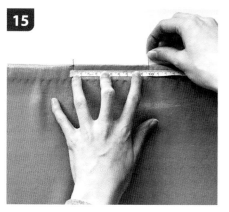

To mark the positions for the buttonholes on the fabric, measure along the folded edge of one of the back pieces and mark 21.5cm (8in) from the edge with a pin. Then mark 9.75cm (3¾in) on either side of the pin.

**16**

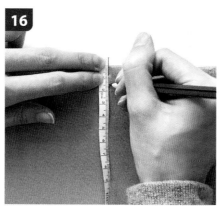

Measure 1.5cm (½in) down from the folded edge at each pin and mark a dot on the fabric at this point with a pencil. Remove the pins.

**17**

Draw a straight line that extends 8.5mm out from each side of the marked dots. The full length of this line should be 1.7cm.

**18**

Mark a short vertical line at the start and end of each line. This marks the start and end of the buttonholes.

**19**

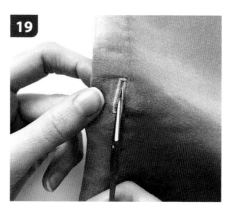

Sew the buttonholes on a sewing machine, making sure you align the machine with the lines you drew on the fabric. Then cut the buttonholes open.

**20**

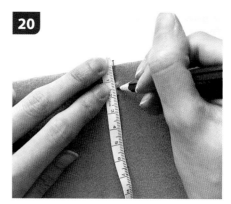

Take the other back piece of the cushion and repeat Steps 15 and 16 to mark the position of the buttons on the fabric.

*continued on the following page…*

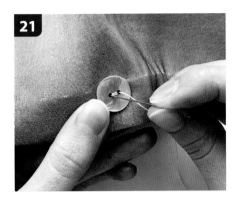

With a double length of sewing thread, in a colour that matches the silk dupion, sew the buttons onto the fabric at the marked dots. Make sure the centres of the buttons sit on top of the marked dots.

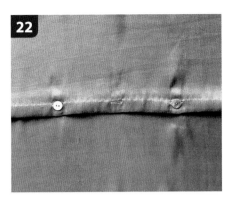

Attach the two back pieces of the cushion together by pushing the first and last buttons through the buttonholes. Leave the middle button undone. This will allow you to turn the cushion the right way round after you have sewn it together.

Turn the fabric over and use a pin to secure both pieces of fabric together on each side of the folded opening.

Lay the front of the cushion right-side up and then on top of this place the back of the cushion right-side down.

Line up the edges of the front and back pieces of the cushion and pin together. Sew around the fabric, 1.5cm (½in) away from the edges.

To turn the cushion the right way round, pull the fabric through the gap in the back of the cushion. Use a thin, blunt object, such as the end of a pencil or crochet hook, to push the corners of the cushion out.

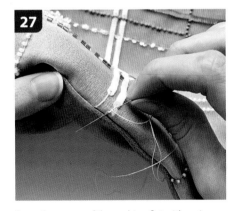

Press the seams of the cushion flat with an iron, using a low heat and covering the embroidery with a cloth to avoid melting the sequins. Sew beads and sequins onto the ends of the lines to fill the edges of the cushion. Undo all the buttons and insert a cushion pad into the cushion cover.

## Removing Fabric Bulk at the Corners

If you have used a heavier fabric than the silk dupion used in this project, you can cut some of the fabric away at each corner of the cushion after you sew the front and back of the cushion together, and while the cushion is still inside out. This will remove the bulk at the corners when the cushion is turned the right way round, which will allow the corners to be turned out into neat right angles.

## Sewing Buttonholes on Unstable Silk Fabric

If your sewing machine struggles to sew accurate buttonholes onto the silk fabric due to its unstable, slippery nature, you can place a piece of cotton calico fabric behind the fabric, underneath the area where the buttonhole is to be sewn. The buttonhole can then be sewn on top of both pieces of fabric. The calico will help to add stability to the silk fabric, allowing the buttonholes to be accurately stitched. The excess calico can be cut away from the back of the fabric close to the buttonhole stitching.

# SUMMER FLOWERS AND FRUIT

This framed design features summer flowers and fruit embroidered with the tambour hook using a variety of threads, beads and sequins. These materials are applied using a range of techniques to create different textures and patterns within the flowers and leaves. The large scale of the embroidery allows more detail to be added to the design and also helps to create a statement framed piece. This is the most challenging project in this book due to several areas of the design requiring you to make decisions about exactly where and at what angle to apply lines of materials. Due to the size of this embroidery, it can only be worked in a slate frame.

The finished summer flowers and fruit design. This ambitious large scale design is a wonderful project in which to challenge your tambour skills. It features many of the techniques covered in this book, including several advanced techniques. The use of these techniques has been focused on creating interesting applications of the materials within the flowers and leaves.

## MATERIALS

Dark blue silk organza, one piece cut to 60cm × 78cm (24in × 31in)
Dark blue opaque silk, one piece cut to 60cm × 78cm (24in × 31in)
Cotton threads in colours that match the beads and sequins
Light, mid and dark green rayon thread

### For the Lemon
Dark green silver-lined round beads 11
Mid-green silver-lined round beads 11
Porcelain mid-yellow cup sequins 3mm

### For the Dog Rose
Light pink porcelain flat sequins 3mm
Cotton thread in a slightly lighter pink than the pink sequins
White rayon thread
Mid-yellow glossy crystal round beads 10
Porcelain light yellow cup sequins 3mm
Yellow rayon thread
Toho mid-green silver-lined beads 15
Toho dark green beads 15

### For the Sweet Violet
Toho silver-lined dark purple beads 15
Toho mid purple lined beads 15
Toho silver-lined milky light gold beads 15
White matt opaque round beads 16
Clear crystal bugle beads 2mm
Pearl mid green flat sequins 3mm
Glossy crystal dark green flat sequins 3mm

### For the Welsh Poppy
Iridescent light orange cup sequins 4mm
Glossy crystal mid-orange cup sequins 3mm
Mid-green crystal tosca round beads 12
Light green tosca round beads 10
Yellow glossy crystal round beads 10
Porcelain light yellow cup sequins 3mm

### For the Strawberry
Toho mid-red silver-lined beads 15
Toho silver-lined milky light gold beads 15
White glossy ceylon round beads 13
White matt opaque round beads 16
Toho silver-lined mid-green beads 15
Toho dark green beads 15

### For the Fuchsia
Glossy crystal deep pink flat sequins 3mm
Mid-purple flat sequins 3mm
Golden yellow rayon thread
Toho silver-lined milky light gold beads 15
Toho dark green beads 15
Matt dark green flat sequins 3mm

### For the Dahlia
Light peach tosca round beads 10
Toho crystal lined with mid pink beads 15
Toho dark green beads 15
Porcelain dark green cup sequins 3mm
Matt metallic gold flat sequins 3mm
Mid pink rayon thread

### For the Cosmos
White glossy Ceylon round beads 13
Clear crystal bugle beads 2mm
White glossy porcelain flat sequins 3mm
Mid-yellow porcelain cup sequins 3mm
Matt white opaque round beads 16
Toho mid green opaque beads 11

## For the Daisy

White matt opaque round beads 16

White glossy Ceylon round beads 13

White rayon thread

Yellow glossy crystal round beads 10

Light green tosca round beads 10

Iridescent light green flat sequins 3mm

## For the Cherry

Glossy crystal deep pink flat sequins 3mm

Glossy crystal mid pink flat sequins 3mm

Dark green with silver heart bugle beads 1 (2mm)

Matt dark green flat sequins 3mm

## CHAIN STITCHING THE STEMS

The first stage of embroidering this design is to embroider the stems with a decorative chain stitch worked on the right side of the fabric. First transfer the design to the wrong side of the fabric and then turn the fabric over so the right side is facing you.

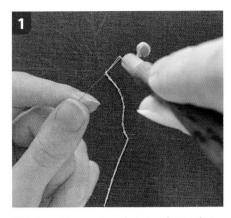

With the mid-green thread, start making a chain stitch from the end of the main stem of the Welsh poppy. When you reach the first stem that extends out from the main stem, make a locking stitch and make chain stitches until you reach the bottom of the leaf. Make a locking stitch and then a small chain stitch sideways.

Working in the opposite direction to the previous line of chain stitch, make another line of chain stitch close to it. Make these chain stitches adjacent to the halfway point of the previous chain stitches. Make a locking stitch when you reach the main stem.

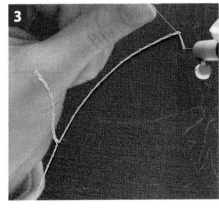

Continue making chain stitches along the main stem until you reach the point where the stem is intersected by a leaf. Make a locking stitch and then a small chain stitch sideways.

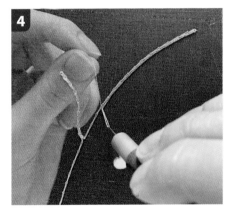

Make another line of chain stitches in the opposite direction, close to the last line of chain stitch. Make a locking stitch at the point where another stem extends out from the main stem.

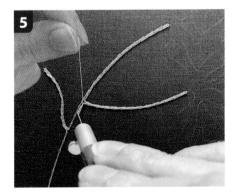

Embroider this stem with chain stitches in the same way as before.

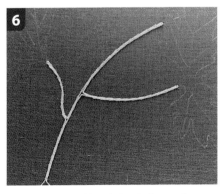

Then continue making chain stitches until you reach the starting point. Make a finishing stitch and cut the thread to complete the first section of the poppy stem.

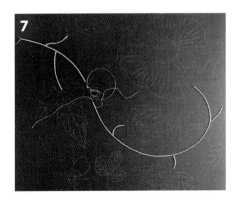

Starting on the other side of the leaf that intersects the Welsh poppy stem, embroider the rest of the stem with chain stitch in the same way as before.

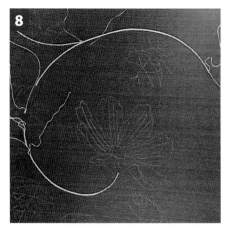

Using the same method, chain stitch the cosmos stem with the mid-green thread.

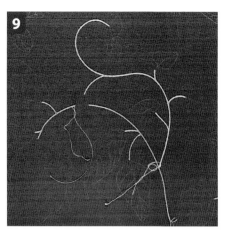

Chain stitch the lemon stem with the mid-green thread. Then chain stitch the sweet violet stem with the light green thread.

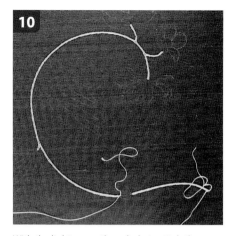

With the light green thread, chain stitch the strawberry stem.

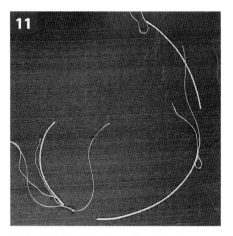

Chain stitch the daisy stem with the light green thread.

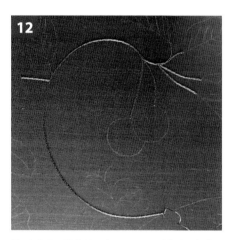

Next chain stitch the cherry stem with the dark green thread.

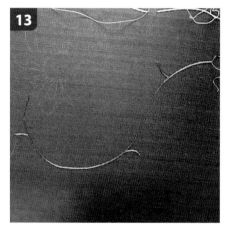

Chain stitch the dahlia stem with the dark green thread.

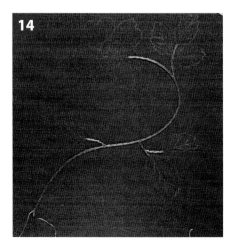

Chain stitch the dog rose stem with the dark green thread.

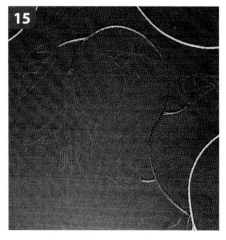

Chain stitch the fuchsia stem with the dark green thread.

# Lemon

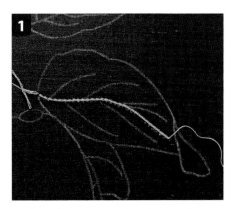

Apply the dark green beads to the central leaf vein.

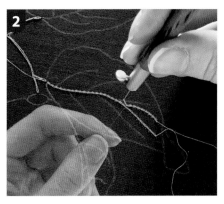

Apply beads to one of the other leaf veins, working from the end of the line towards the central leaf vein, and make a locking stitch after the last bead.

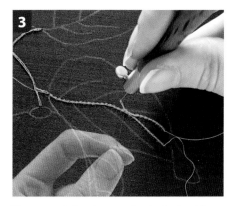

Then to apply beads to another leaf vein without finishing the thread, make several chain stitches very close to the beads at the centre of the leaf and make a locking stitch when you reach the closest leaf vein.

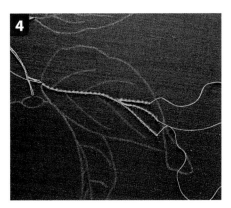

Then apply beads to the leaf vein.

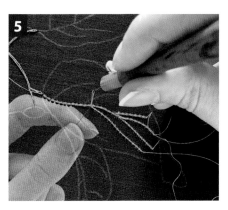

Sometimes after applying beads to one leaf vein, you will need to cross over the beads at the centre to reach the next vein. To do so, make a locking stitch at the end of the line of beads. Then make a small chain stitch between two of the beads in the centre of the leaf.

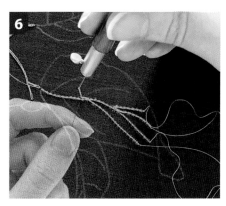

Next make several chain stitches close to the central line of beads and then a locking stitch to reach the next leaf vein.

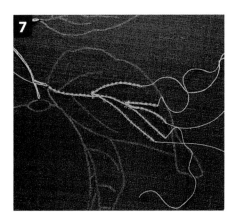

Apply beads to the leaf vein.

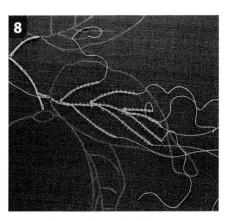

Apply beads to the final leaf vein in the same way as before.

Use the same process to apply beads to all the leaf veins of the lemon leaves and then finish the thread ends.

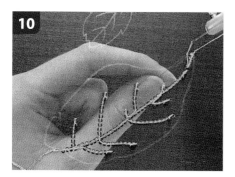

**10**

The mid-green beads are applied in lines to the edges of the leaves. To begin, apply a line of beads starting from the tip of the leaf. Then make a locking stitch at the end of the line of beads and make a diagonal chain stitch back to the edge of the leaf. This chain stitch should be made to the point where you want to start applying your next line of beads. Then make another locking stitch.

**11**

Apply another line of beads, then make a locking stitch followed by a diagonal chain stitch back to the edge of the leaf. Then make a locking stitch.

**12**

Repeat Step 11 to apply more lines of beads, alternating the lengths of the lines of beads so that some are shorter and some longer.

**13**

When the lines of beads become quite long, instead of making one long diagonal chain stitch back to the edge of the leaf, you should make two chain stitches very close to the last line of beads and then make one diagonal chain stitch to reach the edge of the leaf.

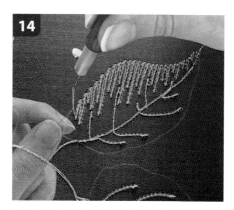

**14**

Continue along the edge of the leaf. Then, when you are a short distance from the end of the leaf, bring the diagonal chain stitch a little bit further away from the last line of beads.

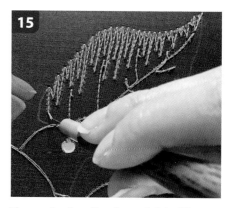

**15**

Then apply a line of beads at a slightly different angle to the last line of beads.

**16**

Then apply more lines of beads in the same way, slightly changing the angle of the line of beads each time.

**17**

Due to shape of the base of this particular leaf, next you need to make a chain stitch diagonally upwards and then make a locking stitch. Then apply one or more beads to meet the stem.

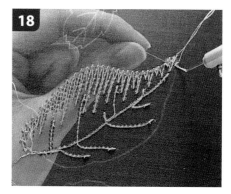

**18**

Now return to the tip of the leaf and apply a bead. Then make a diagonal chain stitch and locking stitch, a little bit more than a bead's width away from the last line of beads.

*continued on the following page…*

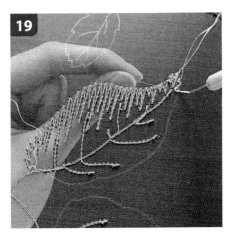

Apply a line of beads at a slightly different angle and then make a diagonal chain stitch and locking stitch; again, make this slightly more than a bead's width away from the last line of beads.

Apply another line of beads, which will establish the angle you will follow down the leaf.

Continue applying lines of beads at the edge of the leaf until you have nearly reached the end of the leaf. Then make the diagonal chain stitch and locking stitch slightly further away from the last line of beads to begin changing the angle of the lines of beads.

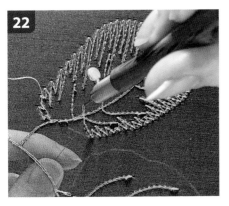

Apply a line of beads at a slightly different angle to the last line and make a locking stitch.

Then make a diagonal chain stitch a little more than a bead's width away from the last line of beads and repeat Step 22.

Continue applying lines of beads to complete the leaf.

Applying beads to the leaf with the folded tip needs to be managed slightly differently. To begin, apply beads around the side and bottom of the folded section and make a locking stitch after the last bead.

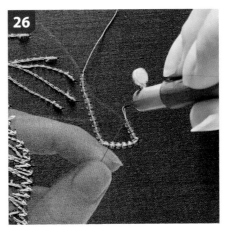

Make a chain stitch backwards to form a corner and apply a line of beads up to the top of the folded section; then make a locking stitch.

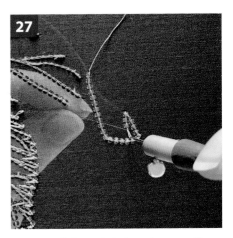

Make a small chain stitch along the top outline and then a locking stitch. Apply a line of beads at a slightly different angle to the last line and make a locking stitch.

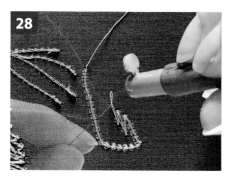

**28** Make a chain stitch and locking stitch back to the top of the outline and then apply another line of beads. Then make a locking stitch. Repeat the process of making a chain stitch back to the top of the outline.

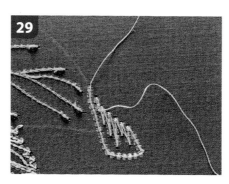

**29** Continue applying lines of beads along the top edge of the folded section, varying the lengths of the lines. Apply the last line of beads at a slightly different angle to fill the space left.

**30** Then begin applying beads along the bottom edge of the leaf. The first line of beads you apply should be at a different angle to the beads you applied to the outline of the folded section.

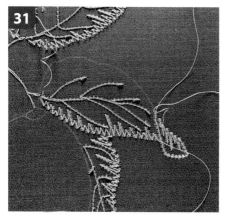

**31** Apply lines of beads all along the bottom edge of the leaf.

**32** Then begin applying beads to the top edge of the leaf, again applying the first line at a different angle to the beads on the outline of the folded section.

**33** Apply lines of beads along the whole of the top edge of the leaf, using the techniques previously described to alter the angle of the lines of beads as you approach the end of the leaf. Then apply beads to the edges of all the other lemon leaves.

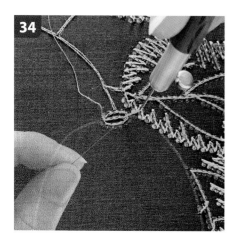

**34** Apply the dark green beads around the oval shape at the top of the lemon and then fill the centre of the shape with beads.

**35** Using the mid-yellow 3mm cup sequins, fill the lemon with the scrunched sequins technique (*see* Chapter 7: Advanced Techniques).

**36** The embroidery of the lemon and the lemon leaves is now complete.

# DOG ROSE

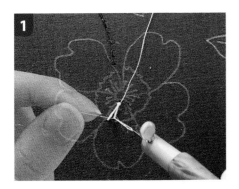

On the wrong side of the fabric, using the white rayon thread, make a starting stitch at the edge of the circle at the centre of the flower. Make a long pulled stitch just beyond the outline of the petal detail. Make a chain stitch back into the same hole. Then make a slightly shorter pulled stitch and make a chain stitch back into the same hole again.

Keep making pulled stitches, alternating the length of the stitches, until you have filled the first petal.

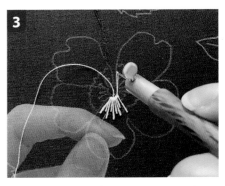

Make a chain stitch sideways to cross over the line separating the petals. Then make a pulled stitch in the next petal.

Repeat Steps 2 to 3 to make pulled stitches into every petal. Then finish the thread ends.

Starting at the edge of the petal on the left side, apply a line of the light pink flat sequins with the light pink thread, stopping just more than halfway down the length of the petal and continuing with several empty chain stitches. Finish the chain stitches just before you reach the white pulled stitches.

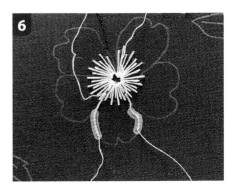

Apply another line of sequins and make several empty chain stitches in the same way on the opposite side of the petal.

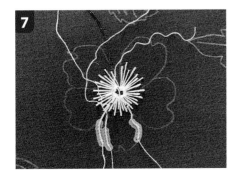

Apply a line of sequins on the left side of the petal to a point just below where the sequins finished on the previous line of sequins. Continue with several empty chain stitches.

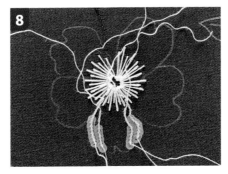

Repeat Step 7 to apply another line of sequins and chain stitches on the right side of the petal.

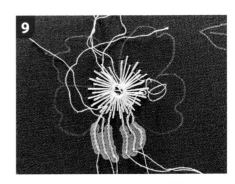

Apply two more lines of sequins and chain stitches on either side of the petal, varying the point where you stop applying the sequins.

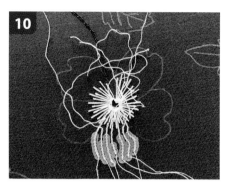

**10** Apply one line of sequins and chain stitches to the left of the petal.

**11** Then apply one more line of sequins and chain stitches to fill the small space left in the centre of the petal.

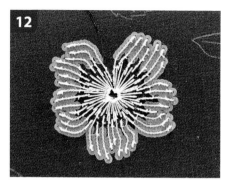

**12** Repeat the process of applying lines of sequins and making chain stitches to fill all the petals of the rose. Then finish the thread ends.

**13** With the yellow rayon thread and yellow beads, make a starting stitch at the edge of the centre of the flower. Then make a chain stitch between the white pulled stitches.

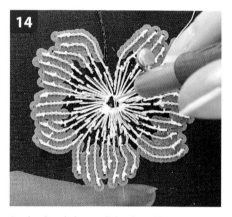

**14** Apply a bead, then pull the thread back to make a pulled stitch with the chain stitch that you used to apply the bead.

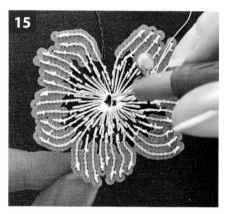

**15** Then make a chain stitch into the same hole as where you made the starting stitch.

**16** Make a chain stitch between the white pulled stitches, a short distance away from your last chain stitch and bead.

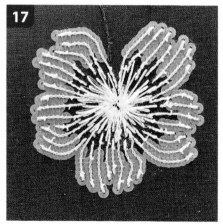

**17** Then repeat Steps 14 to 16 around the centre of the dog rose, varying the length of the chain stitches, until you reach the point where you started. Then finish the thread ends.

**18** Apply one mid-yellow cup sequin to the centre of the flower using the technique of applying sequins on both sides (*see* Chapter 7: Advanced Techniques) to complete the dog rose flower.

*continued on the following page…*

Apply the mid-green silver-lined beads to the leaf veins in the way you applied beads to the lemon leaf veins. Apply a line of the dark green beads along the outline at the bottom of one side of the leaf. Then make a locking stitch followed by a chain stitch sideways and then several chain stitches to the next point on the edge of the leaf.

Apply a line of beads towards the centre of the leaf. Then make chain stitches up to the next point at the edge of the leaf.

Apply another line of beads along the edge of the leaf until you meet the end of the leaf vein. Then make chain stitches until you reach the centre of the leaf.

Apply a line of beads to fill the space between the leaf veins and then make a small locking stitch when you get to a point about halfway along your previous line of beads.

Then changing the direction, apply more beads, stopping a little before the end of the previous line of beads. Make a locking stitch.

Then make chain stitches up to the next point at the edge of the leaf.

Apply a line of beads back towards the centre of the leaf and then make chain stitches up to the point at the top edge of the leaf.

Apply a line of beads until you reach the centre of the leaf and then make a locking stitch and a chain stitch followed by another locking stitch close to the central leaf vein.

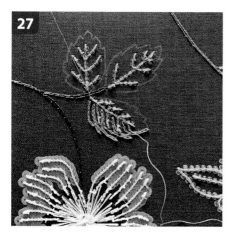

Apply one bead towards the previous line of beads and then make a finishing stitch.

Fill the other side of the leaf with lines of beads in the same way, making the last line so that it meets the bead at the top point of the leaf.

Then apply a line of beads to fill the space on one side of the leaf and make chain stitches close to the beads back up to the top of the leaf.

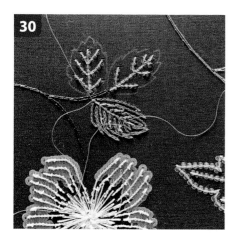

Apply a line of beads to fill the space left on the other side of the leaf.

Fill the other leaves in the same way by making lines of beads and then chain stitches back to the points at the edge of the leaf. At times you will need to break up the lines of beads to best fill the leaf.

## Sweet Violet

Apply the mid-green flat sequins to the leaves using the diagonal sequin filling technique (*see* Chapter 7: Advanced Techniques). Make sure to apply one sequin at the tip of each leaf to create a point.

Fill the turned-over sections of the leaves with the dark green flat sequins. Apply the sequins around the outline of the shape first and then fill the centre of the shape.

With the clear bugle beads and mid-green thread, make a starting stitch through the hole in the sequin at the tip of each leaf and apply a line of beads in the centre of each leaf.

*continued on the following page…*

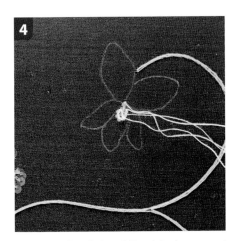

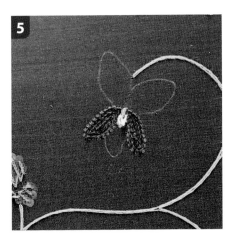

Apply two of the light gold beads in the centre of the flower and then apply the matt white beads around the shape in the centre of the flower. Then fill the gap left underneath the gold beads.

Outline and then fill the two petals on either side of the centre of the flower with the dark purple beads.

Apply the dark purple beads to the outline of the top-left petal.

Outline and then fill the top-right petal with the mid purple lined beads. Then fill the top-left petal and outline and fill the remaining petal at the bottom of the flower with the same beads. Finish all the thread ends to complete the sweet violet flower and leaves.

## WELSH POPPY

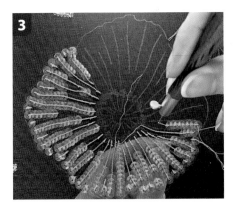

Apply the mid-green beads to the leaf veins using the same process that you used to apply beads to the lemon leaf veins.

Apply the light green beads around the outlines of all the leaves.

Start applying the light orange sequins from the edge of the petals, applying the sequins in lines between the lines drawn on the petals.

**4**

When the sequins reach a point where they cannot fit in between the lines without overlapping them, continue the line with empty chain stitches up to the centre of the poppy.

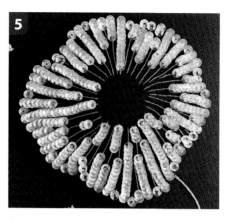

**5**

Continue applying lines of the light orange sequins to fill all the petals, making sure not to cover the lines drawn on the petals.

**6**

Apply the mid-orange sequins to all the lines on the petals using the technique of attaching sequins on both sides.

**7**

On one of the lines that separates the petals, apply a line of chain stitch on the right side of the fabric with the same orange thread that you used to apply the mid orange sequins. Make a bend in the line and then make two more chain stitches.

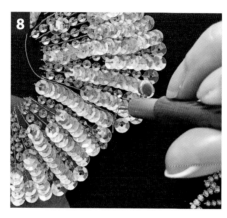

**8**

Pull the last chain stitch back to make a pulled stitch.

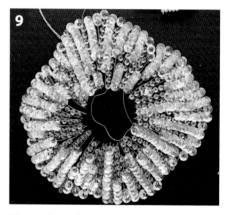

**9**

Then apply another line of chain stitch very close to the previous line. Make each chain stitch next to the centre of the chain stitches in the previous line.

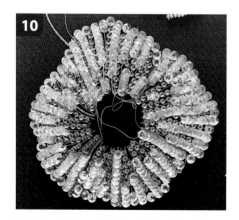

**10**

Make double lines of chain stitch on the other lines between the petals in the same way.

**11**

Using yellow thread, make a long chain stitch over one of the lines at the centre of the poppy.

**12**

Then pull the chain stitch back to make a pulled stitch and make a chain stitch back into the same hole as the starting stitch.

*continued on the following page…*

Make a small chain stitch sideways then make another long chain stitch to the end of the next line.

Pull the chain stitch back to create a pulled stitch and make a chain stitch into the same hole as the beginning of the long chain stitch.

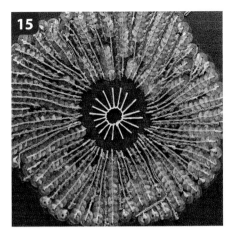

Repeat Steps 13 and 14 to make pulled stitches over all the lines in the centre of the poppy.

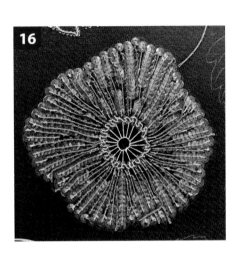

Apply the yellow beads in a vermicelli pattern in the space between the petals and pulled stitch lines. Change the direction of the chain stitch each time you apply a bead.

To complete the poppy, apply the light yellow sequins to fill the small circle at the centre of the poppy.

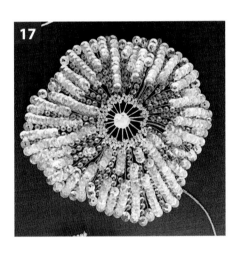

## Strawberry

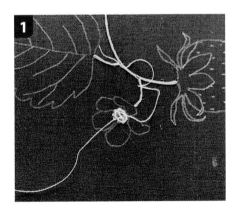

Apply the light gold silver-lined beads just inside the outline of the centre of the strawberry flower. Then fill the centre with beads.

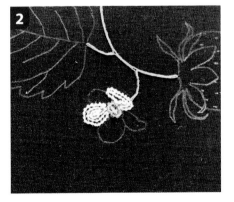

Using the matt white beads, apply beads to the outline of two of the petals and then fill the petals with the beads.

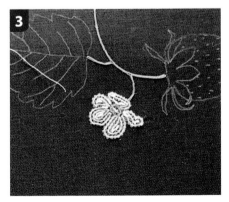

Fill the other petals in the same way with the glossy white beads.

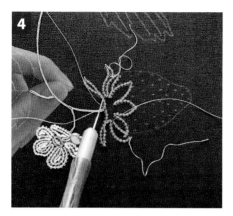

Starting at the bottom of the stalk, apply the mid-green beads to the outlines of the leaves at the top of the strawberry. You will need to finish and restart the outline at a few points because it is not a continuous outline.

Then fill the leaves with the same green beads. You will also need to finish and restart at several points to be able to fill the centre of some of the leaves.

Apply the red beads to the outline of the strawberry. Then, using the red thread with the gold beads, apply the beads to the dots on the strawberry, making chain stitches between them. Make sure you apply each bead in the same direction.

Start filling the strawberry with the red beads in a vermicelli-like pattern so that the beads are applied in all different directions. Apply a circle of beads around each gold bead. Then fill the spaces in between the circles of beads, before moving on to make a circle of beads around the next gold bead.

Continue applying the red beads until you have completely filled the strawberry.

Apply the dark green beads to the leaf veins.

Starting from the base of the leaf on one side of the stem, apply a line of the mid-green beads to the outline until you reach the point at the edge of the leaf. Make a locking stitch and then make several chain stitches backwards to the point where you want to start applying the next line of beads.

Apply another line of beads until you reach the point at the edge of the leaf. Then make a locking stitch.

*continued on the following page…*

**12**

Make several chain stitches backwards close to the beads and then make a chain stitch diagonally across followed by a locking stitch to reach the point where you want to start applying the next line of beads.

**13**

Apply another line of beads until you reach the outline then make a locking stitch.

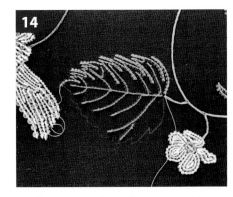

**14**

Continue applying lines of beads and making chain stitches back to reach the point where you want to start applying the next line of beads, all the way along one side of the leaf. The beads should be positioned close together at the edge of the leaf but can move away from each other towards the centre of the leaf.

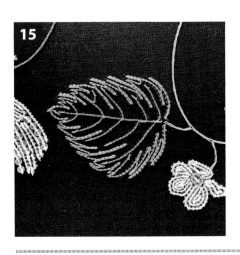

**15**

Apply lines of beads to the other side of the leaf in the same way.

Apply the mid-green beads to the other two leaves.

**16**

---

## FUCHSIA

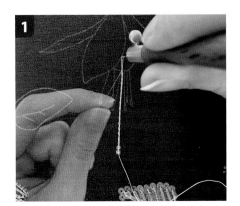

**1**

With the golden yellow thread and gold beads, start from the bottom of the central stamen and apply two beads. Then continue up the stamen with chain stitches until you reach the petal. Then make a locking stitch.

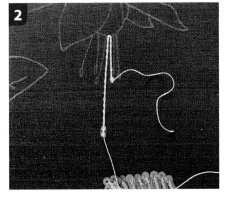

**2**

Make a chain stitch sideways, followed by a locking stitch, and then chain stitch down the next stamen and apply a bead at the end.

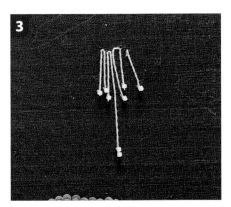

**3**

Embroider the other stamens with beads and chain stitch in the same way.

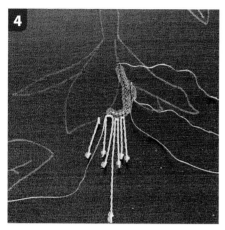

Apply a short line of the mid-purple sequins to fill the small petal at the centre of the fuchsia. Then apply more of the mid-purple sequins to outline the next petal.

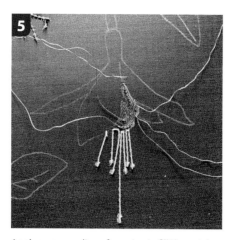

Apply one more line of sequins to fill the petal. Apply this line of sequins in the same direction as the outline.

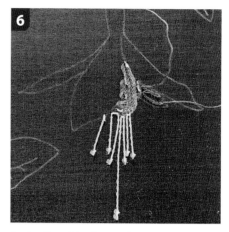

Apply a line of the deep pink sequins to the small petal and then make several chain stitches backwards and apply a second line of sequins in the same direction to the first line.

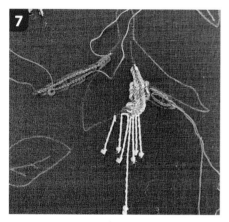

Fill the long thin petal with two lines of sequins applied in the same direction.

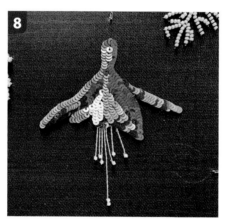

Apply sequins just inside the outlines of the rest of the flower and then fill the centre of the shape with sequins.

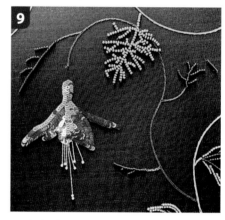

Apply the dark green beads to the leaf veins.

Starting at the point above where the leaf folds over, apply the dark green sequins just inside the outline of the leaf. When you reach the central leaf vein, make several chain stitches in the opposite direction to the point where you will begin to apply the next line of sequins.

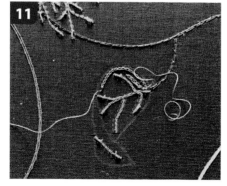

Then apply another line of sequins to fill the space between your previous line of sequins and the beaded leaf vein.

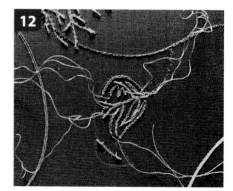

Fill the other sections of this part of the leaf with the sequins in the same way, using empty chain stitches between the lines of sequins you apply to ensure that the sequins are all applied in the same direction.

*continued on the following page…*

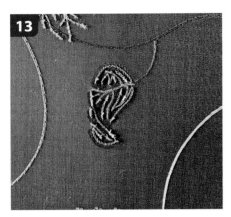

Then, starting from the tip of the leaf, fill the folded-over part of the leaf with sequins, again making sure that you apply all of the sequins in the same direction.

Fill the other fuchsia leaves with the dark green matt sequins in the same way.

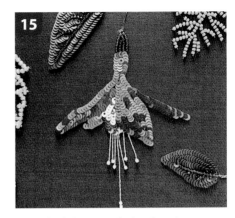

Apply the dark green Toho beads to the outline of the shape above the flower. Then fill the shape.

# DAHLIA

Fill some of the petals at the centre of the dahlia with the mid-pink beads. On the petal that has a turned-over section at the top, fill the bottom part of the petal but only outline the top part.

On the right side of the fabric, fill the other petals at the centre of the dahlia with chain stitch using the mid-pink thread. Also use chain stitch to fill the turned-over part of the petal that you outlined with the mid-pink beads.

Outline and then fill alternate petals with the light peach beads.

Outline the other petals with the mid-pink beads, including the turned-over section at the edge of one of the petals you filled with the light peach beads.

Then, on the right side of the fabric, fill all three of the turned-over sections of the petals with chain stitch using the mid-pink thread.

Next, use the light peach beads to fill the petals that you outlined with the mid-pink beads.

You should now have completely filled all the petals with beads and chain stitch.

Then apply the matt gold sequins to the centre of the flower using the scrunched sequins technique.

The dahlia flower is now complete.

Apply the dark green Toho beads to the leaf veins.

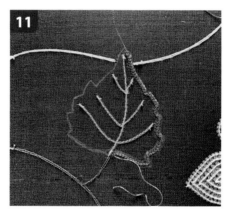

Starting from just below the tip of one of the leaves, apply the dark green cup sequins to the outline of one half of the leaf.

Starting just above the first sequin that you previously applied, begin applying sequins to the other half of the leaf. Continue applying sequins along the outline of the leaf.

Apply sequins to the other dahlia leaves in the same way.

## Cosmos

After you have applied the clear bugle beads to the lines on the cosmos petals in Step 1 of the instructions, there are no lines drawn on the design to indicate where the other beads and sequins should be applied to each petal. These materials are applied randomly but you should avoid placing more than two lines of the same beads next to each other, and the lines of sequins should not touch each other.

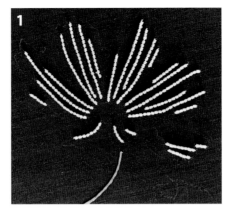

Apply the clear bugle beads to the lines on the petals and then finish the thread ends.

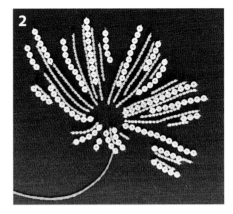

Apply lines of the white flat sequins to the petals using the technique of attaching sequins on both sides. Apply the sequins between the lines of beads and at the edges of some of the petals.

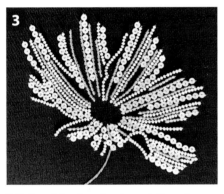

With the white glossy beads, apply lines of beads in the spaces between the lines of beads and sequins. Apply lines of beads at all of the edges of the petals that have not had sequins applied to them and around the outlines of the folded petals.

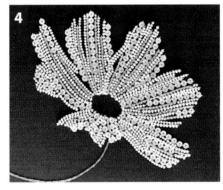

Apply the matt white beads in lines to fill most of the rest of the space left in the petals. Fill the folded petal detail on the bottom-left petal (when you have the wrong side facing you) completely with the matt beads.

Fill any remaining spaces with the white glossy beads.

Apply the mid-yellow cup sequins to the centre of the flower using the scrunched sequin technique.

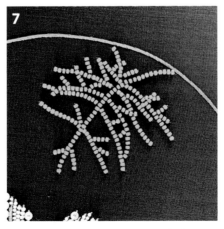

Apply the opaque mid-green beads to the leaves. Apply the beads to the central line first; then apply beads to the other lines using the same process of crossing over the line of beads with empty chain stitches that you used for the lemon leaf veins.

# DAISY

**1**

Apply the matt white beads to every other petal of the daisy by outlining each petal with beads first and then filling the centre of the petal.

**2**

On the right side of the fabric, using the white rayon thread, chain stitch around the edge of a petal.

**3**

Then make chain stitches around the inside edge to fill the petal. You can make a pulling stitch to change direction when the shape left to fill has pointed ends.

**4**

Fill the rest of the petals with chain stitch.

**5**

Fill the centre of the daisy with the yellow beads. Outline the daisy centre first and then fill the space left in the centre.

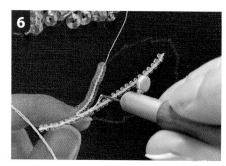

**6**

Apply the light green beads to the leaf veins. Starting from the edge of one of the leaves, apply the light green sequins just inside the outline. Stop applying sequins when there is no more room to fit a sequin between the beads and the outline of the leaf. Make chain stitches close to the beads until you reach half a sequin's width away from the sequins you just applied.

**7**

Then make chain stitches towards the edge of the leaf, finishing just before the next point at the edge of the leaf. This line of chain stitch must be positioned exactly in the middle of where you want to apply the next line of sequins because the sequins are semi-transparent.

**8**

Then apply another line of sequins, making your chain stitches in the middle of the chain stitches you just made.

**9**

Apply more lines of sequins, using empty chain stitches to travel between the start and ends of the lines of sequins. When there is just a small space left to fill between the previous line of sequins and the beads, make chain stitches up to the point where you want to apply the first sequin in the line.

*continued on the following page…*

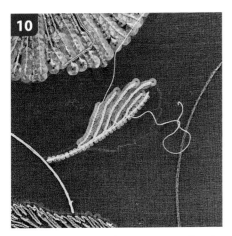

Then apply a final line of sequins to complete the filling of one half of the leaf.

Fill the other half of the leaf with sequins in the same way, making sure that you start each line of sequins from the edge of the leaf.

Fill the other daisy leaves with sequins, positioning the start of each line so that they highlight the points at the edge of the leaf and curve around sections where there are no points at the edge.

## CHERRY

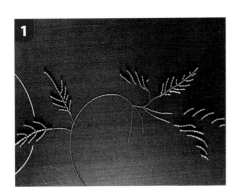

Apply the dark green bugle beads to the leaf veins in the same way as the lemon leaf veins.

For the folded leaves, start from the tip of the leaf and begin applying a line of the dark green matt sequins just inside the outline of the straightest edge of the leaf. When you reach the first leaf vein, make a chain stitch close to the beads and then make another chain stitch into the same hole as the end of the beads.

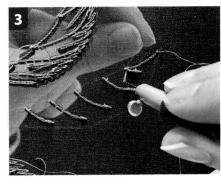

Then make a chain stitch close to the beads to bring the thread just inside the outline.

Make a chain stitch about half the diameter of a sequin along the edge of the leaf and then apply sequins up to the next leaf vein.

Apply a line of sequins all the way along the top edge of the leaf, repeating the process used in Steps 2 to 4 to break the line of sequins when you reach a leaf vein.

Make several chain stitches to bring the thread to just inside the other edge of the leaf.

Then apply sequins back towards the previous line of sequins, making sure the last sequin overlaps the previous sequins.

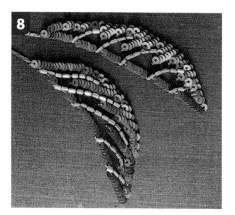

Continue the process of making chain stitches towards the edge of the leaf and then applying a line of sequins in the opposite direction, varying the lengths of the lines of sequins. Repeat Steps 2 to 8 to fill the other folded leaves in the same way.

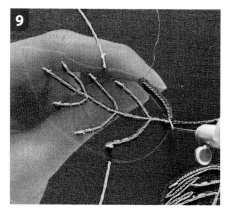

For the full leaves, start applying a line of sequins from the edge of the leaf, at the base of the leaf, just inside the outline.

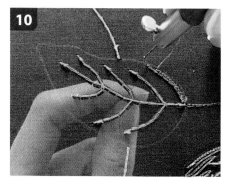

Make chain stitches back to the edge of the leaf, close to the sequins, so that the edge of the sequins overlaps the chain stitches on the right side.

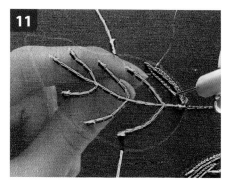

Then apply another line of sequins, making sure there is no gap between the lines of sequins. Stop applying sequins a little before you reach the central leaf vein.

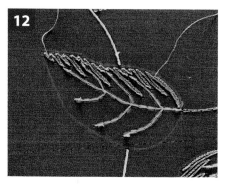

Repeat Steps 10 and 11 to apply more lines of sequins along the leaf, varying the lengths of the lines of sequins, until you have reached the tip of the leaf.

Then apply lines of sequins to the other side of the leaf in the same way.

Fill the other full leaves in the same way to complete all the cherry leaves.

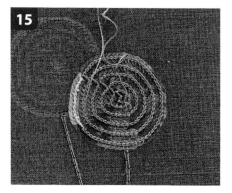

Apply a short line of the mid-pink sequins just inside the outline of the cherry. Then apply the deep pink sequins just inside the rest of the outline of the cherry, making sure there are no gaps in the outline where the two different sequins meet. Then fill the cherry with sequins; apply each circle of sequins in the same direction.

*continued on the following page…*

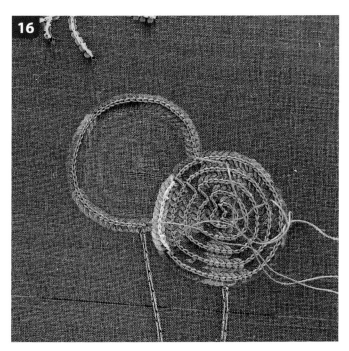

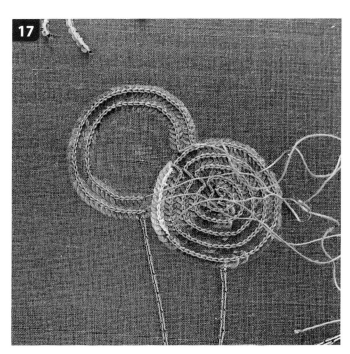

Starting a short distance away from the sequins on the completed cherry, so that the first sequin meets but does not overlap the previous sequins, apply the deep pink sequins just inside the outline of the other cherry. Finish the line of sequins close to the sequins on the completed cherry.

Repeat Step 16 to apply another line of sequins inside the previous line. Ensure that you start the sequins next to the start of the previous line of sequins so that the sequins are applied in the same direction.

Start another line of sequins, again ensuring these sequins are applied in the same direction as previous ones. Instead of stopping the sequins next to the completed cherry as before, continue applying the sequins in a spiral.

Continue applying the sequins in a spiral until you have completely filled the cherry.

## MOUNTING THE EMBROIDERY

You can now mount your finished embroidery for framing. To do this, you can follow the instructions for mounting embroidery included in the 'Flock of Geese' project. For this project, you will need to cover the mount board with a layer of dark blue silk first and then mount the embroidery on top of this.

The finished summer flowers and fruit embroidery, mounted and ready to be framed.

# CHRISTMAS GARLAND

This garland features Christmas motifs embroidered with beads and sequins. The motifs are embroidered onto organza and then cut out and applied to a stiffer base fabric using the appliqué technique. Instead of embroidering the whole garland, you could also use the motifs to create individual decorations for hanging on a tree.

## MATERIALS

White silk organza, one piece about 30 x 24cm
Cotton threads in colours that match the beads, sequins and wool felt for each decoration
Baker's twine or decorative string
Acid-free medium-weight card

### For the Gingerbread Man
Glossy white round beads 13
Toho light pink Ceylon beads 15
Toho mid-green silver-lined beads 15
Toho light blue silver-lined beads 15
Metallic mid-brown flat sequins 3mm
Toho mid-brown silver-lined beads 15
Mid-brown wool felt, 1mm thick

### For the Star
Silver-lined clear round beads 10
Metallic silver cup sequins 3mm
Ivory wool felt, 1mm thick

### For the Stocking
Toho silver-lined white beads 15
Glossy crystal mid pink flat sequins 3mm
Pearl mid-green flat sequins 3mm
Metallic gold flat sequins 3mm
Metallic silver flat sequins 3mm
Bright green wool felt, 1mm thick

### For the Candy Cane
Toho opaque lustred white beads 15
Toho red silver-lined beads 15
Mid-red wool felt, 1mm thick

### For the Bow
Metallic gold flat sequins 3mm
Toho silver-lined gold beads 15
Deep yellow wool felt, 1mm thick

## PREPARATION

To start, trace all of your designs onto your fabric, leaving at least 4cm (1½in) of space between the edges of each motif so you have plenty of fabric to leave as borders when you cut them out. Now follow the instructions to make each decoration for the garland.

The finished Christmas garland project. This joyful garland features a festive choice of bead and sequin colours and finishes that are used to embroider the Christmas motifs. Each motif is individually finished by being stiffened with card and backed with felt before being combined with the other motifs to make the garland.

# GINGERBREAD MAN

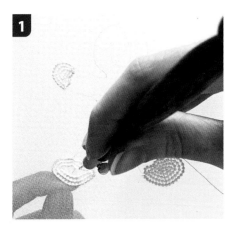

Using glossy white beads, fill the hands and feet of the gingerbread man.

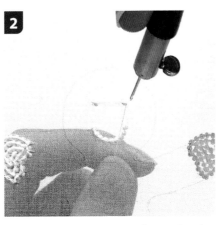

Apply the same white beads to the mouth and eyes. Apply only one bead to each eye and carry the thread between them with a long chain stitch.

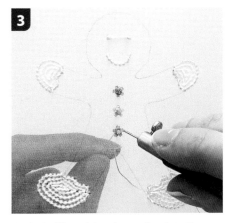

Apply the blue, pink and green beads to the buttons. Use six beads for each button; apply the first five beads in a small circle and then apply the last bead in the centre of the circle. Finish the thread ends.

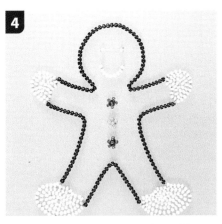

Apply the brown beads to the outlines of the gingerbread man, positioning the beads so they meet the white beads.

On the inside edge of the beaded outline, apply the brown sequins. Make sure you position the sequins so that there is no gap between the edge of the sequins and the beads.

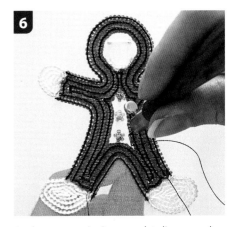

Apply more sequins in a complete line around the shape so they sit next to the previous line of sequins. Then make a starting stitch to fill the spaces left in the centre of the gingerbread man.

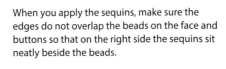

When you apply the sequins, make sure the edges do not overlap the beads on the face and buttons so that on the right side the sequins sit neatly beside the beads.

# Star

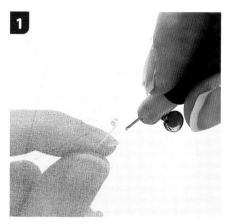

**1**

Make a starting stitch just before one of the inner corners of the star and apply a silver-lined clear bead so the centre of the bead intersects the outline of the star.

**2**

Apply the silver-lined beads all around the outline of the star. Form corners at each point of the star.

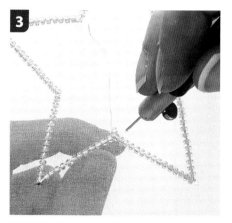

**3**

Make a locking stitch at the end of the line of beads and then make a small chain stitch upwards and then another locking stitch. Then apply a bead above the corner of the star.

**4**

Apply beads down to the next corner so they sit next to the previous line of beads. Then make a locking stitch and a chain stitch backwards at a slight angle and apply a bead.

**5**

Continue applying beads around the inside of the outline of the star, repeating Step 4 to form the corners at each point of the star. Then finish the thread ends.

**6**

Using the same beads, embroider a vermicelli pattern within the star, spacing the beads apart with some chain stitches between each one.

**7**

Using the vermicelli technique, apply silver cup sequins around the beads in the centre of the star. The sequins should cross over the chain stitches made when applying the beads, to cover the thread.

Finish the thread ends on the wrong side of the embroidery. The centre of your star should now be completely filled with the sequins.

**8**

# STOCKING

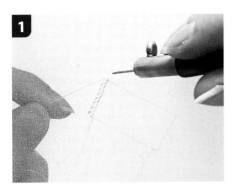

Using the white beads, apply a line of beads at the edge of the top section of the stocking.

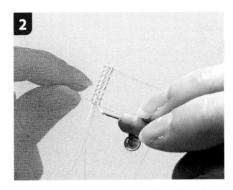

Make a chain stitch sideways and apply another line of beads next to the previous line. Make sure this line of beads is applied close to the last one.

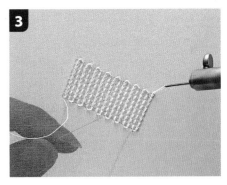

Repeat Step 2 to continue applying lines of beads until you have filled the shape.

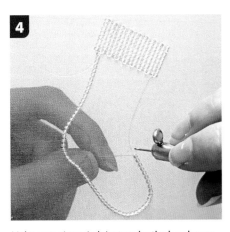

Make a starting stitch just under the beads you just applied to the top of the stocking, and apply the white beads around the outline. Finish the thread ends.

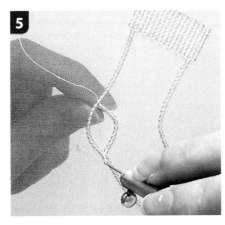

At the heel of the stocking, apply the white beads around the curved outline.

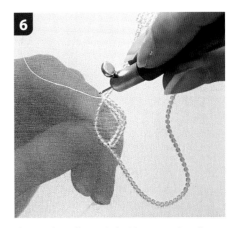

Then make a chain stitch sideways and apply beads inside the curved outline.

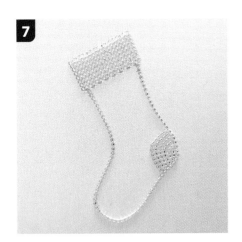

Apply more curved lines of beads to fill the shape with beads, working inside the previous line of beads until the shape is filled.

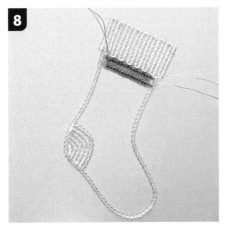

Apply a straight line of pink sequins at the top of the stocking underneath the beads. The sequins should meet each edge of the beaded outline. Then apply a second line of pink sequins in the same direction underneath the previous line.

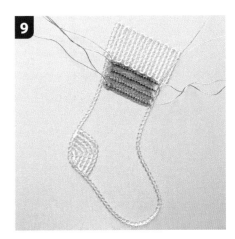

Switch to the gold sequins and apply two lines of them underneath the pink sequins.

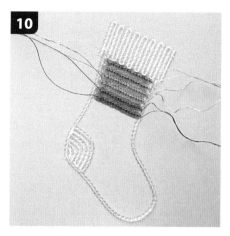

Apply two lines of green sequins.

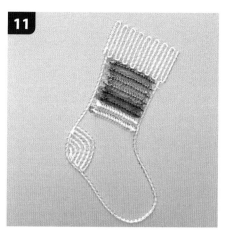

Apply two lines of silver sequins.

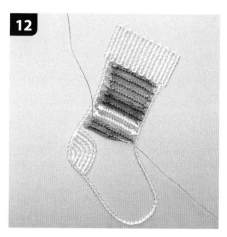

Apply one line of pink sequins then make several long chain stitches back to the other side of the stocking. Apply another line of sequins, stopping before the end of the previous line and angling the line to overlap the previous sequins.

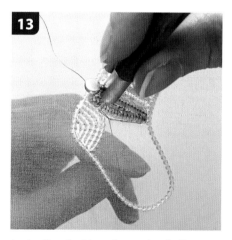

Apply a line of gold sequins, curving the line slightly so that it overlaps the pink sequins. Make several chain stitches backwards and then make a locking stitch to just before the beads on the heel.

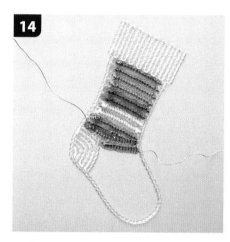

Apply another line of gold sequins at a slightly different angle to the last line to meet the beaded outline on the other side of the stocking.

Apply a line of green sequins up to about halfway along the previous line of sequins. Make several chain stitches backwards and then make a locking stitch just before the beads.

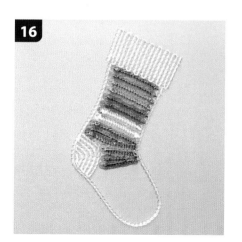

Apply a line of green sequins to meet the beaded outline on the other side of the stocking, angling the line to overlap the end of the previous line of sequins.

Then apply a half line and then a full line of silver sequins. Next, apply a full line of pink sequins. Make chain stitches backwards and apply another line of sequins, stopping before the end of the previous line and angling the line to overlap the previous sequins.

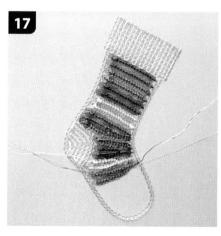

*continued on the following page…*

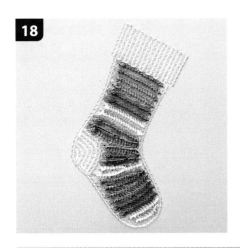

**18**

Then apply two lines of gold sequins and two lines of green sequins, followed by two lines of silver sequins to complete the filling of the shape. Finish all the thread ends.

On the right side you can see how the use of the fan-filling technique has changed the angle of the sequins at the bend in the middle of the stocking.

**19**

# CANDY CANE

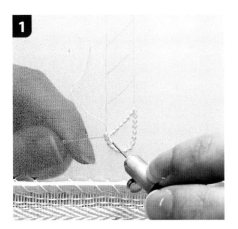

**1**

Using the white beads, outline the first stripe at the bottom of the candy cane.

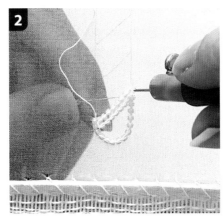

**2**

Make a chain stitch downwards then apply a line of beads following the curve of the beads at the top of the outlined section.

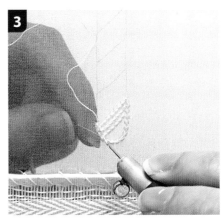

**3**

Make a locking stitch at the end of the line of beads and then make a chain stitch downwards. Apply another line of beads.

**4**

Repeat Step 3 until the shape has been completely filled with lines of beads.

**5**

Switch to the red beads and outline the next stripe of the candy cane with the beads.

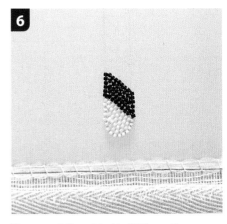

**6**

Then repeat Steps 2 to 4 to fill the section with beads.

**7**

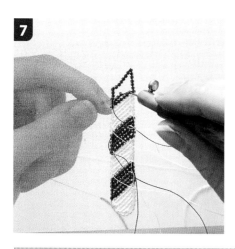

Continue outlining and filling each stripe of the candy cane with beads, alternating the white and red beads until the whole candy cane has been filled.

Finish all the thread ends on the wrong side of the embroidery to complete your candy cane.

**8**

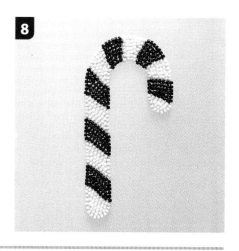

## Bow

**1**

Outline and then fill the centre of the bow with the gold beads.

**2**

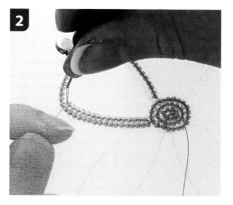

Apply beads to the outline of one half of the top section of the bow. Then make a chain stitch upwards and apply beads along the inner edge of the outline.

**3**

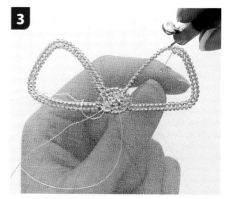

Repeat Step 2 on the other side of the bow.

**4**

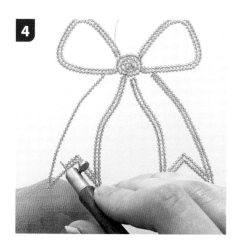

On one half of the bottom section of the bow, apply beads to the outline. Then make a chain stitch sideways and apply beads along the inner edge of the outline. Repeat on the other side of the bow.

**5**

On the right side of the fabric you should now have double lines of beads applied to the outlines of the bow, and the centre of the bow should be completely filled with beads.

**6**

Apply a line of the gold sequins to one of the top sections of the bow, next to the beads. Repeat this on the other side of the bow.

*continued on the following page…*

**7** On one of the bottom sections of the bow, apply a line of sequins starting and finishing at the top of the shape. Repeat on the other side of the bow.

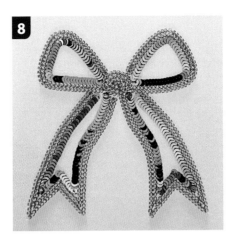

**8** On the right side, you can now see how the sequins have been applied. When you are applying your sequins in the bottom points of the bow, you will not be able to completely fill the points with sequins; do not worry about this – just apply the sequins as far down the points as they will fit.

**9** Apply beads around the inside edge of the sequins in the bottom and top sections of the bow.

**10** Apply sequins around the inside edge of the beads in the top sections of the bow.

**11** Starting at the bottom of one of the points of the bow, apply a short line of sequins next to the inside edge of the beads; apply the sequins as far up the bottom section of the bow as they will fit. Repeat on the other side of the bow.

**12** On the right side of the embroidery, you should now only have small gaps left in the centre of each section of the bow.

**13** Fill these gaps with beads and finish the thread ends to complete your bow.

# FINISHING THE DECORATIONS TO MAKE THE GARLAND

Cut around the embroidered motifs, leaving a border of about 1cm (⅓in) of fabric. Apply glue along the edge of any parts of the motif where you will need to make cuts in the fabric to allow the border to be turned over. Thread a sewing needle with a single length of sewing thread and stitch the fabric border to the wrong side of the motif using the same technique shown in the appliqué instructions in Chapter 7: Advanced Techniques.

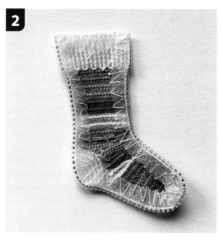

Continue making stitches to secure the fabric border until you have worked your way around the whole motif.

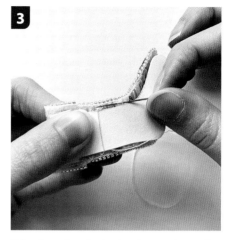

Cut a piece of card out using the template and secure a single length of sewing thread to the back of the motif. Start making stitches across the card by making small stitches through the fabric on either side of the card.

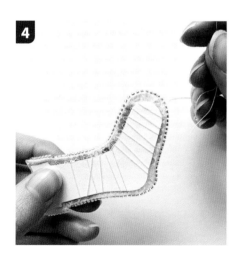

Continue making stitches over the card to secure it to the back of the motif until you reach one end of the piece of card.

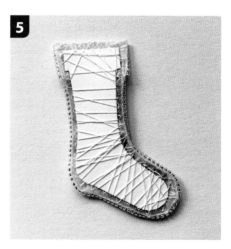

Then work back up the motif, making more stitches until the whole piece of card is securely attached to the motif. The piece of card should be secured so that it is not able to move around.

Cut out a piece of wool felt using the template and trim it down to match the edges of the motif, if necessary.

*continued on the following page…*

**7**

Cut a 5cm (2in) length of baker's twine and fold it in half to create a loop. Thread a needle with a double length thread in a colour that matches the felt backing and tie a knot in the end. Bring the needle through the baker's twine just over 1cm down from the top of the loop.

**8**

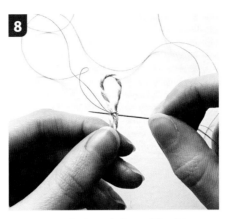

Bring the needle through the middle of the baker's twine again to make a stitch over one side of twine. Then insert the needle into the twine again. Make two stitches on each side of the baker's twine.

**9**

Position the twine loop on the felt backing at the point you want to hang the decoration from. On the stocking motif, this should be positioned at the corner. The loop should extend about 1cm (⅓in) beyond the edge of the piece of felt. Make a stitch through the back of the felt (this stitch should not show on the right side of the felt).

**10**

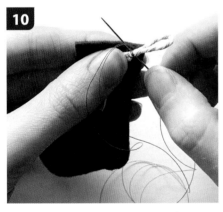

Then make a stitch over the twine loop by inserting the needle into the back of the felt again, underneath the twine. Make two stitches over the twine like this.

**11**

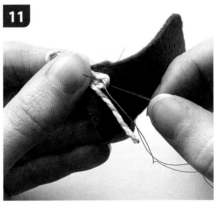

Then fold one end of the twine back on itself and make a stitch over the fold, through the back of the felt. Then make a second stitch over the fold.

**12**

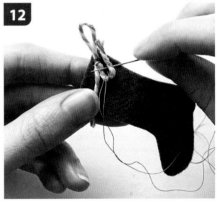

Then make a stitch a short distance away from the fold in the twine, over the twine.

**13**

Make another stitch over the twine at the same point as previously and then cut off the excess twine.

**14**

Repeat Steps 11 to 13 to fold over and secure the other end of the twine.

**15**

Position the felt on the back of the embroidered motif and bring the needle through the fabric border on the back of the motif to bring the thread to the edge of your decoration.

**16**

Bring your needle through the felt on one side of the twine loop and then catch the fabric border with your needle; angle the needle to bring it out through the edge of the fabric border a short distance away.

**17**

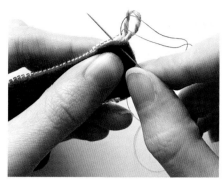

Make a stitch on the other side of the twine loop by bringing your needle through the felt and then back out through the edge of the fabric border, a short distance away.

**18**

Keep making stitches through the felt and the edge of the fabric border. Try to keep these stitches an even distance apart and make them as straight as possible on the back of the felt.

**19**

Continue making stitches around the felt to secure the felt backing to the front of the decoration until you reach the point where you started. Then make two stitches through the edge of the fabric border. Then make a longer stitch in between the layers and bring the needle up through the felt backing. Then cut the thread close to the felt.

**20**

Now you have completely finished the backing for the decoration, repeat Steps 1 to 19 to finish the other decorations for your garland.

**21**

For the gingerbread, star and candy cane motifs, you should position the twine loops at the top centre of the motif. For the bow motif, you should position two twine loops at the top of each side of the bow.

---

### Check the Sizing of the Card and Felt Backing

You need to check the size of the pieces of card and the felt backing because the size of the embroidered motifs may have shrunk a little when they were removed from the tension of the frame or hoop. Check the size of each piece against the corresponding embroidery and trim the pieces down to fit the size of the motif. The card should be just smaller than the embroidery so that you have a border of fabric still visible around the edges of the card, and the felt backing should match the edges of the embroidery.

# Assembling the Garland

## 2

Cut a long length of baker's twine and thread it through the twine loops on the bow. Position the bow so that it is in the centre of the length of twine. Thread a needle with a double length of thread and knot the end. Bring the needle through the top of one of the twine loops.

Then bring the needle down through the top of loop, a short distance away from where you brought the needle up, and then bring it down through the long length of baker's twine.

## 3

Make several stitches through both pieces of twine to secure them together. Then make three small stitches through the twine to secure the thread end; then cut it close to the twine. Stitch the other loop to the length of twine in the same way to secure the bow.

**4**

Then position the candy cane 10cm (4in) away from the right loop of the bow and stitch in place. Then position the stocking 10cm (4in) away from the left loop of the bow and stitch in place.

**5**

Position the star to the right of the candy cane, 12.5cm (5in) away from the twine loop, and stitch in place.

**6**

Then position the gingerbread man to the left of the stocking, 12.5cm (5in) away from the twine loop, and stitch in place.

**7**

Tie a knot in both ends of the length of twine to complete the garland. The long ends of twine can be used to secure the garland to two objects or nails to display it.

# PATTERNS FOR THE PROJECTS

The following pages contain the designs for all the projects in this book. These can be traced and transferred onto fabric. Where appropriate, the designs have been reflected so that you can apply the design onto the wrong side of the fabric and the design will be the correct way round on the right side.

Some of the designs will need to be enlarged; this can be done with a photocopier. Set the photocopier to enlarge the copied image by the appropriate percentage. To help you enlarge the designs accurately, the designs that have been scaled down state what percentage of their original size they are, and a blue square has been included at the edge of the design. The square will measure 1cm ($\frac{1}{3}$in) when the design has been correctly enlarged. If this is not the case, adjust the scaling of the design up or down.

# PRACTICE SHAPES FOR THE TECHNIQUES IN CHAPTERS 4, 5, 6 AND 7

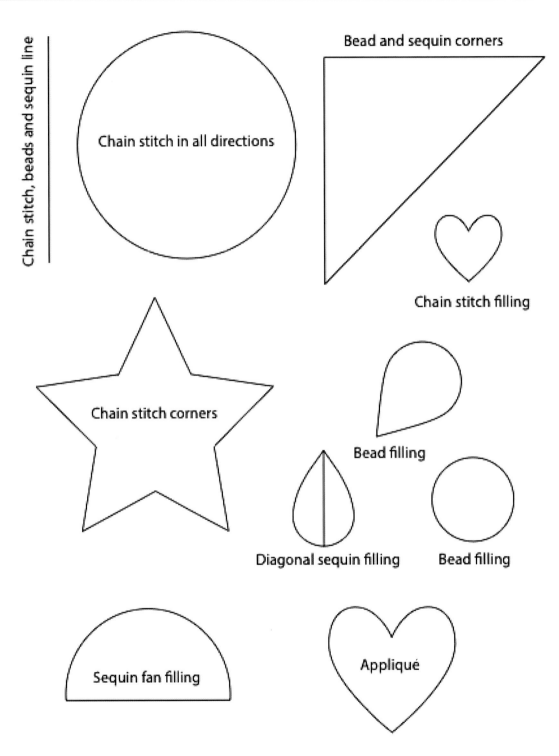

Practice shapes for Chapters 4, 5, 6 and 7.

Designs for practising vermicelli with a drawn guide on the fabric. Transfer to the wrong side of the fabric.

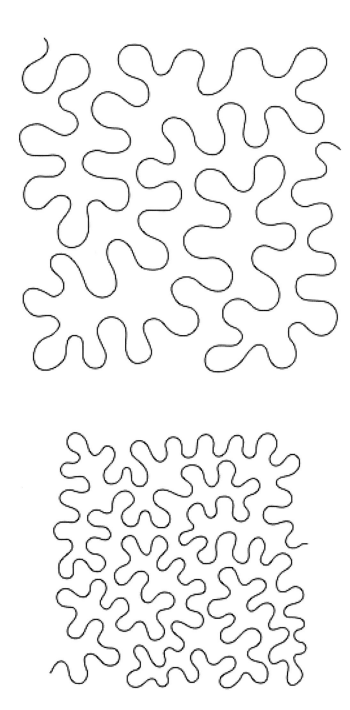

Patterns for vermicelli.

# SPRING FLOWERS PRACTICE DESIGN FROM CHAPTERS 4, 5 AND 6

This design is included at its actual size. Transfer to the wrong side of the fabric.

Pattern for the three spring flowers
practice design.

# PROJECT 1: LEAF CLUTCH BAG

This design is scaled down to 60 per cent of its original size. Transfer to the wrong side of the fabric.

Pattern for the leaf clutch bag.

# PROJECT 2: FLOCK OF GEESE

These designs are included at their actual sizes, which measure 148mm × 210mm (6in × 8in). Transfer to the wrong side of the fabric

Pattern for the top three geese layer.

Pattern for the middle skein of geese layer.

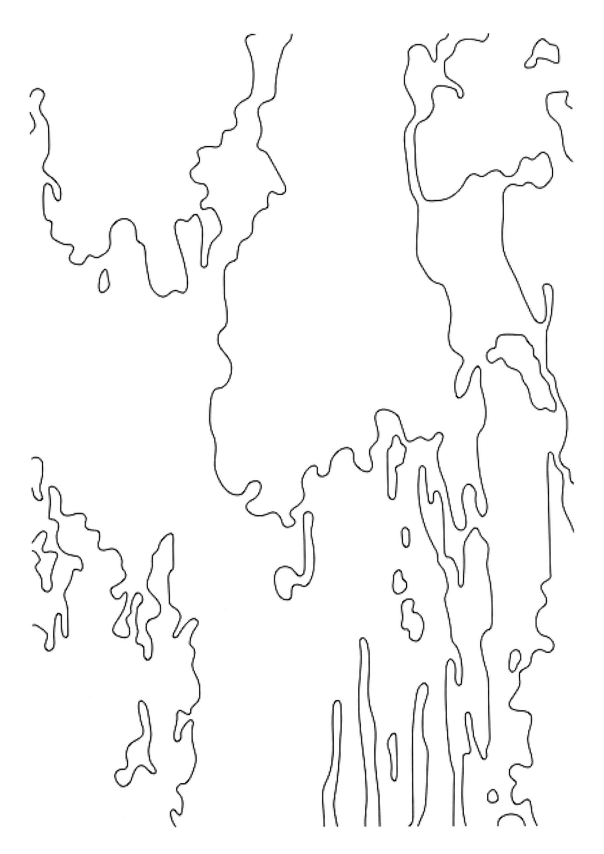

Pattern for the bottom cloud layer.

# PROJECT 3: SPRING FLOWERS SCULPTURE

These designs are included at their actual sizes.

Transfer the designs for the sequin fronts to the wrong side of the fabric.

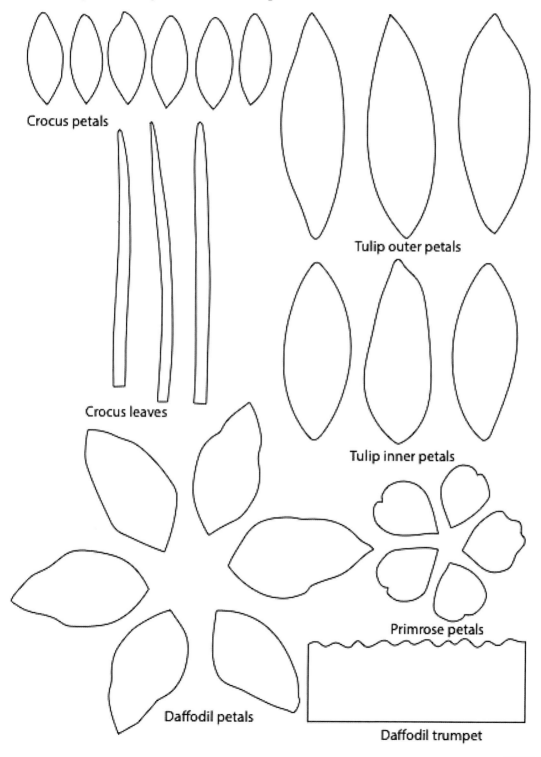

Crocus petals

Crocus leaves

Tulip outer petals

Tulip inner petals

Primrose petals

Daffodil petals

Daffodil trumpet

Transfer the designs for the sequin leaf fronts to the wrong side of the fabric.

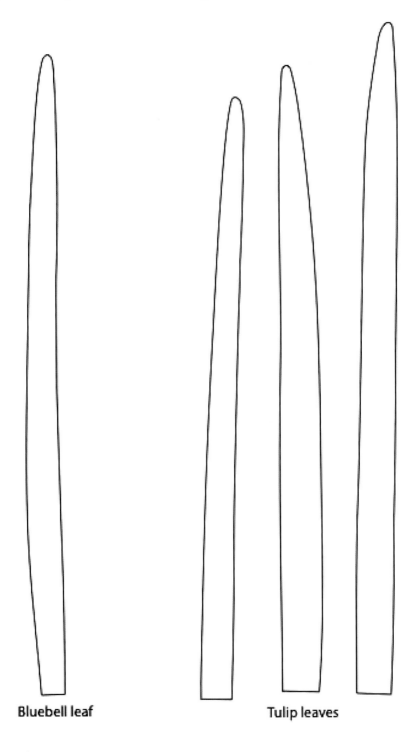

**Bluebell leaf**                    **Tulip leaves**

Patterns for the sequin leaf fronts.

Transfer the designs for the chain stitch fronts to the right side of the fabric.

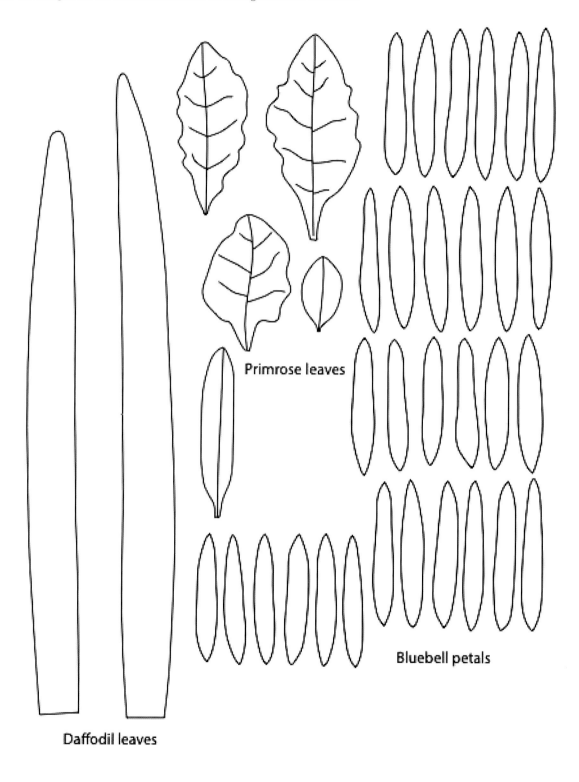

Primrose leaves

Bluebell petals

Daffodil leaves

Patterns for the chain stitch fronts.

Transfer the designs for the sequin backs to the wrong side of the fabric.

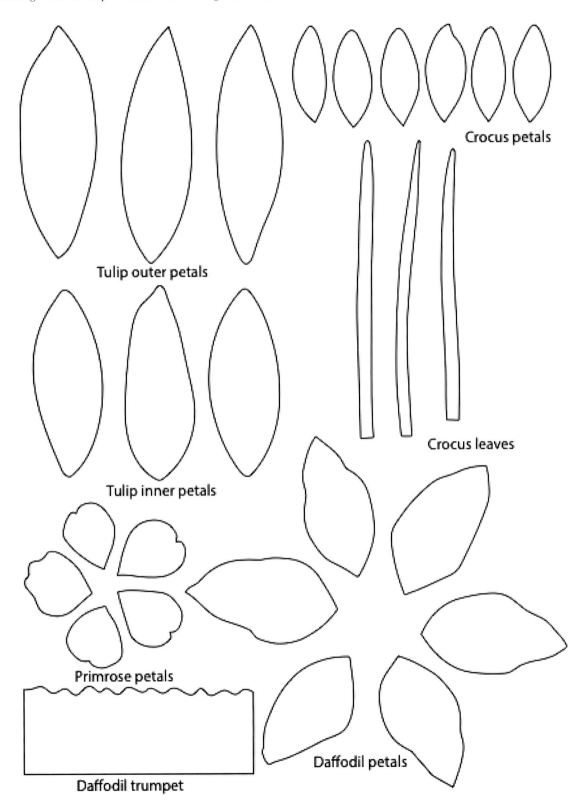

Crocus petals

Tulip outer petals

Crocus leaves

Tulip inner petals

Primrose petals

Daffodil petals

Daffodil trumpet

Patterns for the sequin backs.

Transfer the designs for the sequin leaf backs to the wrong side of the fabric.

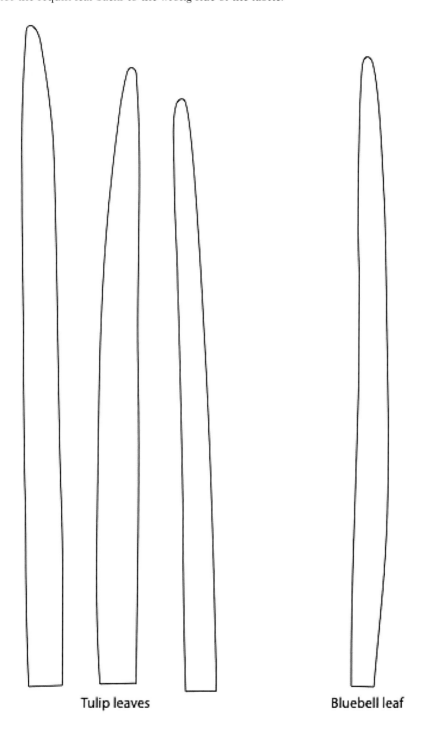

Tulip leaves

Bluebell leaf

Patterns for the sequin leaf backs.

Transfer the designs for the chain stitch backs to the right side of the fabric.

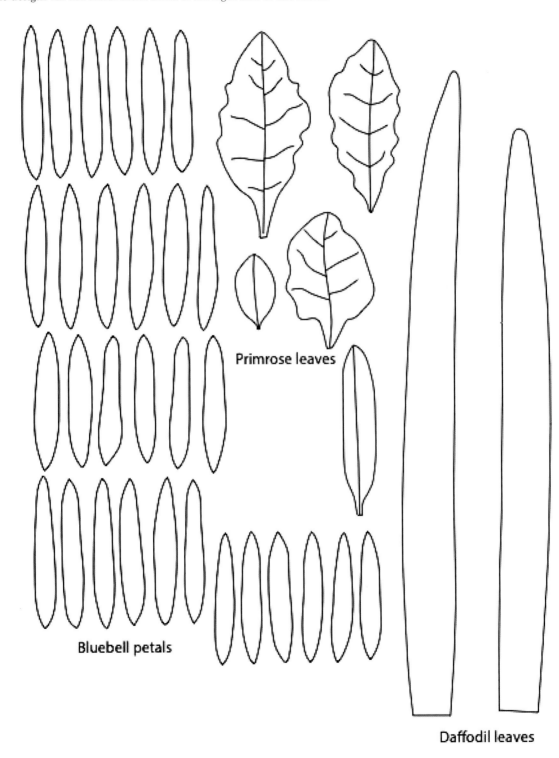

Primrose leaves

Bluebell petals

Daffodil leaves

Patterns for the chain stitch backs.

# PROJECT 4: APPLIQUÉ BUTTERFLY AND CLOVER

This design is included at its actual size. Transfer to the wrong side of the fabric.

Pattern for the appliqué butterfly and clover project.

# PROJECT 5: CHECK CUSHION

This design is scaled down to 40 per cent of its original size. At its actual size it measures 40cm × 40cm (16in × 16in). Transfer to the wrong side of the fabric.

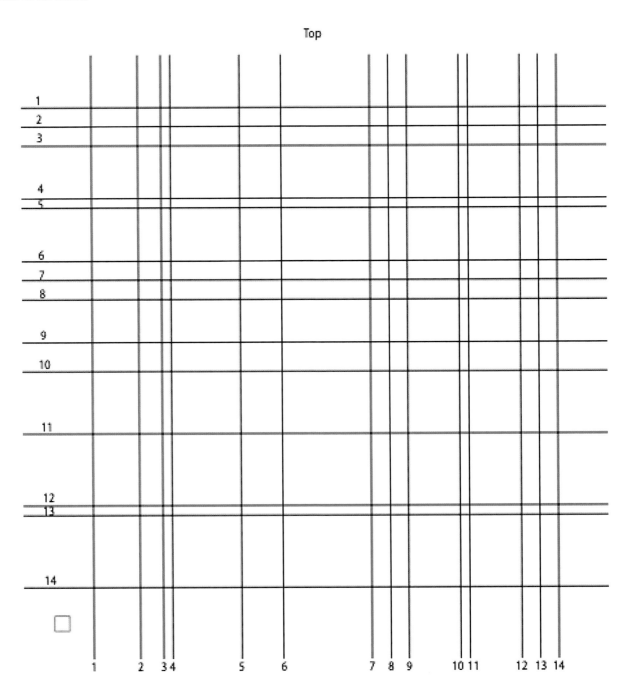

Pattern for the check cushion project.

# PROJECT 6: SUMMER FLOWERS AND FRUIT

This design is scaled down to 35 per cent of its original size. At its actual size it measures 420mm × 594mm. Transfer to the wrong side of the fabric.

Pattern for the summer flowers and fruit project.

# PROJECT 7: CHRISTMAS GARLAND

These designs are included at their actual sizes. Transfer to the wrong side of the fabric

Patterns for the Christmas garland project.

Templates for the card to go in between the embroidery and felt backing.

Templates for the card.

# STOCKISTS

Gütermann, the author's preferred brand of sewing thread for applying beads and sequins.
https://consumer.guetermann.com/en/

Sajou, the manufacturer of *Fil à gant* (gloving) thread and metallic threads. These products can be also be bought on a wide variety of websites selling embroidery supplies.
https://sajou.fr/en/

Paillettes et Broderie, the website from which you can order the French-made Langlois Martin pre-strung sequins and beads.
https://www.paillettesetbroderie.com

Brodely, a French company that sells smaller quantities of pre-strung sequins and beads.
https://www.brodely.com

Fried Frères, a long-established supplier of beads and sequins for tambour beading. You can only order by a digital catalogue or visit the shop in Paris to purchase items.
https://friedfreres.fr/en

Broderie Plaisir, a French company selling strung and loose beads and sequins.
https://www.broderieplaisir.com

I-beads, a stockist of a large range of the Japanese-manufactured Toho and Miyuki loose seed beads.
https://www.i-beads.co.uk

Pongees, silk specialists selling silk organza in a wide range of colours, as well as many other types of silk fabrics.
https://www.pongees.co.uk

Beckford silk, a specialist in silk fabrics, many of which are available in a large range of colours.
https://beckfordsilk.co.uk

Wool Felt Company, a company selling 100 per cent wool felt in a wide variety of colours and several thicknesses.
https://www.woolfeltcompany.co.uk

Hand & Lock, seller of tambour hooks and haberdashery.
https://www.handembroideryshop.com

Sarah Homfray, tambour hooks sold with a variety of different sized hooks.
https://www.sarahhomfray.com

Jenny-Adin Christie, traditional slate frames.
https://jennyadin-christieembroidery.com

Royal School of Needlework, traditional slate frames.
https://royal-needlework.org.uk

DMC, one of the few companies from which you can purchase a high-quality hardwood seat clamp and hoop.
https://www.dmc.com

John James Needles, seller of good-quality needles and pins.
https://www.jjneedles.com

Preservation Equipment, conservation materials and equipment for protecting textiles including neutral pH PVA glue.
https://www.preservationequipment.com

advanced filling with sequins
    fan filling  100–101
    filling a leaf shape  99–101
appliqué  93–95
appliqué butterfly and clover project
    147–150
applying beads  51, 54–55
    filling with beads  58–60
    to a corner  56–57
    transferring beads to thread
        51–53
applying sequins  69–71
    filling  75
    to a corner  73–74
    transferring sequins to thread  69

beads
    pre-strung beads  13–14
    bead shapes, finishes and sizes
        14–15
bricking stitch  86–88

chain stitch  33, 36, 40–42
    corners  43
    filling with chain stitch  44

check cushion project  151–164
choosing colours  108–109
Christmas garland project  189–201
creating a tambour design  103–106
cutwork  83–85

decorative chain stitch  13

English style sequin application  97

fabric  16
    opaque fabrics  17
    silk organza  16–17
finishing stitch  37
finishing the thread ends  37–39
flock of geese project  117–126
frames and hoops  17–19
    setting up a slate frame  23–26
    setting up an embroidery hoop  27

leaf clutch bag project
    111–116

mounting embroidery for framing
    122–126

point tiré/pulled stitch  95–96
practice design
    beads  61–67
    chain stitch  45–49
    sequins  75–81

scrunched sequin texture  91
sequin flowers  92
sequins applied on both sides  98–99
sequins
    pre-strung sequins  13–14
    sequin shapes, finishes and sizes
        15–16
spring flowers sculpture project  126–146
starting stitch  34–35
summer flowers and fruit project  165–189

tambour hook  12
thread
    fil à gant  13
    metallic thread  13
    sewing thread  12–13
transferring a design  29–31

vermicelli  88–91

First published in 2024 by

The Crowood Press Ltd

Ramsbury, Marlborough

Wiltshire SN8 2HR

**enquiries@crowood.com**

**www.crowood.com**

**British Library Cataloguing-in-Publication Data**

A catalogue record for this book is available from the British Library.

ISBN 978 0 7198 4341 9

Cover design by Sergey Tsvetkov

Photography for the cover, projects and chapter openers by Sam Lucas

Typeset by SJmagic DESIGN SERVICES, India

Printed and bound in India by Thomson Press Ltd

# BIBLIOGRAPHY

Bentley, G.V., The History and Development of Tambour Embroidery. *The Costume Society.* 9 May 2021  https://costumesociety.org.uk/blog/post/the-history-and-development-of-tambour-embroidery

Mauriès, P., *Maison Lesage* (Thames & Hudson, 2020)

# ACKNOWLEDGEMENTS

The first people to thank have to be my number one support team, my parents, who have always encouraged me to follow my passion for embroidery. Without you both, I would not be where I am today.

Thank you to my wonderful sister, Katherine, a doctor of English literature, for using your skills to proofread my drafts.

Thank you to my lovely friend Jessica for your excitement and enthusiasm about this book.

Thank you to Justine Bonenfant for teaching me tambour beading many years ago – clearly your teaching skills made an impression on me!

Thank you to Lesley Coidan for sharing your tambour beading knowledge and helping me to advance my tambour skills when I visited your inspirational studio several years ago.

Thank you to Sam Lucas for taking the beautiful photos of the projects and embroidery samples.

Thank you to Rich Edwards for the care you put into creating beautiful frames for the two framed projects.

Finally, thank you to the team at The Crowood Press for the wonderful opportunity to write this book.